IMAGES
of America

The Chicago Movie Palaces of Balaban and Katz

On the cover: This 1925 photograph features the Uptown Theatre, Balaban and Katz's largest movie palace. Located on Chicago's North Side, it seats more than 4,300. (Courtesy of Theatre Historical Society of America.)

IMAGES
of America

THE CHICAGO MOVIE PALACES OF BALABAN AND KATZ

David Balaban
Foreword by Joseph R. DuciBella

ARCADIA
PUBLISHING

ISBN 978-0-7385-3986-7

Published by Arcadia Publishing
Charleston, South Carolina

Printed in the United States of America

Library of Congress Catalog Card Number: 2005936216

For all general information contact Arcadia Publishing at:
Telephone 843-853-2070
Fax 843-853-0044
E-mail sales@arcadiapublishing.com
For customer service and orders:
Toll-Free 1-888-313-2665

Visit us on the Internet at www.arcadiapublishing.com

Balaban and Katz Timeline

1906	Architectural firm of C. W. and George L. Rapp is established in Chicago.
1908	Balaban family rents and manages the Kedzie, a storefront nickelodeon at Twelfth Street and Kedzie Avenue with 103 seats.
1909	Balaban family builds the Circle Theater at 3241 West Roosevelt Road with 707 seats.
1916	A. J. and Barney Balaban, with Sam Katz, form the Balaban and Katz Corporation.
1917	On October 27, Balaban and Katz opens the Central Park Theatre at Central Park Avenue and West Roosevelt Road with 1,780 seats.
1918	On September 19, Balaban and Katz opens the Riviera Theatre at Broadway Street and Lawrence Avenue with 1,943 seats.
1921	On February 6, Balaban and Katz opens the Tivoli Theatre at Sixty-third Street and Cottage Grove Avenue with 3,520 seats.
1921	On October 26, Balaban and Katz opens the Chicago Theatre at 175 North State Street with 3,861 seats.
1925	On August 17, Balaban and Katz opens the Uptown Theatre at 4814 Broadway Street just off of Lawrence Avenue with 4,320 seats.
1926	On May 9, Balaban and Katz opens the Oriental Theatre at 20 West Randolph Street with 3,217 seats.
1926	On June 17, Balaban and Katz opens the Norshore Theatre at 1748 North Howard Street with 3,017 seats.
1926	On June 30, Famous Players Lasky Corporation buys a controlling interest in Balaban and Katz Corporation.
1949	Paramount splits into two separate corporations: Paramount Pictures and United Paramount Theatres. Balaban and Katz Corporation becomes a wholly owned subsidiary of United Paramount Theatres.
1953	On February 9, United Paramount Theatres merges with the American Broadcasting Company.
1970	On July 31, Balaban and Katz, now a subsidiary of American Broadcasting Company, is officially dissolved.

This Balaban and Katz timeline is based in part on a timeline in *Marquee* 27, no. 2, "Paradoxes in Paradise: Elements of Conflict in Chicago's Balaban and Katz Movie Palaces" (1993). *Marquee* magazine is a publication of the Theatre Historical Society of America.

CONTENTS

ACKNOWLEDGMENTS

Special thanks goes to the following individuals and organizations who made this book possible: John Peters, Chicago Area Theatre Organ Enthusiasts, Paul Jannusch, Barbara Balaban, Daniel Balaban, Samuel Balaban, Max Balaban, Roslyn Balaban, Cherry Robins, Rachel Balaban, Gail Scalamonti, Tony Robins, Leonard Balaban, Micki Balaban, Judy Balaban Quine, A. C. Lyles, Adolf Zukor, David Dinerstein, Gloria and Mike Stern, Jean Siegel, Joseph R. DuciBella, Betty Blair, Mathew Balaban, Adelaide Balaban, Michael Balaban, Steve Balaban, Ida Scully, Bob Balaban, Lynn Grossman, Richard Balaban, Kathi Balaban Douglas Gomery, Gordon Parks, Andy Pierce, Larry Wechsler, Alan Gresik, Theatre Historical Society of America, Karen Colizzi-Noonan, Richard Sklenar, Kathy McLeister, Chicago Historical Society, Rob Medina, Chicago Transit Authority, Joyce Shaw, Noelle Gaffney, Chicago Loop Alliance, Laura Jones, Ty Tabing, Spertus Jewish Institute, Joy Kingsolver, Jewish Historical Society of Chicago, Howard Schwartz, Theatre Dreams Chicago LLC, Lawrence Wilker, Javier Ayala, Maxwell Street Historic Preservation Coalition, Steven Balkin, Shuli Eshel, Roger Schatz, Arcadia Publishing, John Pearson, Melissa Basilone, Cinema Treasures, Ross Melnick, Georgetown University Library Special Collections Division, Heidi Rubenstein, Ashlee Harris, Broadway in Chicago, Central Park, House of Prayer Church of God in Christ, Rene Rabiela Jr., Brian Wolf, and Ken Roe.

FOREWORD

Anyone who does research into the development and evolution of commercial film exhibition and marketing worldwide will come across the distinctive Balaban name. For years, that name, coupled with the entire corporate name Balaban and Katz, resounded in the industry, and especially in Chicago. Balaban and Katz developed many of the systems by which we experience commercial cinema to this day.

A fairly large, very inventive, and business wise lot, they developed several adjacent corporations and branches relating to theaters. Now many corporate evolutions can be traced back to the Balaban family's Chicago roots. David Balaban, grandson of one of the original seven brothers, has pulled together a history of the family, together with illustrations of how quickly this family business developed and succeeded with ever-increasing style and class.

For generations, Chicagoans like me saw theaters downtown and in every neighborhood with the Balaban and Katz corporate logo lighted prominently above the theater name. For years, Balaban and Katz had virtually no competition in Chicago. Institutional advertisements promoted the consistent quality of the Balaban and Katz entertainment experience. Quickly theirs became the high mark of the industry—and we had it all within our backyard.

Their theaters were a separate, comfortable, affordable, and distinctive environment that entertained generations. As a reward and or distraction, as they may have been from our daily lives, the public became very enamored—and faithful. Many of their theaters were virtually palaces by any description.

Born on Chicago's West Side, my earliest memories are going to the "movies" in Balaban and Katz's Senate Theatre. By chance, the nearest theater to my boyhood home was Balaban and Katz's most lavish: the Paradise. The very day I turned 16 to qualify, I applied and became employed as an usher at their nearby Marbro (of some 4,000 seats). I immersed myself in what then remained of the sense of show business yet available.

I settled into studying architecture, and that evolved into design as my life's employ. Over the years, my design business has been involved in a few dozen of these theaters I enjoyed. The early inspirations continue today. I renovate, restore, design, write, and lecture about the theaters—and share my archives of photographs and information.

Starting in my school years, understanding the buildings, and especially those who made the system into what it was, continues as my passion. My acquaintances with many of those vintage folks were a tonic and an invaluable education. I got a call last year from David Balaban. He told me he was pulling together the story of the Balaban family for a book and television documentary. This excited me, as I knew only a family member could succeed in this pursuit as David has here.

Any student of the evolution of American culture in the 20th century should have some understanding of how this very unique, comprehensive, and, therefore, important business, as developed by the Balabans, affected our society—and influenced the world.

—Joseph R. DuciBella, Chicago area director
Theatre Historical Society of America

INTRODUCTION

The journey to write this book began three years ago with research of my family's history. Making great discoveries of family accomplishments, I became very proud of my roots. My research has taken me to a dozen states from Wisconsin to Rhode Island, to near forgotten attic chests and mildewed basement treasures.

I discovered 80-year-old photographs and documents in those dusty, cobwebbed boxes—evidence that my family's business evolution from corner grocery store owners to operators of immense movie palaces paralleled evolution of the American chain store. My family's innovations centered on implementation of marketing techniques that were utilized in other business, such as supermarkets and drugstores, in their movie theaters. The Balaban and Katz Corporation was founded in 1916 by my great-uncles, A. J., Barney, John, Max, and their friends Sam and Morris Katz. Who actually started the family in the film-display business is hard to determine, but it is said that the allure of the nickelodeon business was that patrons paid cash "on the way in." What is indisputable is that the fish and grocery market that my great-grandfather Israel, his wife Gussie, and their eight children owned and lived behind on Chicago's South Side did not make much money. In fact, the family claimed bankruptcy several times from having extended credit to too many of their neighbors.

Balaban and Katz, or B and K as it was affectionately known, perfected a holistic entertainment concept and used the movie palaces it built as showplaces to feature the concepts it created. From the moment a customer entered a B and K theater, they were treated as a king or queen. Handsomely attired ticket takers sold patrons tickets for 50¢ or less. Ushers dressed in tuxedo-like uniforms brought them to their seats. Their children were entertained in plush, supervised play areas. The show consisted of a mixture of live vaudeville or popular music and the latest movies. Famous organists even played beautiful organ music. Patrons could stay all day and all night if they wanted. To top that off, the air was purified and air-conditioned at a time when nowhere else was. Even the lobby areas were furnished with museum-quality chairs, curtains, and knickknacks.

From the mid-1920s until after World War II, B and K monopolized the movie business in Chicago. However, the Balabans were not the first to get into the theater business in Chicago. In fact, B and K achieved its vast power in just six short years, from 1919 to 1925. In 1919, B and K possessed only five theaters: the Chicago, Tivoli, Riviera, Central Park, and Roosevelt. In contrast, the Ascher Brothers had 21 and Lubliner and Trinz owned 15, and they were already Chicago's largest chains. Douglas Gomery, professor of journalism at University of Maryland, often writes about the strategies my family used to achieve their success. He postulated that B and K grew rapidly because of its excellent theater locations, its use of grand theater architecture, its pioneering of theater air-conditioning, and its implementation of splendid service.

These four distinctive advantages formed the foundation by which the rapidly growing Balaban and Katz marketing strategies were built. Uncle Barney, A. J., John, Max, the Katzs, and Grandpa Dave knew that having excellent movies was not enough to fuel their desired dominant position in the Chicago film business. In 1926, they wrote in their book, *The Fundamental Principles of Balaban & Katz Theatre Management*, "In our organization we have invested many hundreds of thousands of dollars in buildings and equipment, we cannot afford to build up a patronage depending entirely upon the drawing power of our feature films as we display them. We must build up in the minds of our audience the feeling that we represent an institution taking a vital part in the formation of the character of the community."

To achieve this goal of building an entertainment institution, my family developed a system by which every aspect of the theatergoing experience could be controlled and adjusted from the home office. When Adolf Zukor and the Famous Players Lasky Corporation bought a controlling interest in B and K in 1926, Sam Katz traveled to New York City and spread the Balaban philosophy throughout their newly formed motion picture empire. So successful was the micromanagement of the theater palaces that the U.S. government thought it wise to declare that Paramount Publix (and its rivals) had achieved too much power over the movie exhibition business. In 1950, it forced Paramount and its competition to spin off its theaters and Balaban and Katz into a separate company. But what B and K achieved in the movie theater business had not been for naught. It operated hundreds of theaters for several decades under the United Paramount ABC and various other banners. A host of economic factors have contributed to the demise of the giant movie palace as a viable model for movie display today. Most of the glorious movie palaces my family built and managed from 1917 to the 1950s have been demolished. Their elegance and style have been preserved forever in the hearts of Chicagoans and in the beautiful pictures and stories I have collected here for you to enjoy. As Uncle John used to say, "Come on in, sit back, and enjoy the show!"

—David Balaban
President, Balaban and Katz Historical Foundation

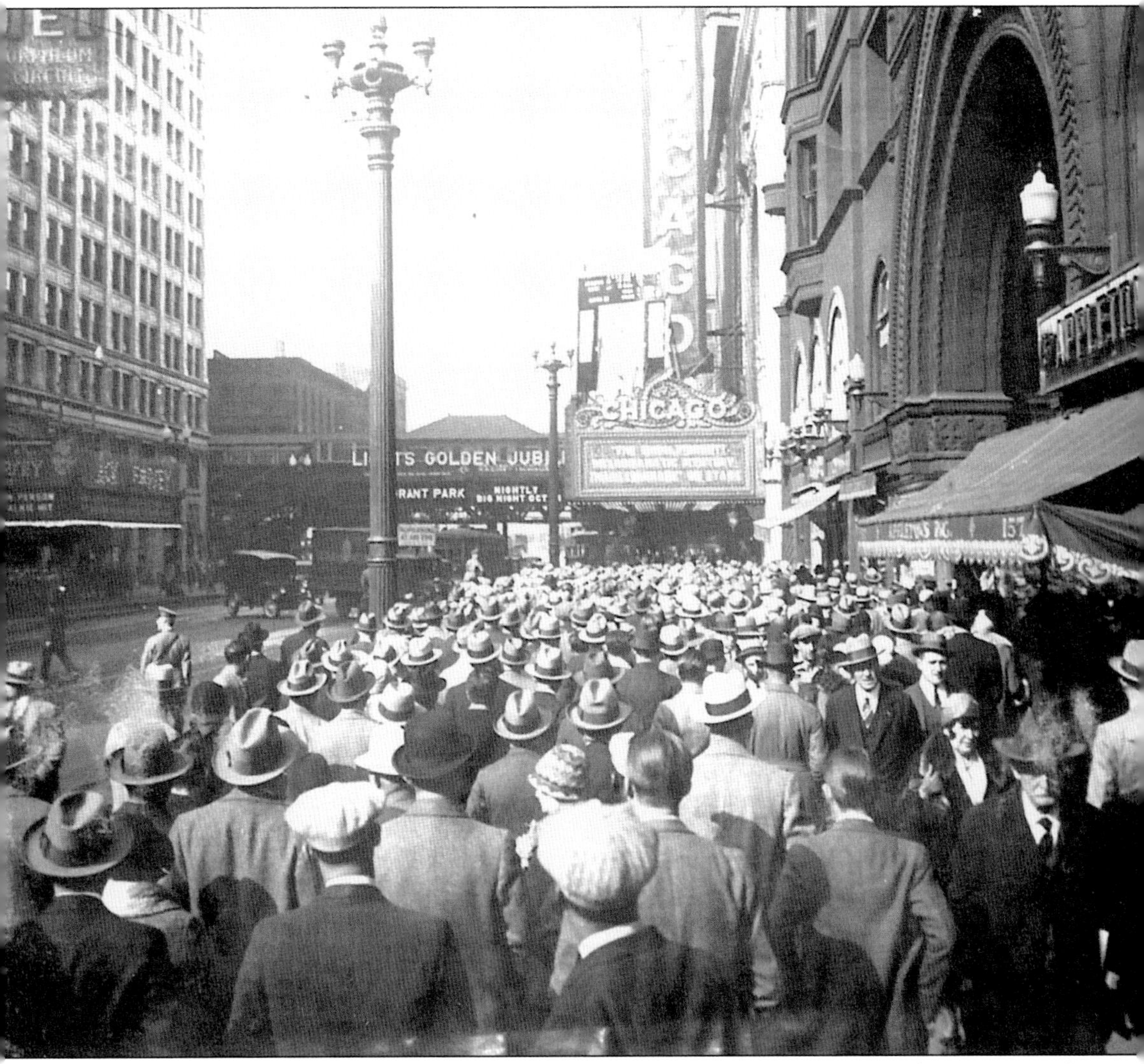

The Balaban and Katz Corporation helped make State Street the center of Chicago. Here the busy, vibrant daily crowds collect outside the Chicago Theatre in the mid-1920s. In 1925, the Chicago Theatre alone hosted more than four million eager patrons. (Photograph courtesy of Chicago Theatre Collection.)

One

The Old Neighborhood

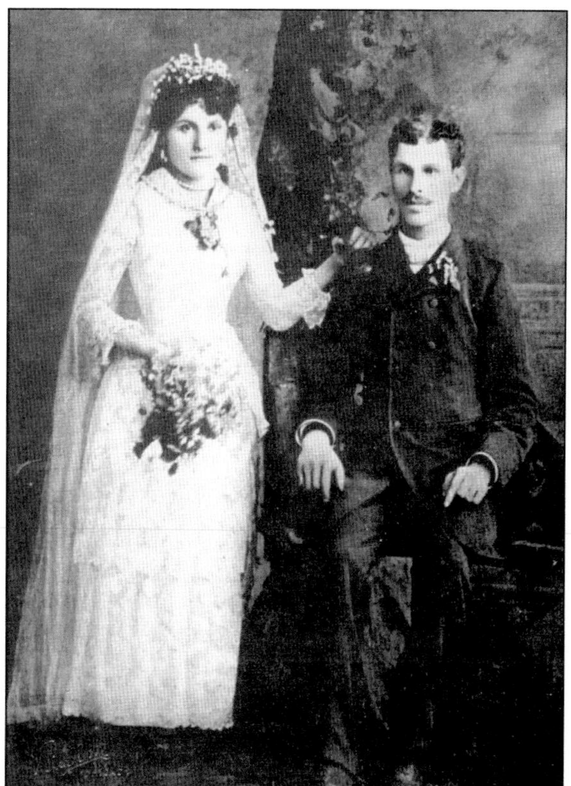

Augusta (Gussie) Mendeburskey married Israel Balaban in Odessa, Russia, in 1886. Israel had been drafted into the czar's army, and they escaped by swimming across a river. They traveled to America by boat, which some say was full of bananas. They moved to Chicago's Maxwell Street neighborhood and opened a small grocery store. They lived in a four-room apartment in the back with their eight children. It was not uncommon for Israel to gently carry one of his children to bed if they had fallen asleep on the pickle barrels in the crowded store. There had actually been ten Balaban children, but Anna died at six months old, and another boy arrived stillborn. Tragically, according to A. J. Balaban's memoirs, Gussie went into labor early with the ninth child after a large case of canned goods fell on her in their food store. (Photograph courtesy of Cherry Robins.)

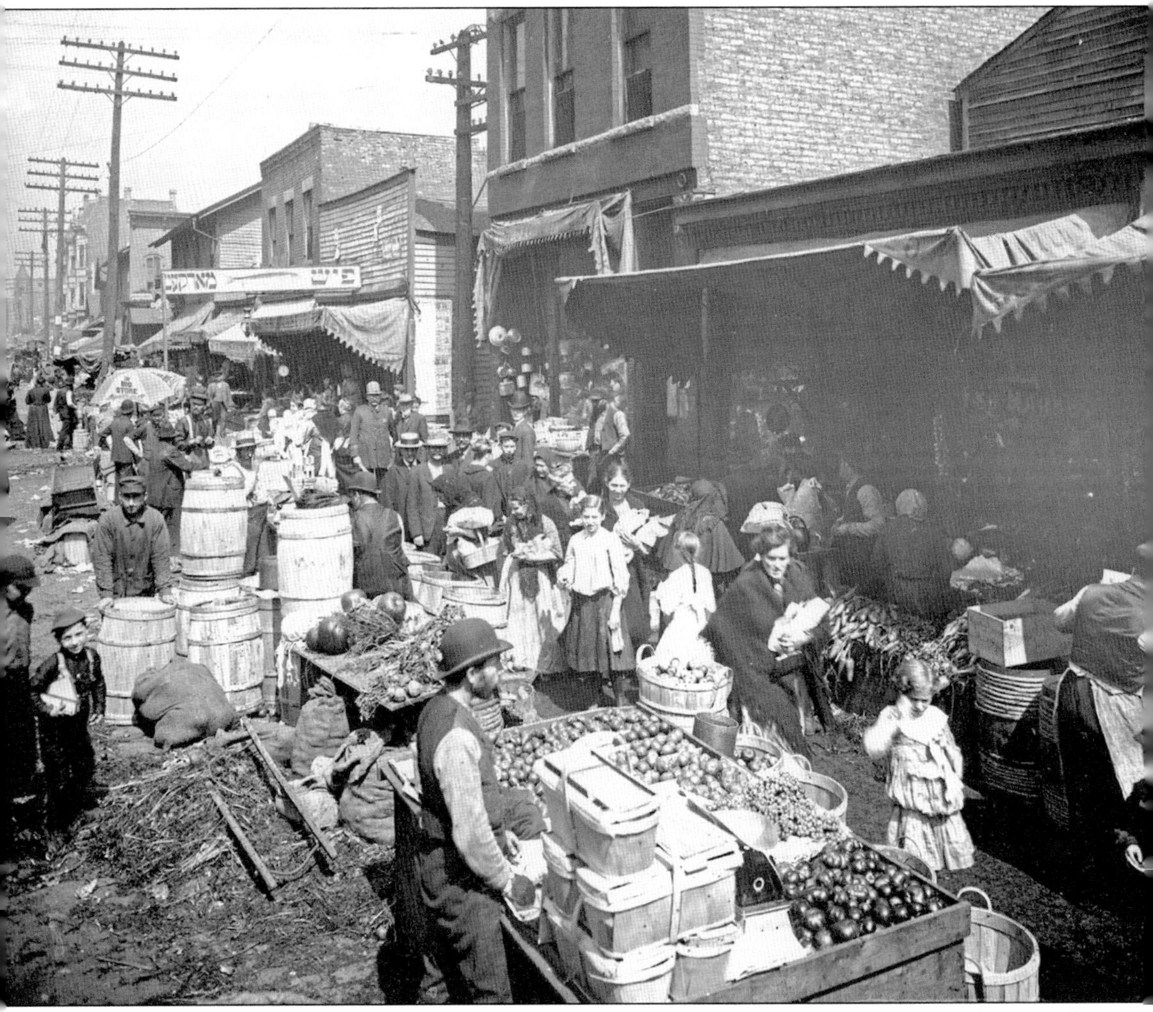

The historic Maxwell Street neighborhood is where the Balaban and Katz story began. The Maxwell Street neighborhood, according to Lori Grove's book *Maxwell Street*, was officially created by a Chicago city ordinance in 1912. Though, the first residences were documented here in the 1860s. It was located on the south side of the city, south of Twelfth Street and west of the Chicago River. It was largely inhabited by Jewish families from Eastern Europe who set up small shops along Maxwell Street, and Jefferson Street in particular, to sell food and dry goods. The Maxwell Street market survived and flourished for nearly a century. As time went on, it became a center for African American culture and music. In the 1950s and 1960s, the Dan Ryan Expressway was built, and a large section of the neighborhood was torn down. In 1990, the University of Illinois decided to expand its south campus into the neighborhood. The market was then moved to nearby Canal Street, and the university began to buy properties and tear them down. The loss of these buildings brought great sadness and was deemed a great loss, especially to those citizens who have traced their heritage to this once vital section of American history. (Photograph courtesy of Chicago Historical Society, ICHi-19155 by Barnes-Crosby.)

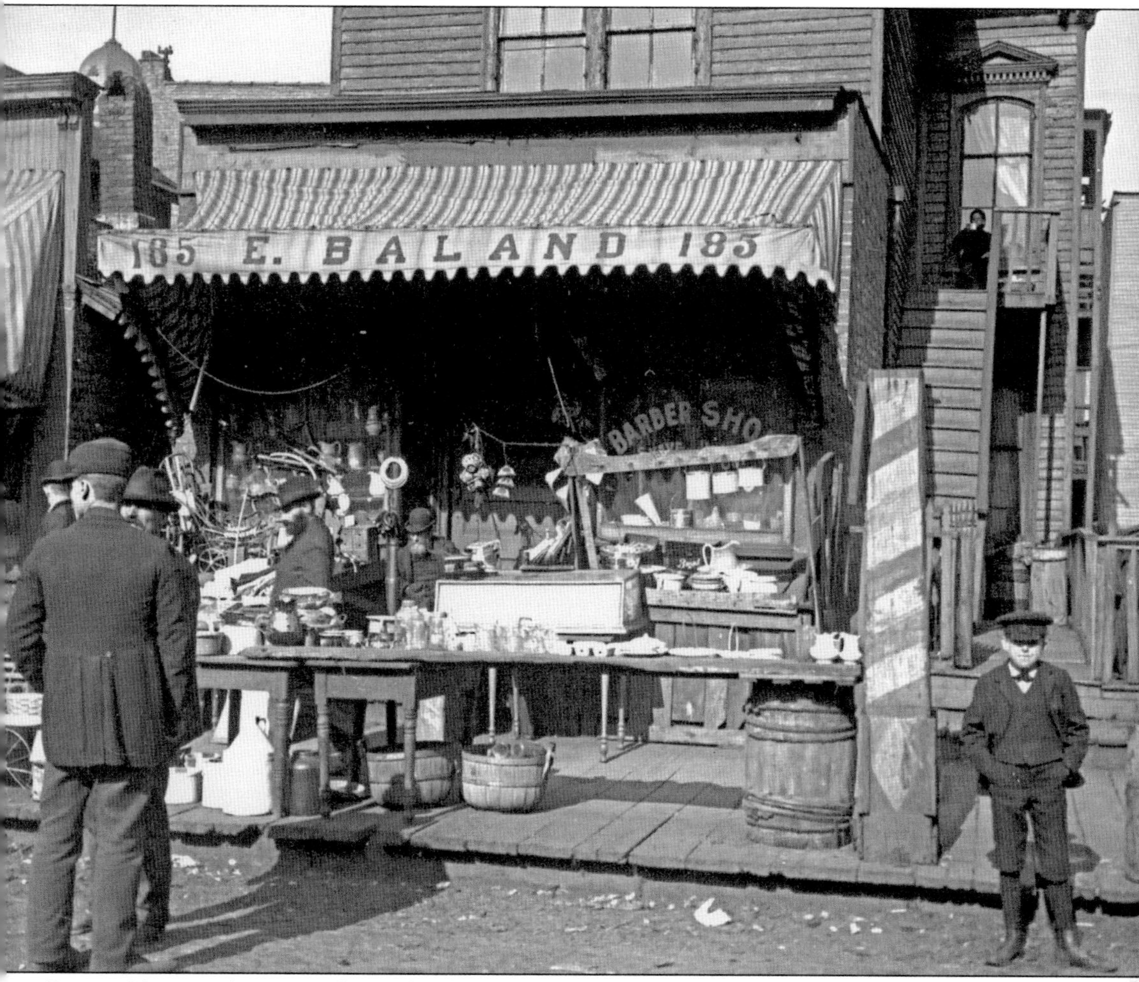

Pictured here is the store of E. Baland at 185 Jefferson Street. Baland built an addition to his wooden home to accommodate the huge crowds at street level. (Photograph courtesy of Chicago Historical Society, ICHi-34418 by Charles R. Clark, 1906.)

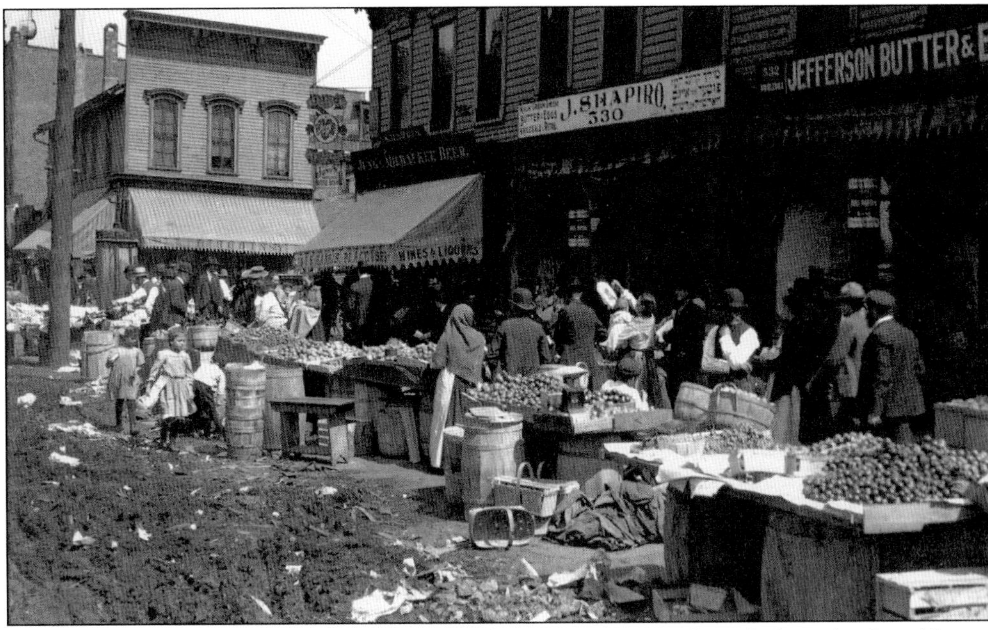

Sam Harris's saloon and the Jefferson butter and eggs store are seen here. Judging by the addresses of these businesses, which are in the 500s, the Balaban store (1137 South Jefferson Street) was about six blocks from here. Notice the crowds squeezing between the on-street fruit stand and the unpaved road—it must have been quite a mess on rainy days. (Photograph courtesy of Chicago Historical Society, ICHi-34422 by Charles R. Clark, 1906.)

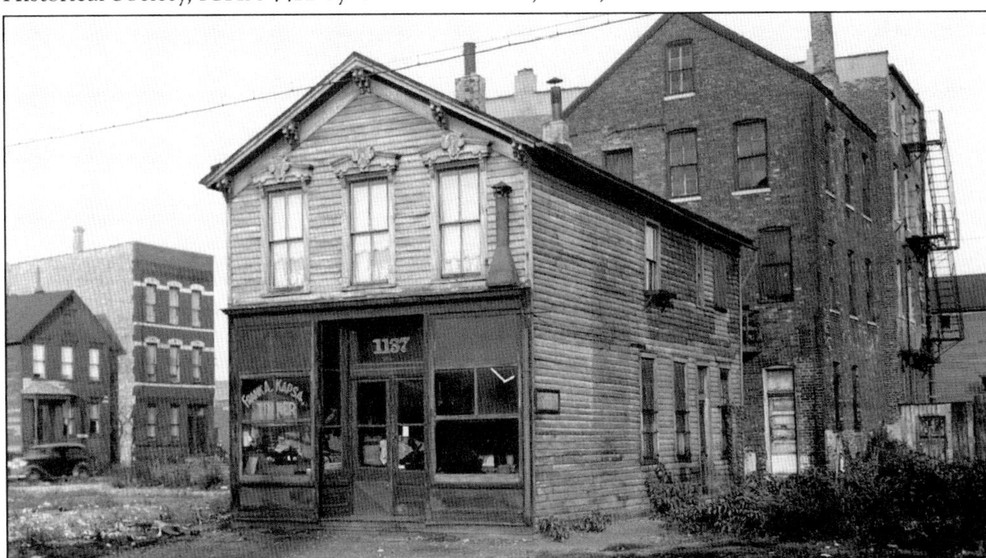

The Balabans lived on the first floor of this two-story clapboard structure at 1137 South Jefferson Street. It was the home of Gussie and Israel Balaban and their eight children: Barney, Abraham, John, David, Max, Elmer, Harry, and Ida. Gussie and Israel Balaban operated a busy grocery and fish store in the front room. Israel had a habit of generously extending credit to his customers, who often ran up tabs they could not pay. Financial problems created a lot of stress for the entire Balaban family, and food vendors were always threatening to stop deliveries. (Photograph courtesy of Theatre Historical Society of America and Rachel Balaban.)

Two

The Balaban and Katz Family Circle

In 1907, Abraham, or A. J., Balaban got a job singing at the Kedzie Nickelodeon on Kedzie Avenue and Roosevelt Road. It was a storefront with 100 creaky folding chairs, a bedsheet for a screen, a piano, and an admission box to put nickels in. One day, his brother Barney and their mother, Gussie, went to the theater. Gussie was impressed with the way customers paid on the way in. She told her sons, "This is a great business . . . the business for us. People pay on the way in. No one can owe us any money!" The Balabans pooled their money—less than \$400—and rented the Kedzie for the month. Each available Balaban had a job: Max and Barney worked the box office, Ida and A. J. played music, John stood outside and announced the shows to the crowds, and Israel cleaned the theater. Seen here is a page from the February 27, 1929, edition of *Variety* magazine, dedicated to A. J. Balaban. Many articles written by A. J.'s closest associates, including Frank Cambria and Morris Sachs, are featured in this issue. (Image courtesy of Reed Business Information.)

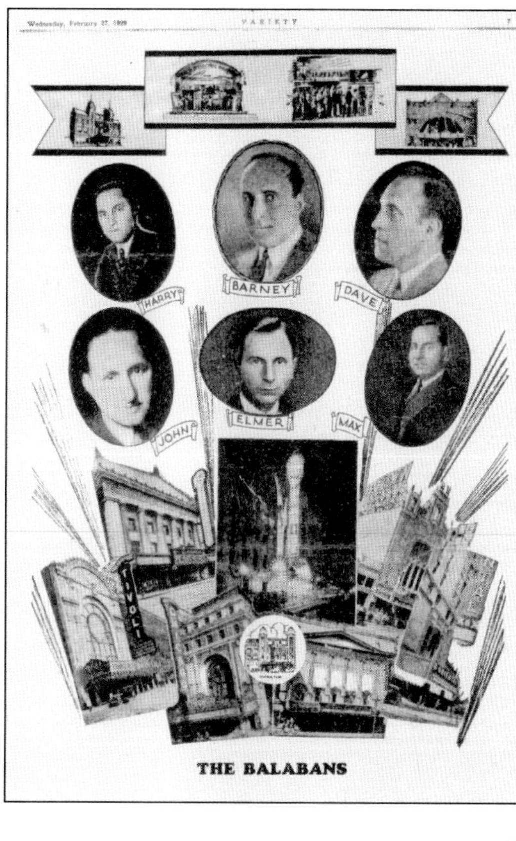

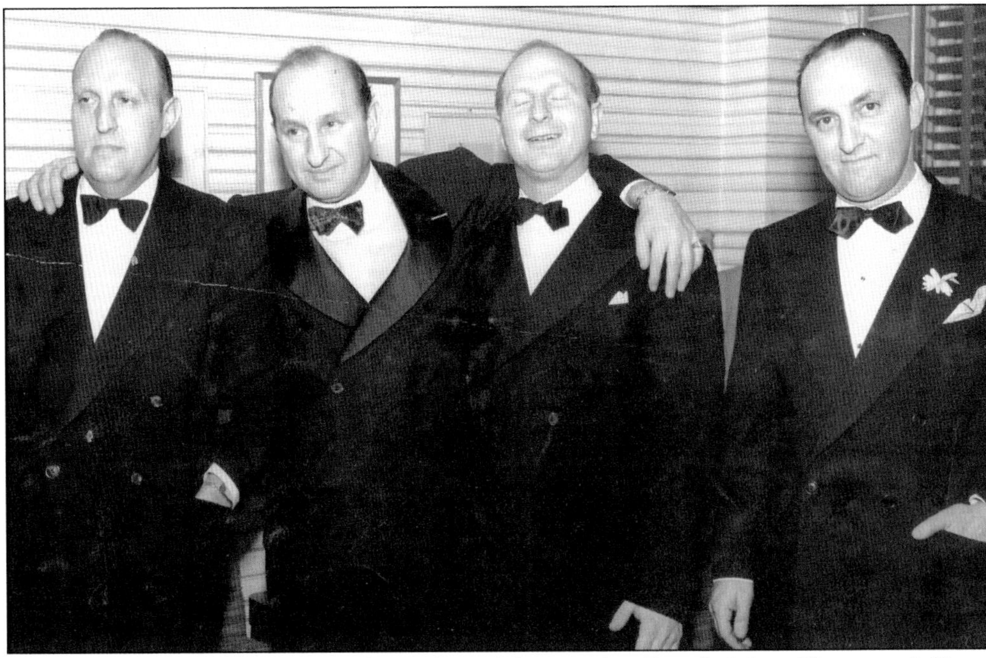

Pictured above are Balaban brothers, from left to right, David, John, Elmer, and Harry. (Photograph courtesy of Bob Balaban.)

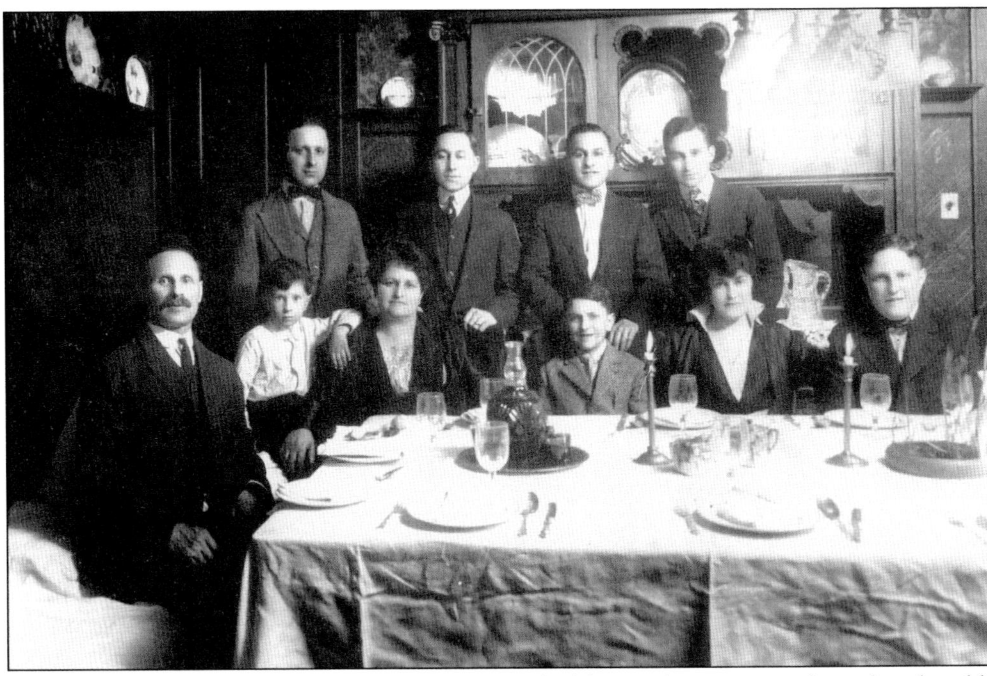

The Balaban family celebrates Passover in 1913. It had been a long journey from their humble beginnings on South Jefferson Street to their relatively luxurious surroundings in their Douglas Boulevard apartment. Pictured from left to right are (first row) Israel, Elmer, Gussie, Harry, Ida, and David; (second row) Barney, Abraham, Max, and John. (Photograph courtesy of Bob Balaban and Chicago Historical Society.)

Israel Balaban was born in 1862 in Odessa, Russia. A very religious Jew, he served as president of the congregation of Beth Hamedrosh Hagodol in Chicago until his death. He was also director of the Union and Orthodox Congregation and a member of the Board of the Hebrew Theological College in Chicago. During his lifetime, Israel experienced tremendous joy as his whole family achieved financial independence and notoriety by virtually controlling the movie theater business in Chicago and the Midwest. He suffered through the incredible loss of his two daughters, Anna and Ida. He died on May 3, 1931, at his home on 3400 Sheridan Road. (Photograph courtesy of Balaban and Katz Historical Foundation.)

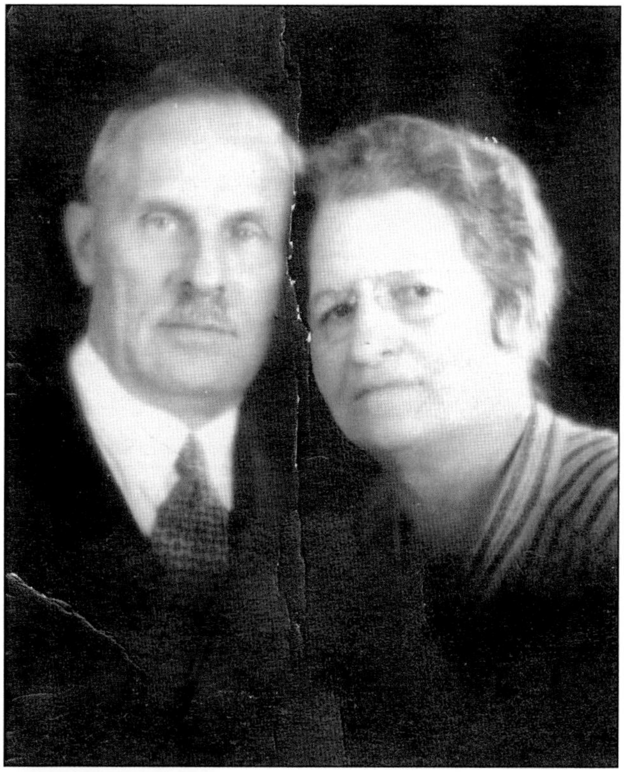

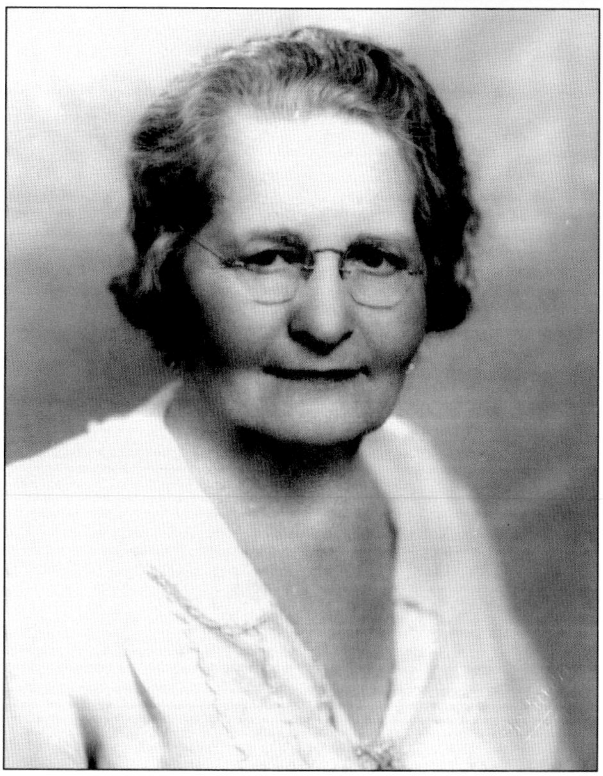

Augusta "Gussie" Balaban (née Mendeburskey) was born in Russia in 1869. She was unwilling to accept a lifestyle of economic suffering in an environment where suffering was the norm. She inspired her children to find creative ways to make money and serve the public need for quality entertainment. Her religious convictions helped her through the tough times and the losses of two of her children. Gussie basked in the light of her children's success. When Israel died in 1931, Gussie moved to Florida. In 1935, she remarried to Max Levin. Gussie returned to Chicago almost every year for the Jewish holidays, and her sons always reserved a spot for her in the temple. She died on February 13, 1936. (Photograph courtesy of Theatre Historical Society of America.)

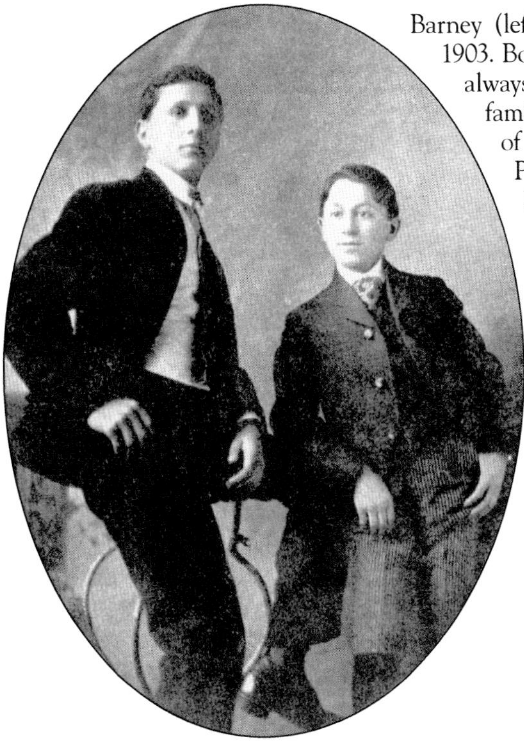

Barney (left) and Abraham Balaban are seen here in 1903. Both Barney and Abraham were very close and always felt a great sense of responsibility for their family's welfare. Barney would become president of Balaban and Katz and later Paramount Pictures. Abraham would lead Balaban and Katz's live entertainment division, become a vice president for Paramount, and head the Roxy Theater in New York City. (Photograph courtesy of Cherry Robins and Theatre Historical Society of America.)

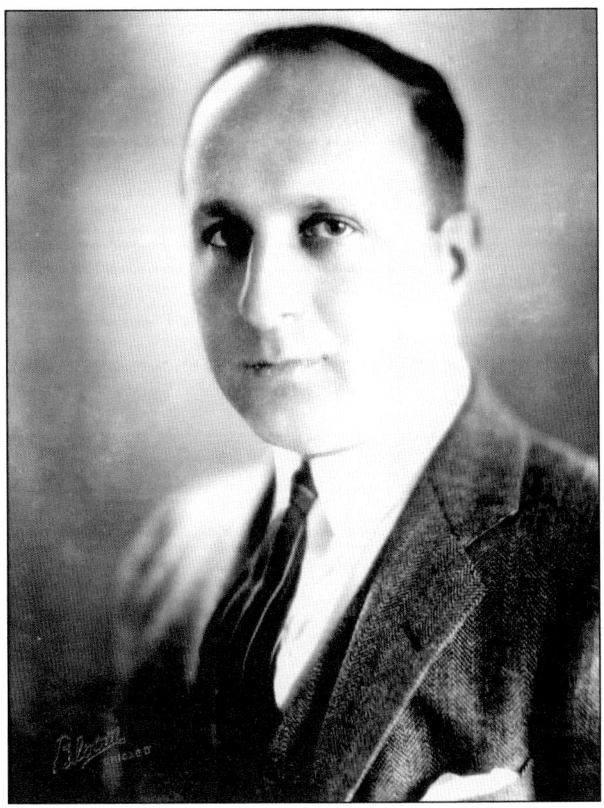

Barney Balaban, born June 8, 1887, was the eldest of the Balaban children. Barney had the privilege of attending school to the seventh grade. At 12, he quit to work as a messenger for Western Union. He also worked as a produce stock boy at a local market and a clerk at a cold storage facility. While Barney worked at the Western Cold Storage facility for $25 a week, his brothers did other jobs to bring money in to the family. It was Barney's idea to use the cooling technology in the meat freezers to cool the patrons at the Balaban movie theaters. (Photograph courtesy of Theatre Historical Society of America.)

Barney loved numbers and budget analysis and had a gift for handling financial matters. He is credited with restructuring the Paramount organization to save it from financial peril. He also loved children and was affectionately referred to as "Mr. Barney." Barney married Tillie Urkov in 1929. They had two children, Judith and Leonard. Tillie also had a son from a previous marriage named Burt. Pictured here are Barney, his wife Tillie, and their son Leonard. Barney was president of Paramount Pictures from 1936 to 1964. He approved all movie projects. He was very patriotic and believed deeply in making films that supported traditional American values. Barney died March 7, 1971, at the age of 83 in Byram, Connecticut. (Photograph courtesy of Rachel Balaban.)

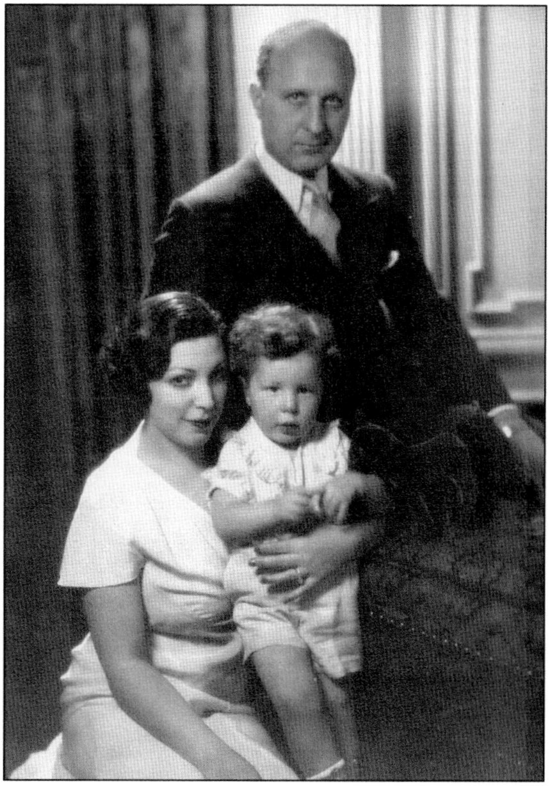

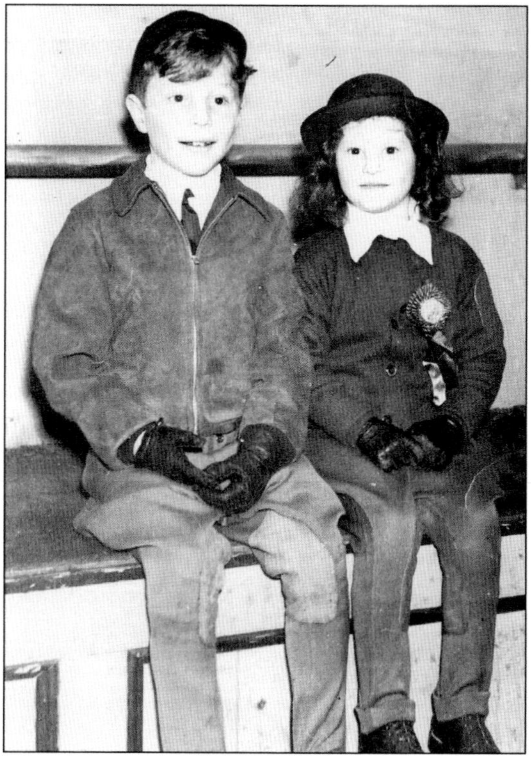

Pictured here are Barney's children Leonard and Judith. Leonard grew up to be a world famous jazz musician. Judith has written several books. (Photograph courtesy of Rachel Balaban.)

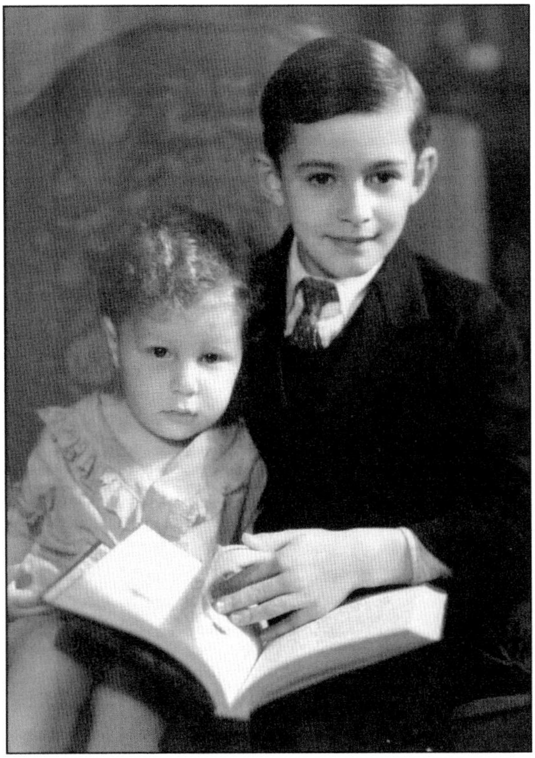

Pictured here are Barney and Tillie's sons Leonard (left) and Burt. Leonard, also known as Red Balaban, owned the jazz club Eddie Condon's in New York City in the 1970s and 1980s. Burt was a film and television producer. (Photograph courtesy of Rachel Balaban.)

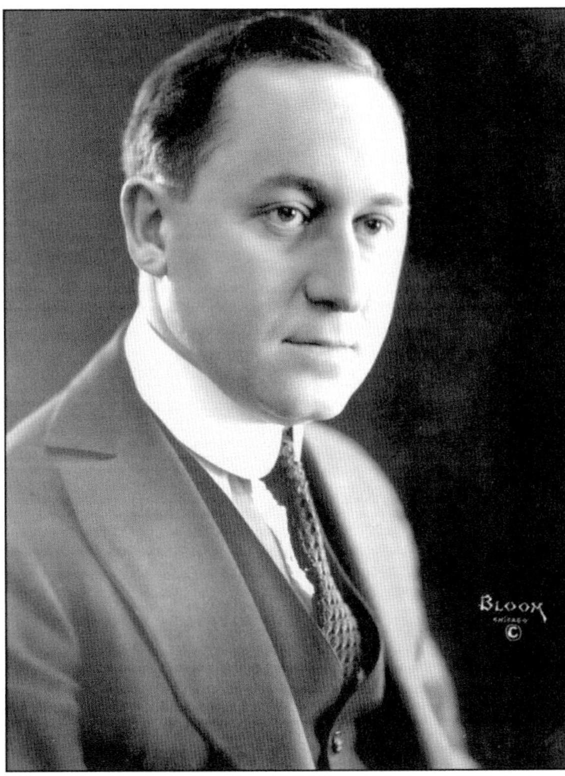

Abraham Joseph Balaban, known as A. J., was born April 20, 1889, the second-eldest son of Gussie and Israel Balaban. He married Carrie, who would always say, "He was such a showman." In her book, *Continuous Performance*, A. J. is revealed as the man behind the Balaban and Katz live shows concept. It was his idea to run live shows and movies continuously from 9:30 a.m. until late at night. He enjoyed the excitement of the curtain rising and the crowd enthusiastically clapping for the beautiful costumes and wonderful performances. A. J. was a purist. He believed that every aspect of the moviegoing experience had to be controlled and perfected. Services like babysitting, convenient show times, and quality stage shows were his vision. He analyzed what the competition was offering and convinced Barney and the others to try different things. (Photograph courtesy of Theatre Historical Society of America.)

Pictured here are A. J. Balaban, his wife Carrie, and an unidentified driver in Florida. After working as a vice president of Paramount in New York for about a year, A. J. decided to leave the business he had helped build. He cashed in a portion of his Paramount stock and moved his family to Geneva, Switzerland, to get back to the simple life. Years later, he returned to America. Though, he did not return to Balaban and Katz or Paramount. He helped his brothers Harry and Elmer build the Esquire Theater, which featured European-style refreshments and short subjects between the standard feature presentations. A. J. became executive manager of the Roxy Theater in New York City. A. J. was a kind and sensitive man. A. J. died in 1962 at his residence in New York City. A. J. was a prime mover in making the movie palace a part of American life. (Photograph courtesy of Cherry Robins.)

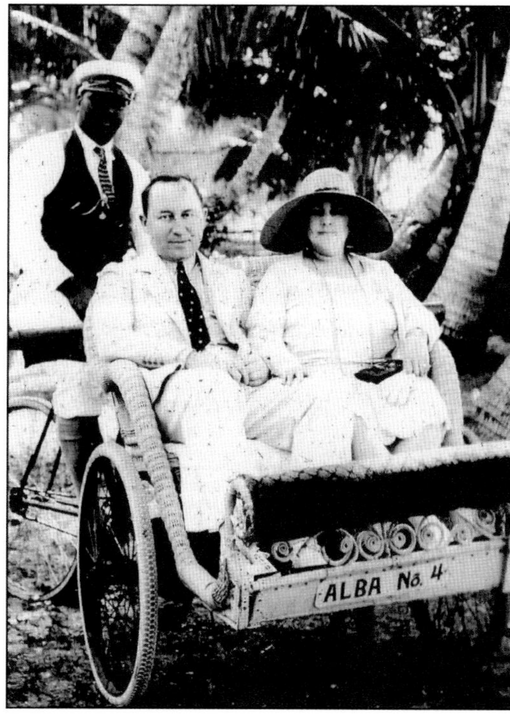

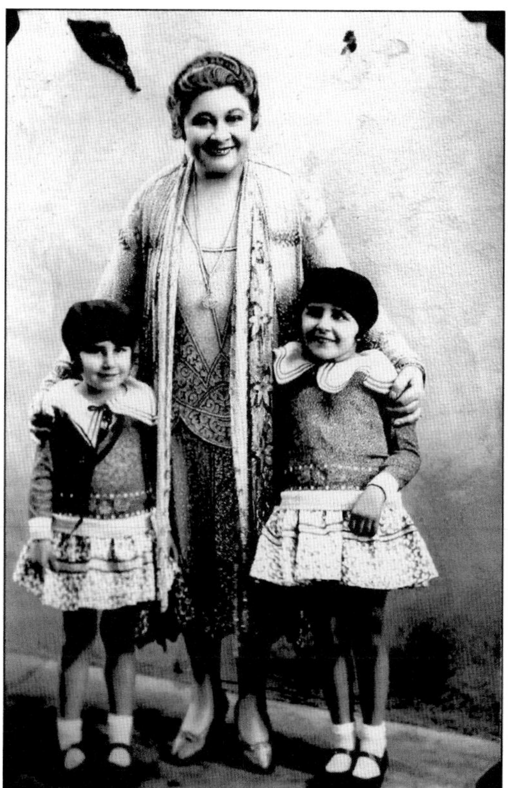

Pictured here in the front are A. J.'s daughters Cherry Blossom (left) and Ida Joy with Sophie Tucker standing in the back. A. J. and Carrie had a son named Bruce a few years later. (Photograph courtesy of Cherry Robins.)

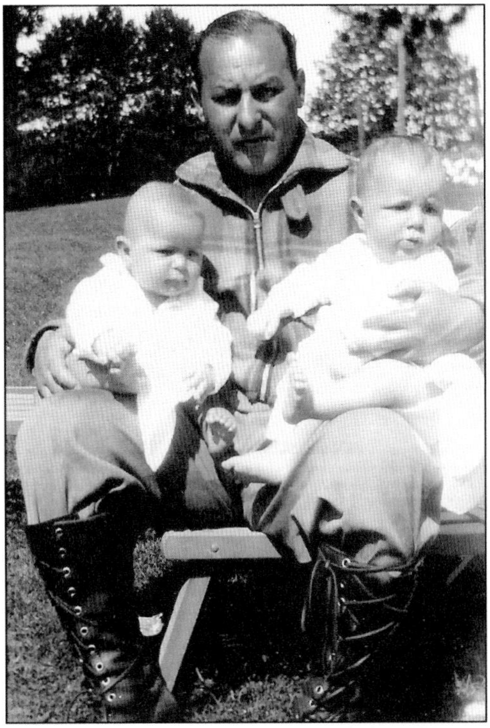

Max Balaban was born in 1893 in Chicago. He was the fourth-oldest child behind Barney, A. J., and Ida. Max loved the movie business. He had helped the family from the very beginning at their first nickelodeon, the Kedzie. Later he was in charge of booking films for a large number of Balaban and Katz theaters. Pictured here, Max holds his daughter Maryann (left) and son Herbert outside their Sheridan Road house in 1931. Herbert grew up to own a well-known restaurant, Balaban's, in St. Louis. (Photograph courtesy of Mathew Balaban.)

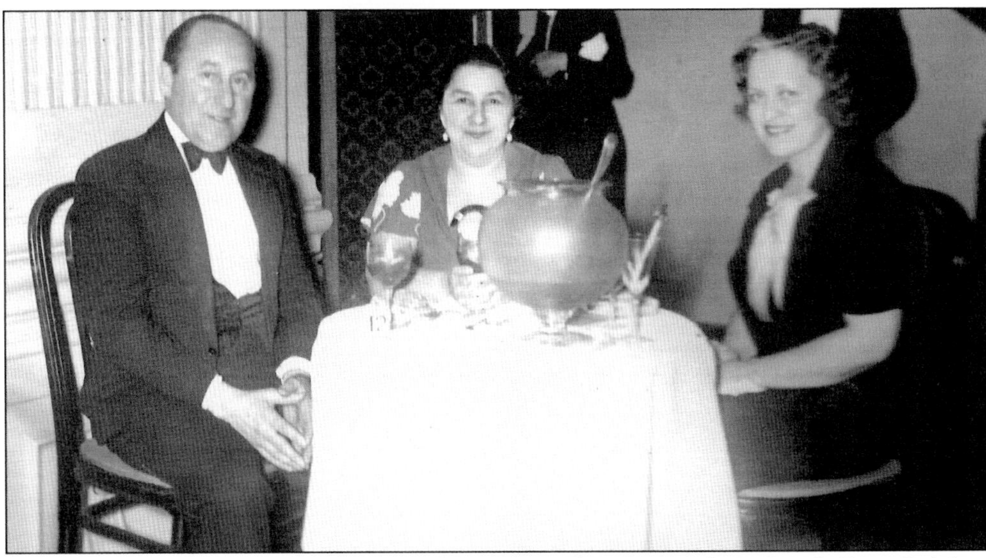

Pictured here from left to right are A. J. Balaban, his wife Carrie, and Max's wife, Dena Balaban. Dena adored Max. She was a professional opera singer. Sadly, Max died on July 18, 1932, from a heart condition when their children were very small. Max was only 39 years old. He and his wife practiced Christian Science and refused most medical treatments. A last-minute operation failed to save his life. A. J. returned from Geneva to be with him during his last month. His passing was an intense shock to the whole Balaban family. He was the first son of Israel and Gussie to pass away. After his death, Dena moved to Europe where she sang professionally. She eventually returned to America when Europe became unstable prior to World War II. (Photograph courtesy of Mathew Balaban.)

John Balaban, born in Chicago in 1894, began his career in 1908 at the Kedzie. He operated a phonograph that played music out onto the street to attract customers. When the family built a small 750-seat theater across the street named the Circle, John worked as an usher. His brothers began to build and operate other theaters, and John became a movie salesman, licensing motion pictures. When the Central Park Theatre was about to open in 1917, his brothers and their partners, Sam and Morris Katz, asked him to manage it. He agreed and remained there until 1920. He then transferred to the Tivoli Theatre and later managed the Southtown Theatre. John became a corporate officer in 1925. His office was in the Chicago Theatre building on State Street with his brothers'. When Barney left for New York in 1936 to become president of Paramount, John was put in charge of Balaban and Katz in Chicago. John was the most visible Balaban, representing the proud Balaban and Katz reputation for elegant movie palaces and exciting live shows. He married Bertha Bruder in 1916. They had two children, Ida and Billy. John Balaban died on April 4, 1957. (Photograph courtesy of Theatre Historical Society of America.)

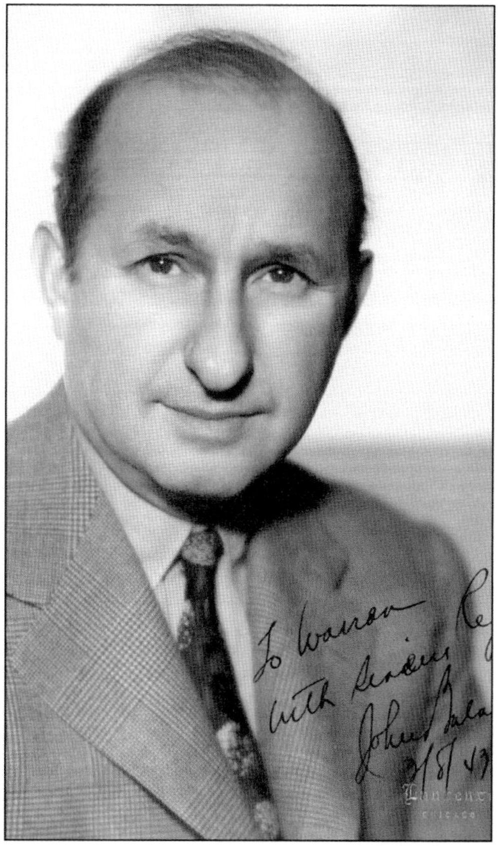

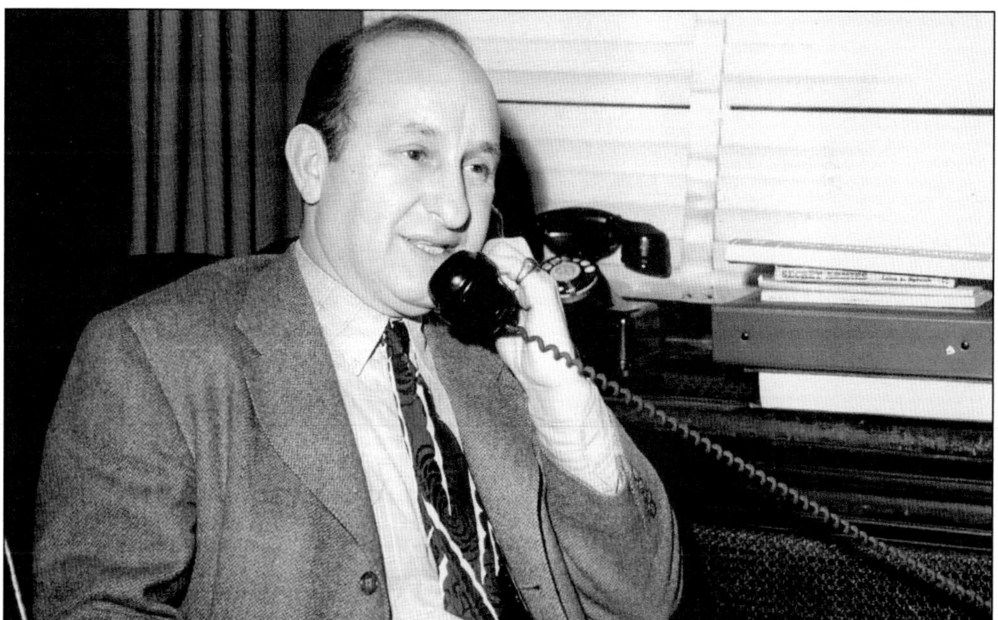

Pictured here is John Balaban conducting important B and K business. (Photograph courtesy of Balaban and Katz Historical Foundation.)

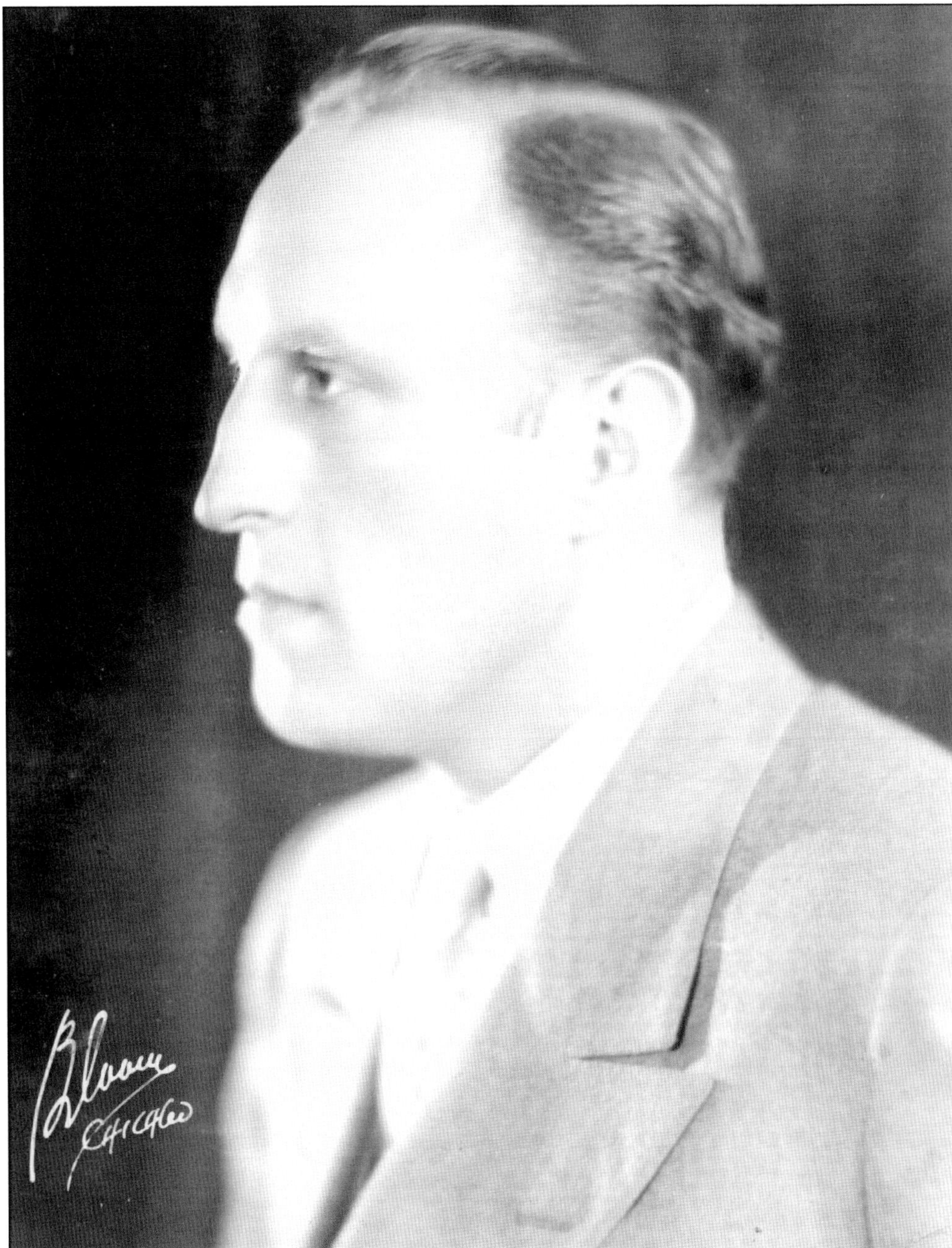

David Balaban had many jobs in the Balaban and Katz organization. He was born in 1897 as the middle child of seven Balaban brothers. He began his career in 1919 as the manager of the Riviera Theatre. He also managed the Uptown a few doors down. Later on, in the 1920s, he managed the Norshore. The last job he had with Balaban and Katz was as director of theater operations for all the Chicago theaters. He died suddenly on June 2, 1949, of a bleeding ulcer in Highland Park, Illinois. David was known for his sense of humor and fairness, and he loved to golf. The author was named after him by his parents, Max and Roslyn Balaban, but unfortunately never got to meet him. (Photograph courtesy of Theatre Historical Society of America.)

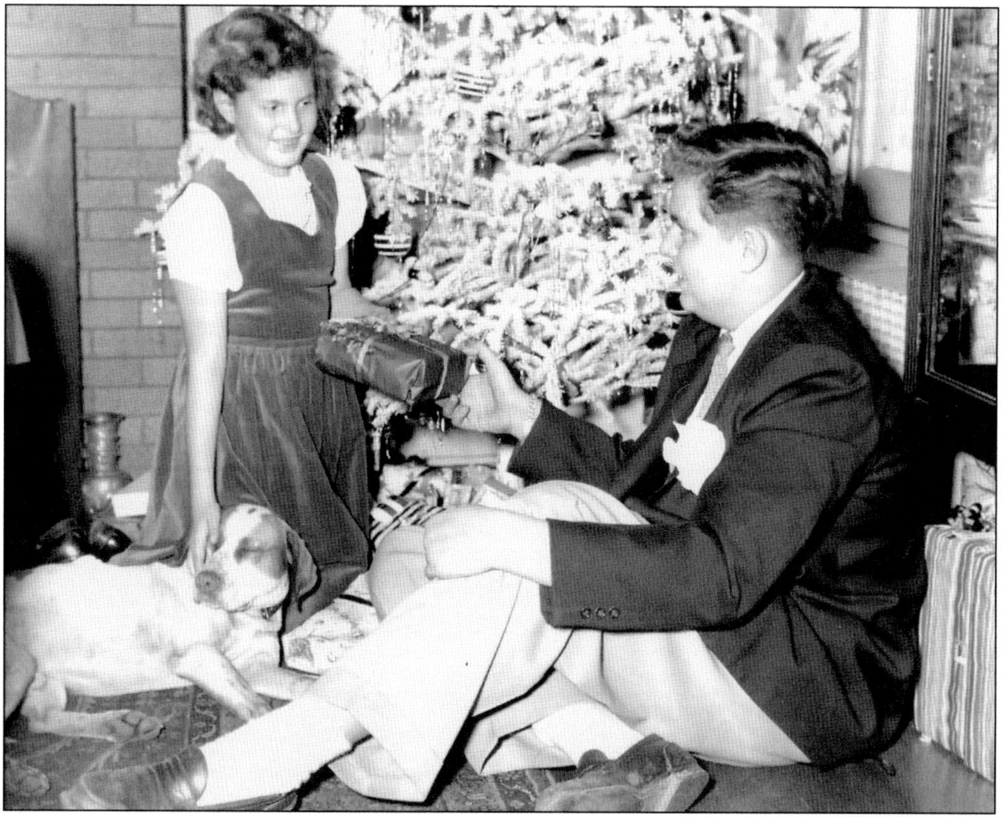

This photograph is of two of David's children, Gail and Max Balaban. (Photograph courtesy of Gail Scalamonti.)

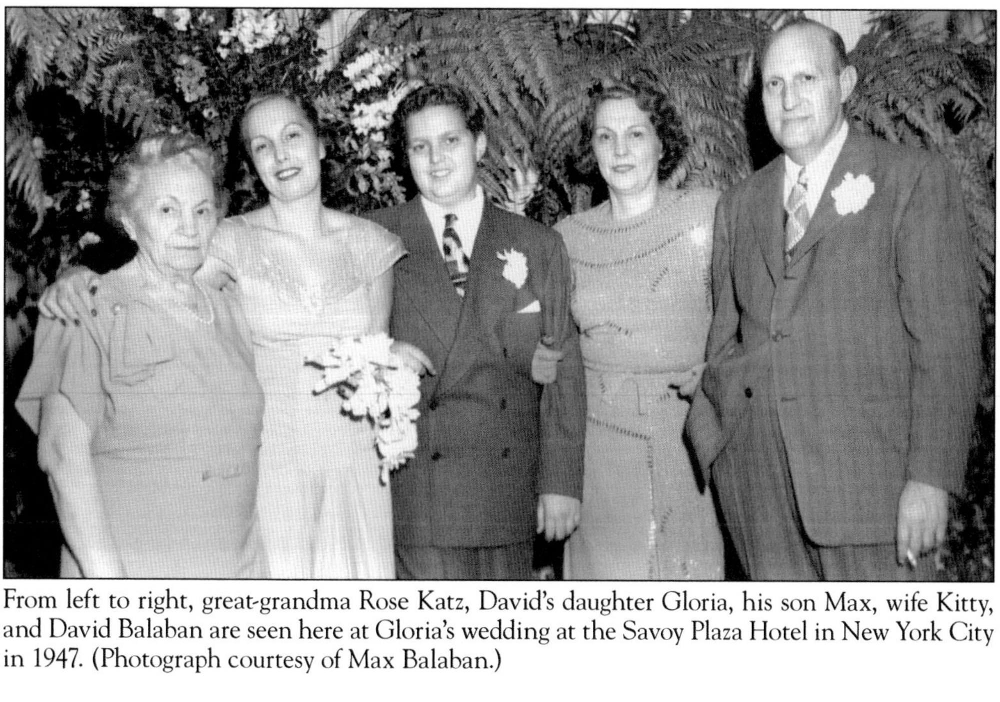

From left to right, great-grandma Rose Katz, David's daughter Gloria, his son Max, wife Kitty, and David Balaban are seen here at Gloria's wedding at the Savoy Plaza Hotel in New York City in 1947. (Photograph courtesy of Max Balaban.)

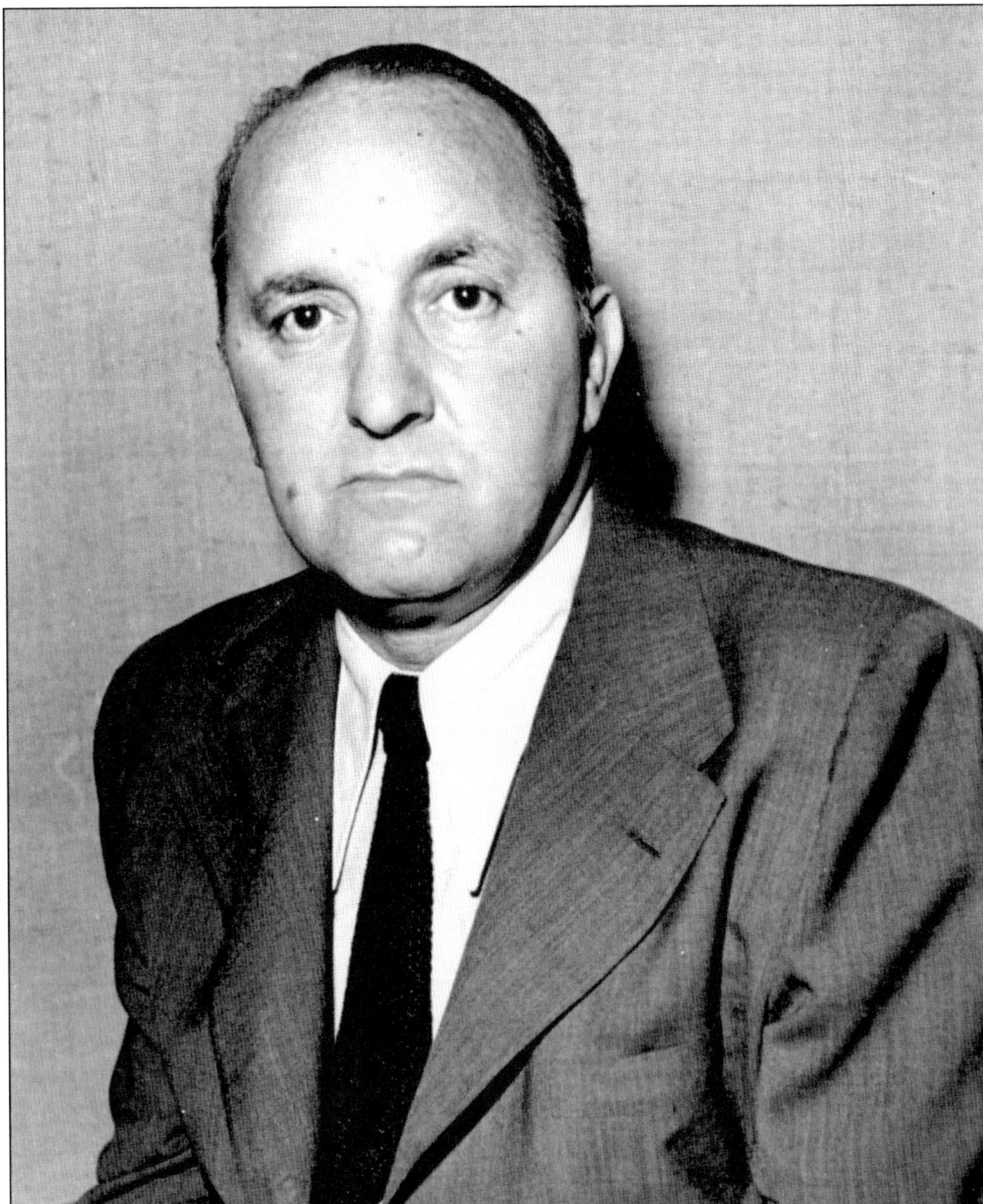

Harry Balaban was born on July 7, 1903, in Chicago. He was the second-youngest child of Gussie and Israel Balaban. He was a partner in H and E Balaban Corporation with his brother Elmer. He was responsible for the building and maintenance of the theaters. He married Marion Rice, who had once been a silent film actress for Universal Pictures. One of her pictures was called *The Call of the Heart*. She used the stage name Joan Alden. Harry and Marion had two children, Richard and Barbara. Richard describes his father as down-to-earth and generous. When his brother David Balaban died in 1949, Harry gave David's son Max his loving support. He was a kind, quiet man, and he also loved to golf. He gave a lot of his time and resources to local Chicago charities, including La Rabida Children's Hospital. Harry died on March 19, 1985. (Photograph courtesy of Quigley Photographic Archive, Georgetown University Library, Special Collections Division.)

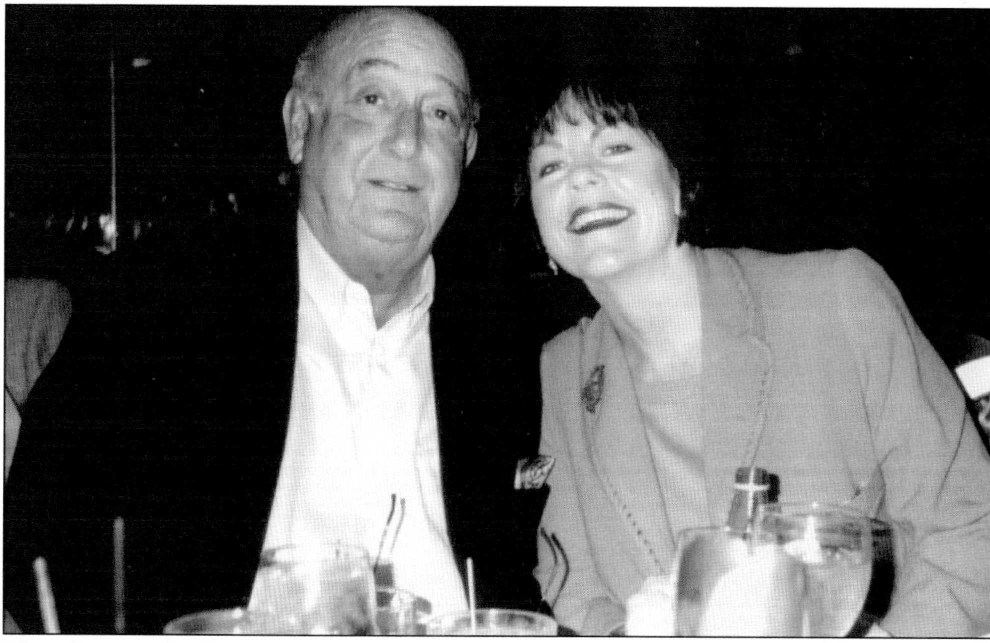

This photograph of Harry's son, Richard (Dick), and his wife Kathi Balaban was taken in the mid-1990s. (Photograph courtesy of Richard Balaban.)

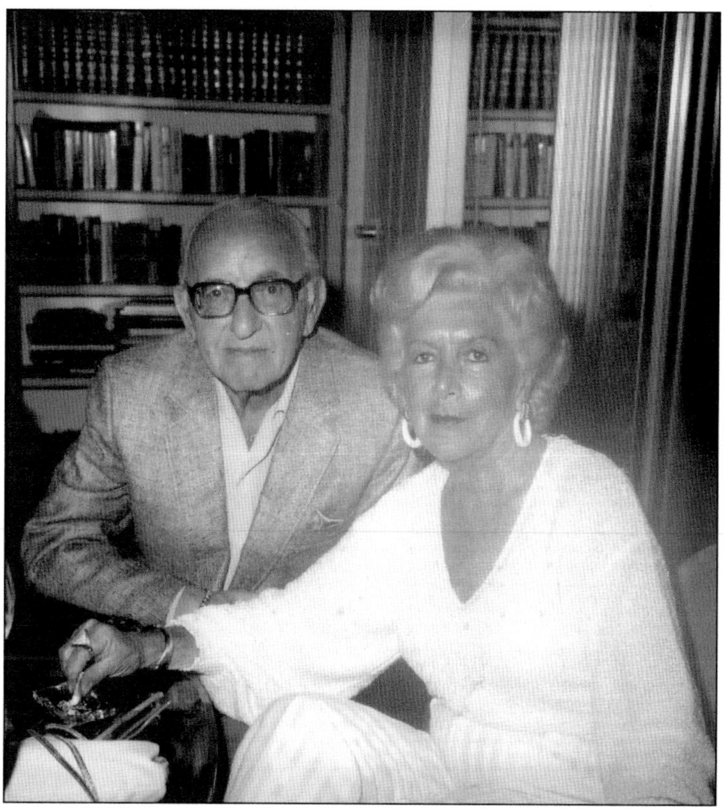

This photograph of Harry and Marion Balaban was taken in the mid-1980s. (Photograph courtesy of Richard Balaban.)

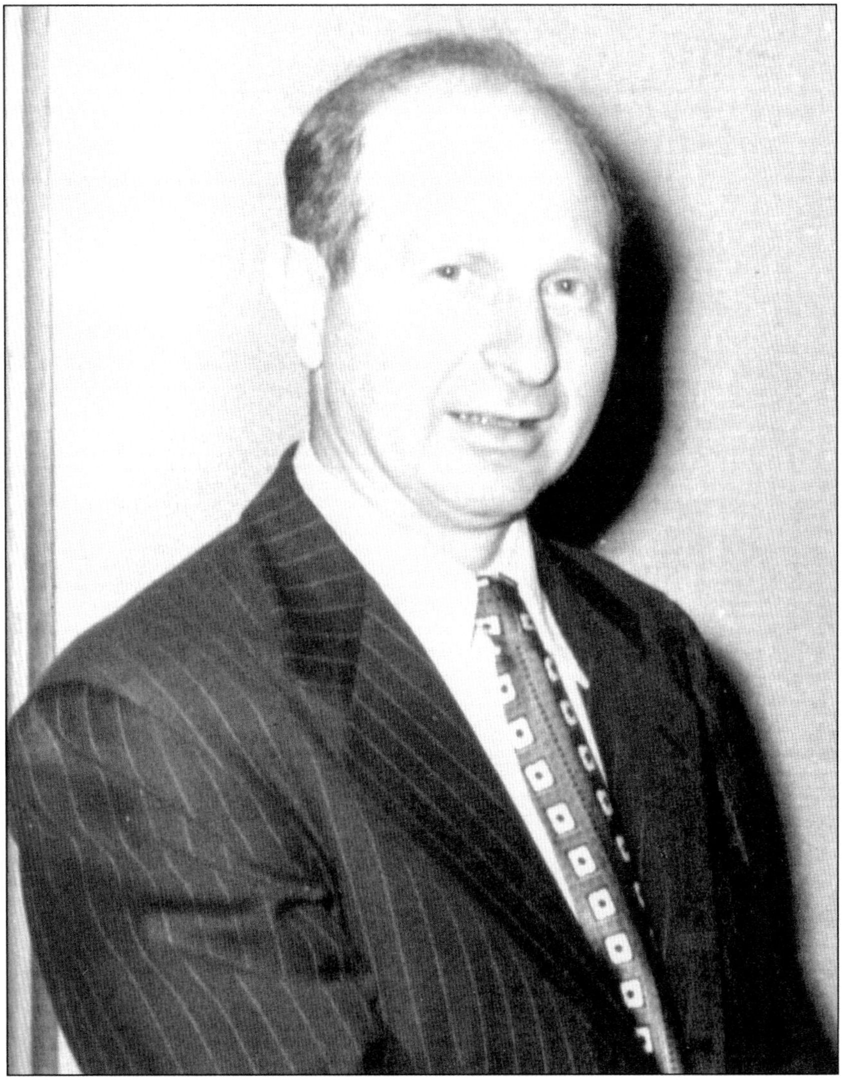

The youngest child of Gussie and Israel Balaban, Elmer Balaban was born in 1909, 22 years after Barney. He was just seven years old when B and K formed in 1916. Elmer owned stock in the family business, but he and his brother Harry were not officially employed by the firm. He graduated from the Wharton School of Business at the University of Pennsylvania in 1931. Elmer and Harry started their own movie theater company, H and E Balaban Corporation, and built or acquired a dozen or so theaters in Illinois and Detroit. Their most famous theater, the Esquire on Oak Street in Chicago, was designed by architect William L. Pereira, who patterned it after buildings erected for the Century of Progress Exposition 1933–1934. In its first year of operation, the Esquire held the Chicago premiere of *Gone with the Wind*. Elmer and Harry also wisely invested in television licenses before many knew what television was. They sold most of their theaters in the 1950s and bought many television and radio stations. Elmer's cable-television company, Plains Television, provided service to remote rural areas of the United States. Elmer's wife Elenore died in 1987. They had two daughters, Susan and Nancy, and a son named Bob, who is now a well-known actor, film director, author, and producer. Elmer died on November 2, 2001, in Chicago at the age of 92. (Photograph courtesy of Quigley Photographic Archive, Georgetown University Library, Special Collections Division.)

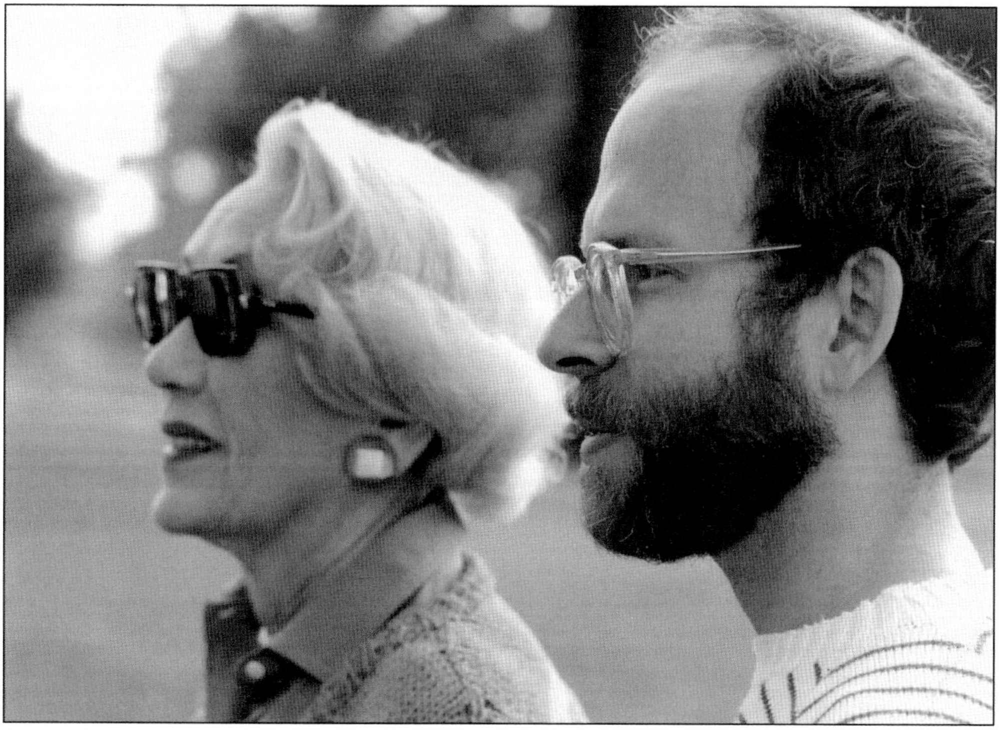

Pictured here is Elmer's wife, Elenore, with their son, Bob. (Photograph courtesy of Bob Balaban.)

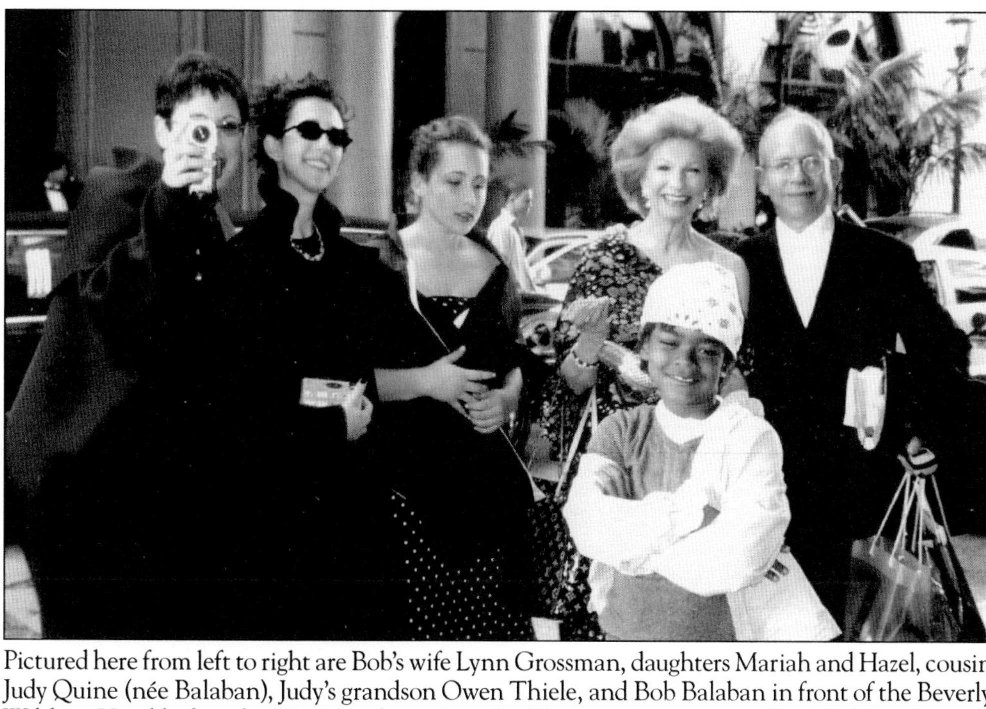

Pictured here from left to right are Bob's wife Lynn Grossman, daughters Mariah and Hazel, cousin Judy Quine (née Balaban), Judy's grandson Owen Thiele, and Bob Balaban in front of the Beverly Wilshire Hotel before the 2002 Academy Awards. (Photograph courtesy of Bob Balaban.)

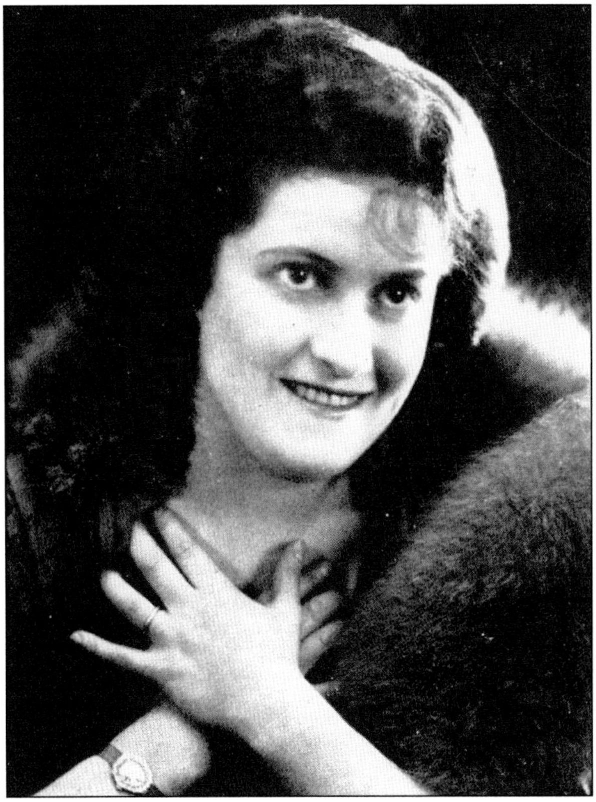

Ida Balaban, the third child of Gussie and Israel, was born in 1891, a year and a half after A. J. As a young lady, she would accompany her brother on the piano while he sang on jobs at parties in Chicago. Sam Katz fell in love with Ida when they first met, and they were married. She died from tuberculosis soon after in 1922. The family was devastated. (Photograph courtesy of Cherry Robins, as it appeared in *Continuous Performance*.)

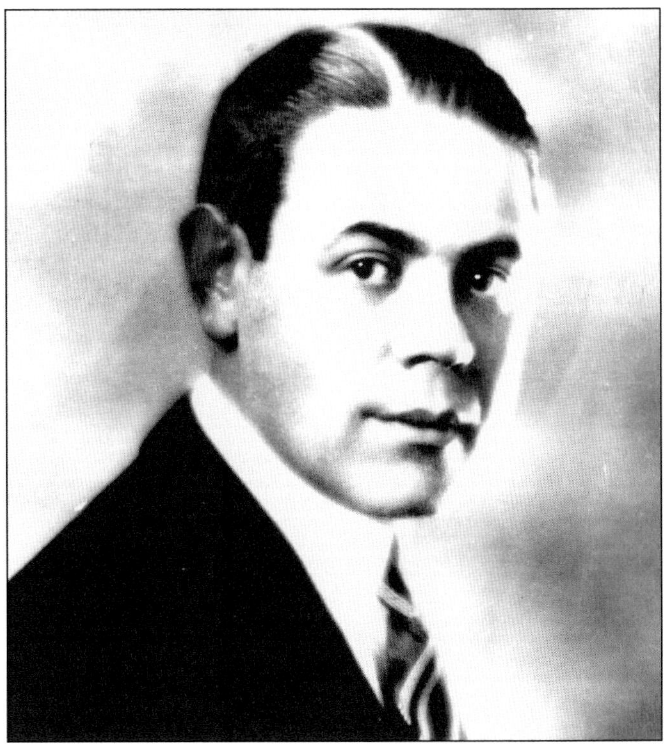

Sam Katz was born in Chicago in 1893. As a teenager, he worked odd jobs, including repairing telephone systems. He frequented nickelodeons, including one on Twelfth Street owned by Carl Laemmle, who eventually founded Universal Studios in Los Angeles. Sam saved enough money to open up his own nickelodeon in an abandoned grocery store, and even though he loved the movie business, he never thought it would be a dependable form of income. He wanted to be a lawyer and financed his way through Northwestern University. (Photograph courtesy of Theatre Historical Society of America.)

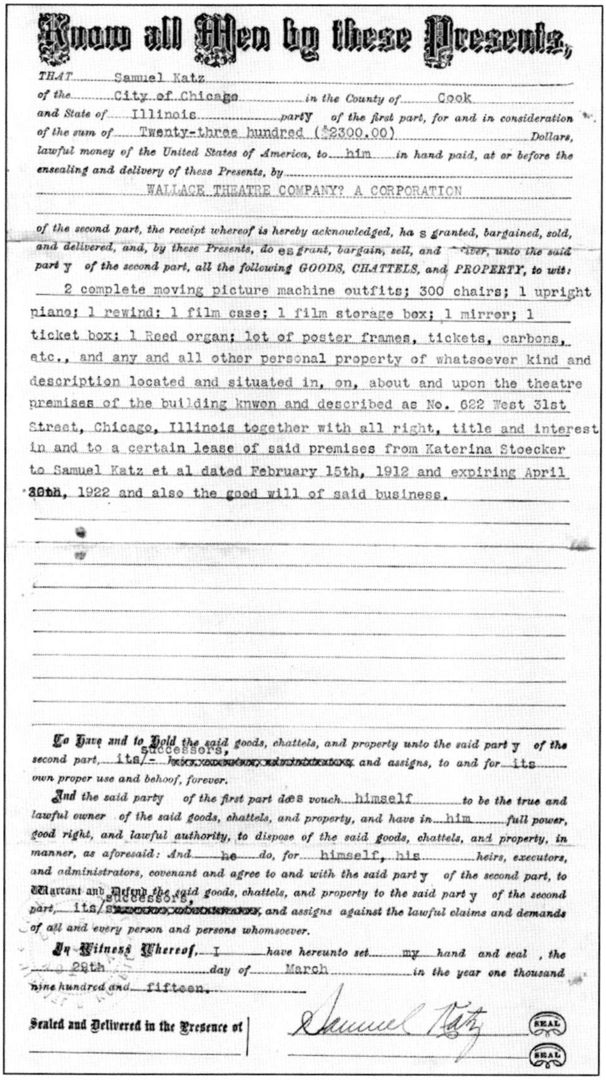

Know all Men by these Presents,

THAT Samuel Katz
of the City of Chicago in the County of Cook
and State of Illinois party of the first part, for and in consideration of the sum of Twenty-three hundred ($2300.00) Dollars,
lawful money of the United States of America, to him in hand paid, at or before the ensealing and delivery of these Presents, by
WALLACE THEATRE COMPANY? A CORPORATION
of the second part, the receipt whereof is hereby acknowledged, has granted, bargained, sold, and delivered, and, by these Presents, does grant, bargain, sell, and deliver, unto the said party of the second part, all the following GOODS, CHATTELS, and PROPERTY, to wit:
2 complete moving picture machine outfits; 300 chairs; 1 upright piano; 1 rewind; 1 film case; 1 film storage box; 1 mirror; 1 ticket box; 1 Reed organ; lot of poster frames, tickets, carbons, etc., and any and all other personal property of whatsoever kind and description located and situated in, on, about and upon the theatre premises of the building knwon and described as No. 622 West 31st Street, Chicago, Illinois together with all right, title and interest in and to a certain lease of said premises from Katerina Stoecker to Samuel Katz et al dated February 15th, 1912 and expiring April 30th, 1922 and also the good will of said business.

To Have and to Hold the said goods, chattels, and property unto the said party of the second part, its/successors, and assigns, to and for its own proper use and behoof, forever.
And the said party of the first part does vouch himself to be the true and lawful owner of the said goods, chattels, and property, and have in him full power, good right, and lawful authority, to dispose of the said goods, chattels, and property, in manner, as aforesaid: And he do, for himself, his heirs, executors, and administrators, covenant and agree to and with the said party of the second part, to Warrant and Defend the said goods, chattels, and property to the said party of the second part, its/successors, and assigns against the lawful claims and demands of all and every person and persons whomsoever.
In Witness Whereof, I have hereunto set my hand and seal, the 29th day of March in the year one thousand nine hundred and fifteen.

Sealed and Delivered in the Presence of

Samuel Katz (SEAL)

(SEAL)

Above is the lease for one of Sam Katz's early theaters in 1915. According to *Continuous Performance*, "A. J. had befriended Sam Katz, who he had met at the offices of the Western Vaudeville agency offices. A. J. and Sam developed the habit of sharing breakfast at a place called Deutches and discussing their dreams. Sam Katz already operated several small theaters with his father." A. J. and Sam brought the idea of merging forces to the rest of their families. The Balaban and Katz partnership was cemented in 1916. Sam Katz was a vice president of Balaban and Katz. Morris Katz, Sam's father, sat on the board of directors. Sam met with bankers and local businessmen to find investors for B and K's newest theater projects. William Wrigley of the famed chewing gum company and John Hertz of the taxicab concern were among those who provided capital for the expansion. Adolf Zukor's Famous Players Lasky Corporation from New York bought a controlling interest in Balaban and Katz in 1926, and Sam moved to New York to head the Publix Theatres Division of the company. Barney Balaban became president of Balaban and Katz. In 1931, Sam offered A. J. a position in New York as a vice president in the Paramount Publix houses to produce movie shorts. Sam managed all aspects of theater operations from the Paramount building in Times Square until 1932 when he was forced to resign. (Lease courtesy of Chicago Jewish Archives of the Spertus Institute of Jewish Studies.)

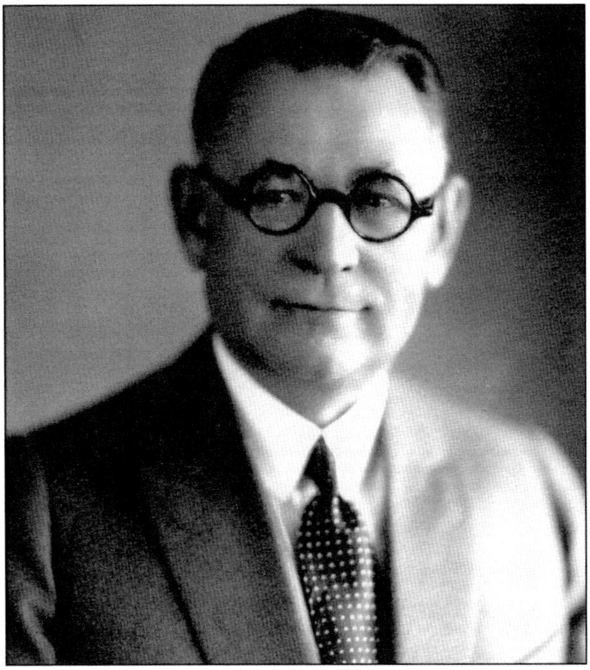

Morris Katz was born July 8, 1869, in Russia. He was the father of Sam Katz and served on the board of directors of Balaban and Katz for the first few years of its existence. (Photograph courtesy of Chicago Jewish Archives of the Spertus Institute of Jewish Studies.)

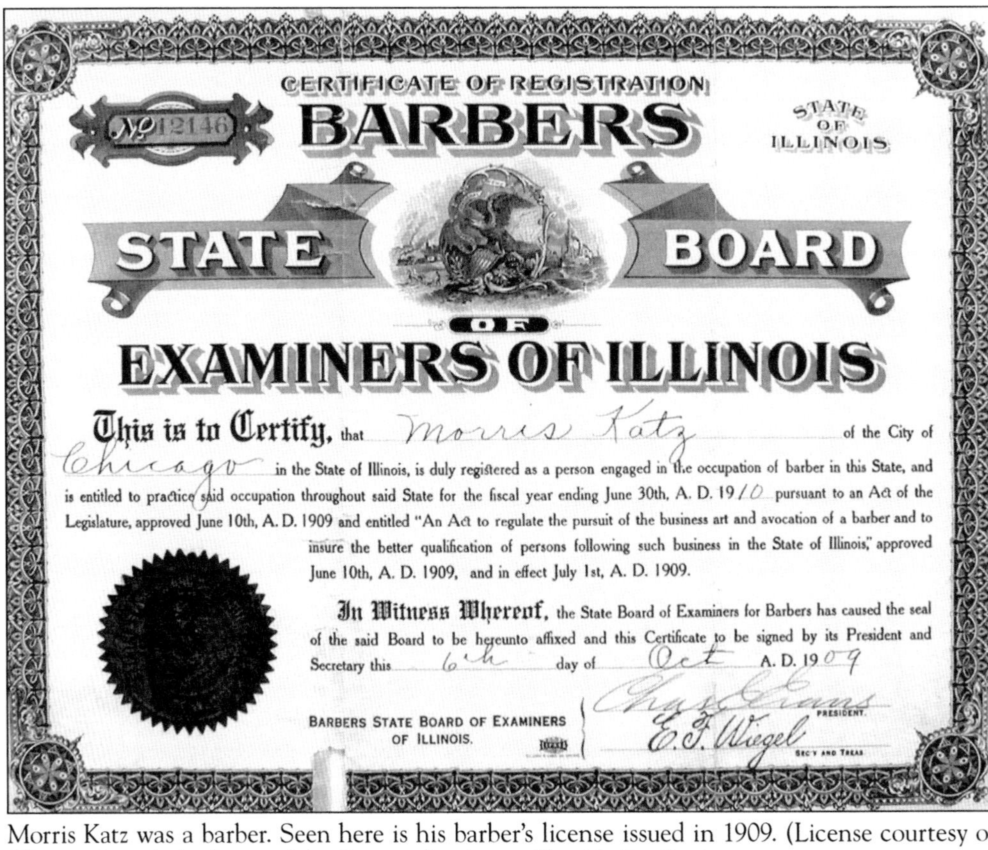

CERTIFICATE OF REGISTRATION

No 12146

BARBERS

STATE OF ILLINOIS

STATE BOARD OF EXAMINERS OF ILLINOIS

This is to Certify, that Morris Katz of the City of Chicago in the State of Illinois, is duly registered as a person engaged in the occupation of barber in this State, and is entitled to practice said occupation throughout said State for the fiscal year ending June 30th, A. D. 1910 pursuant to an Act of the Legislature, approved June 10th, A. D. 1909 and entitled "An Act to regulate the pursuit of the business art and avocation of a barber and to insure the better qualification of persons following such business in the State of Illinois," approved June 10th, A. D. 1909, and in effect July 1st, A. D. 1909.

In Witness Whereof, the State Board of Examiners for Barbers has caused the seal of the said Board to be hereunto affixed and this Certificate to be signed by its President and Secretary this 6th day of Oct A. D. 1909

BARBERS STATE BOARD OF EXAMINERS OF ILLINOIS.

Chas. Evans, PRESIDENT.

E. F. Wiegel, SEC'Y AND TREAS.

Morris Katz was a barber. Seen here is his barber's license issued in 1909. (License courtesy of Chicago Jewish Archives of the Spertus Institute of Jewish Studies.)

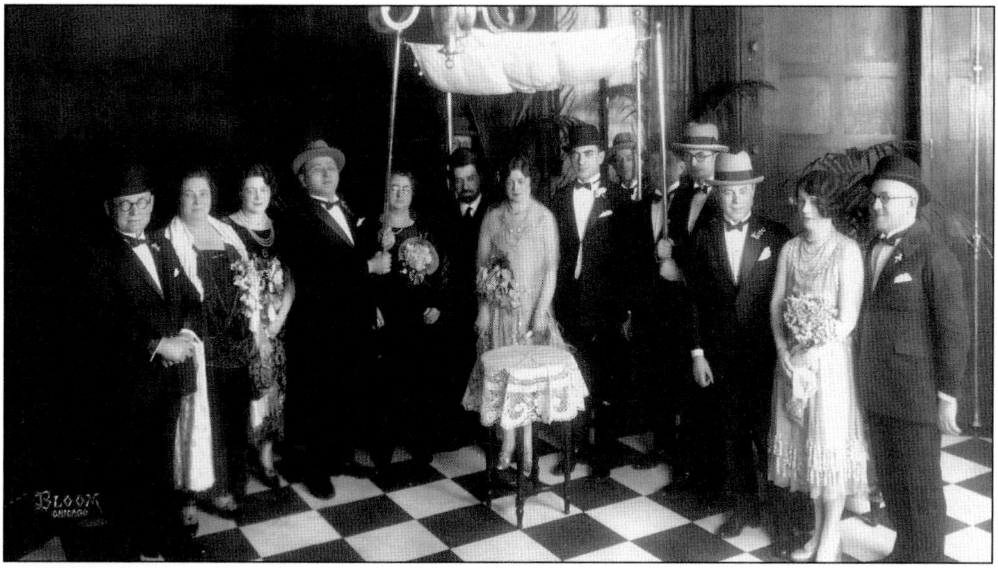

This photograph is of a Katz family wedding. Morris Katz is on the far left, and Sam Katz is the third person from the right. (Photograph courtesy of Chicago Jewish Archives of the Spertus Institute of Jewish Studies.)

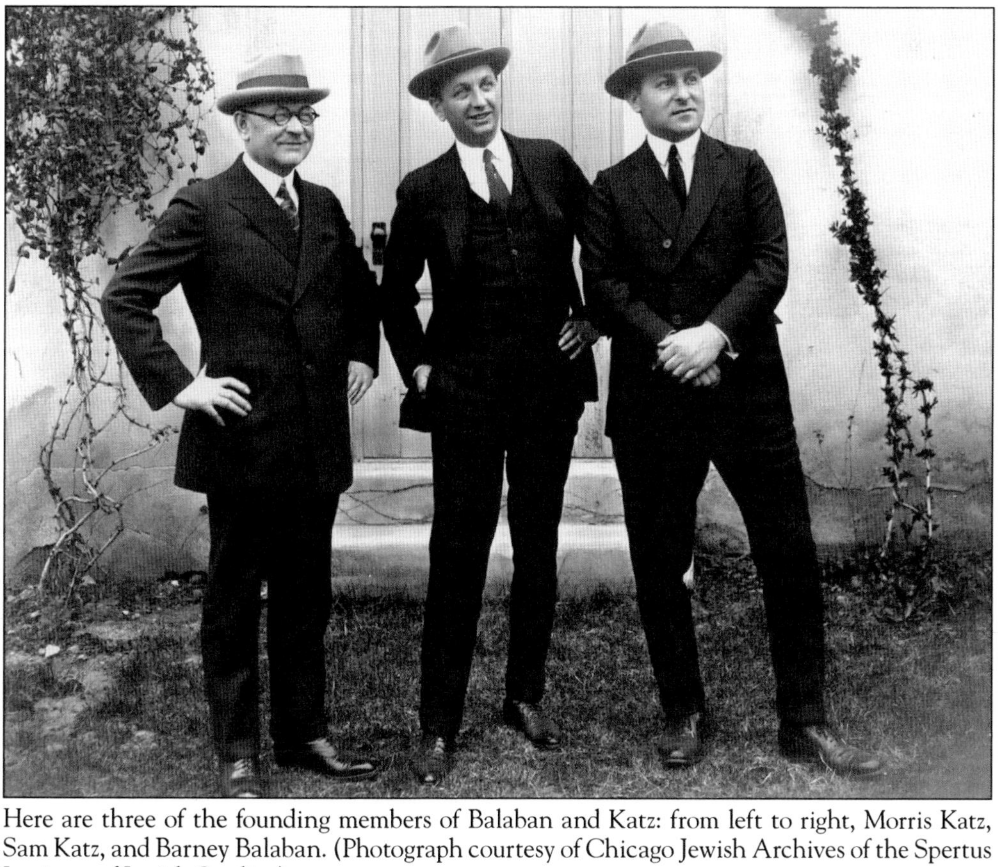

Here are three of the founding members of Balaban and Katz: from left to right, Morris Katz, Sam Katz, and Barney Balaban. (Photograph courtesy of Chicago Jewish Archives of the Spertus Institute of Jewish Studies.)

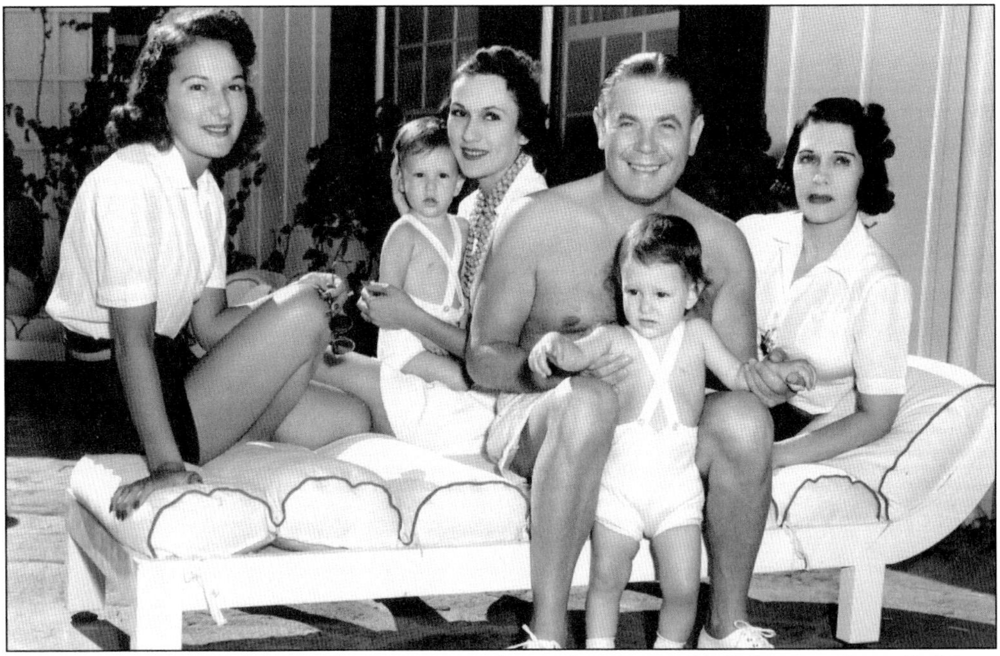

Pictured here are, from left to right, Jeanne Spiegleman (née Pottasch), Bob's sister Susan Balaban, Bob's mom Elenore (née Pottasch), Sam Katz, Sam's wife Belle, and, in front, Bob's sister Nancy Magidson (née Balaban) in Beverly Hills in the 1940s. (Photograph courtesy of Bob Balaban.)

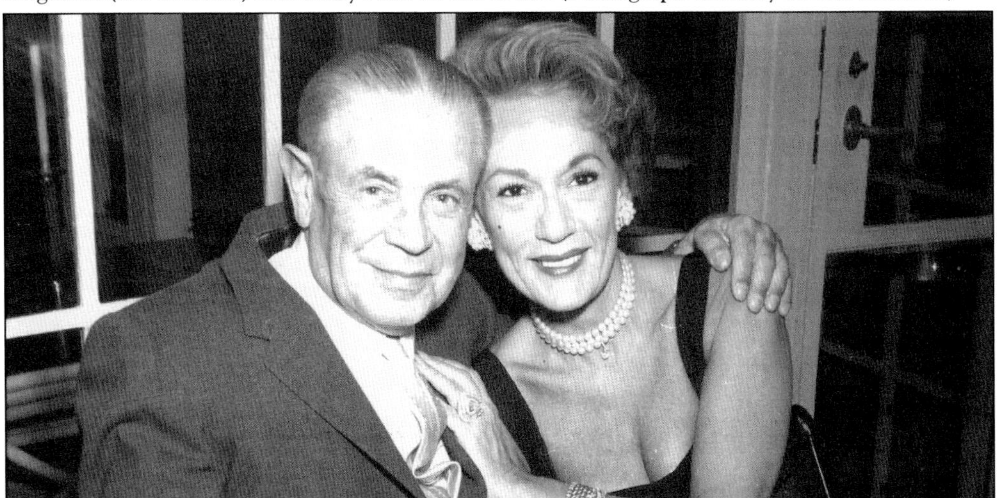

Pictured here is Sam Katz and Elenore Balaban (Elmer's wife). Sam expanded Paramount's theater holdings to over 800 theaters in just a few years. Paramount Publix controlled a large portion of the movie theaters in the United States with a guaranteed audience for the movies it produced. The economy was booming into the late 1920s. When the Depression hit in 1929, the movie industry was hit hard, and the stage shows that were the mainstay of Balaban and Katz and Paramount were all but eliminated. Blamed for the deteriorating financial condition of Paramount, Sam left and went to MGM from 1936 to 1949. He is credited with hiring Judy Garland for the part of Dorothy. Sam married back into the Balaban family to Belle Pottasch. Belle was Bob Balaban's maternal grandmother. Sam Katz died on January 12, 1961, in Beverly Hills. His son William, wife Belle, and his two sisters survived him. (Photograph courtesy of Bob Balaban.)

Three

The First Balaban Theaters

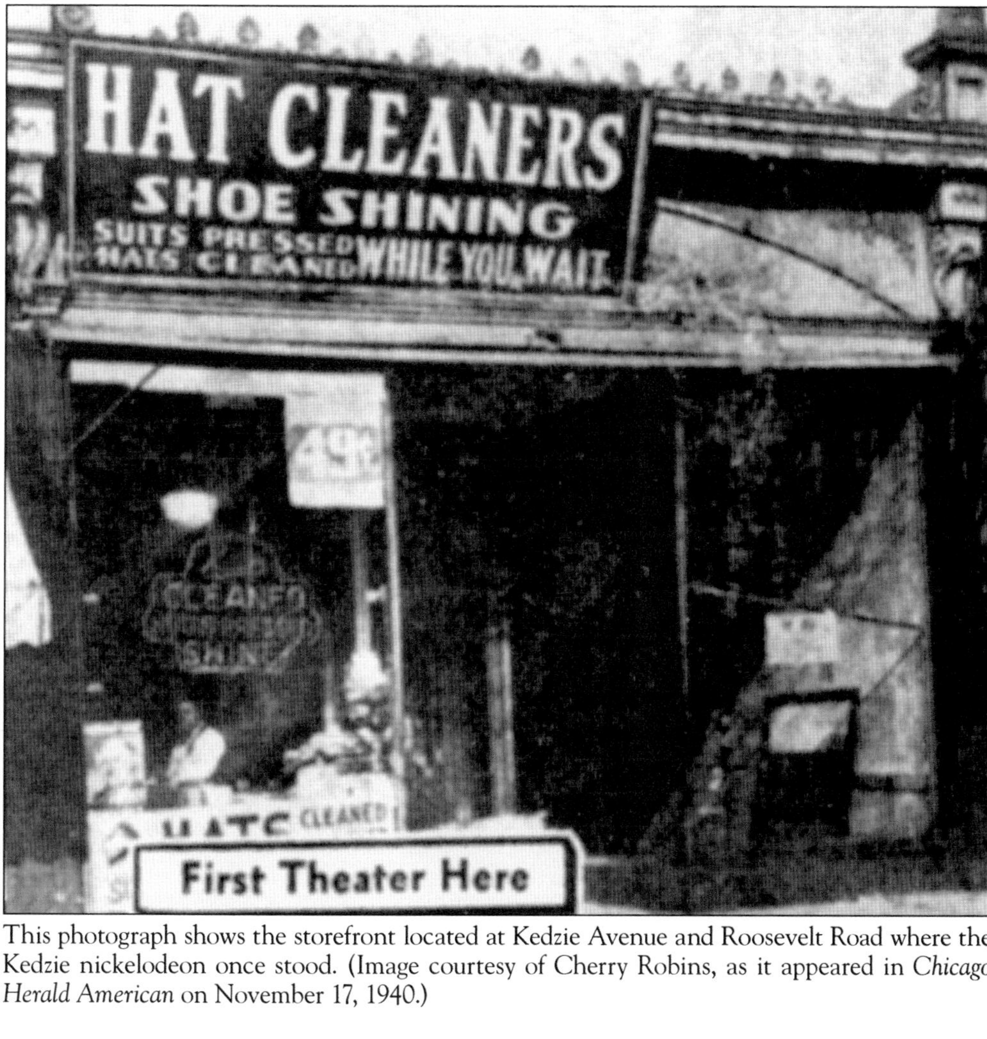

This photograph shows the storefront located at Kedzie Avenue and Roosevelt Road where the Kedzie nickelodeon once stood. (Image courtesy of Cherry Robins, as it appeared in *Chicago Herald American* on November 17, 1940.)

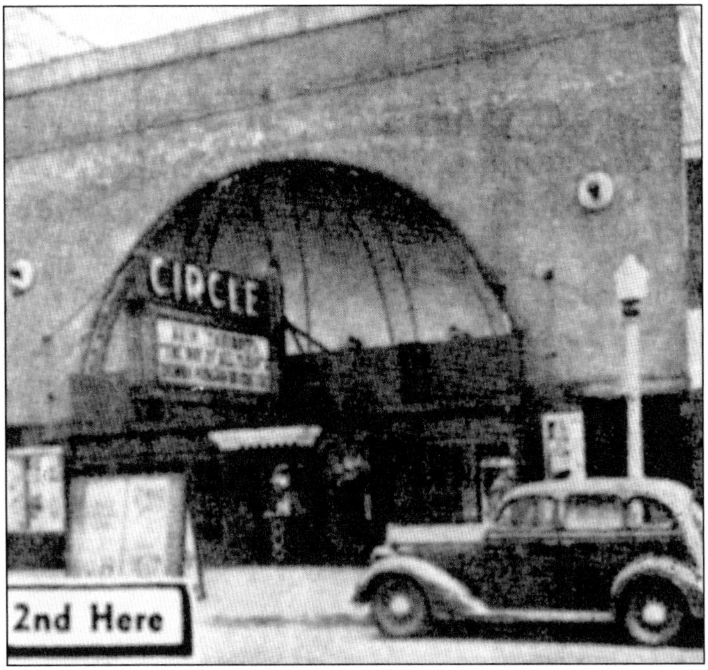

This photograph is of the Circle Theatre. (Image courtesy of Cherry Robins, as it appeared in *Chicago Herald American* on November 17, 1940.)

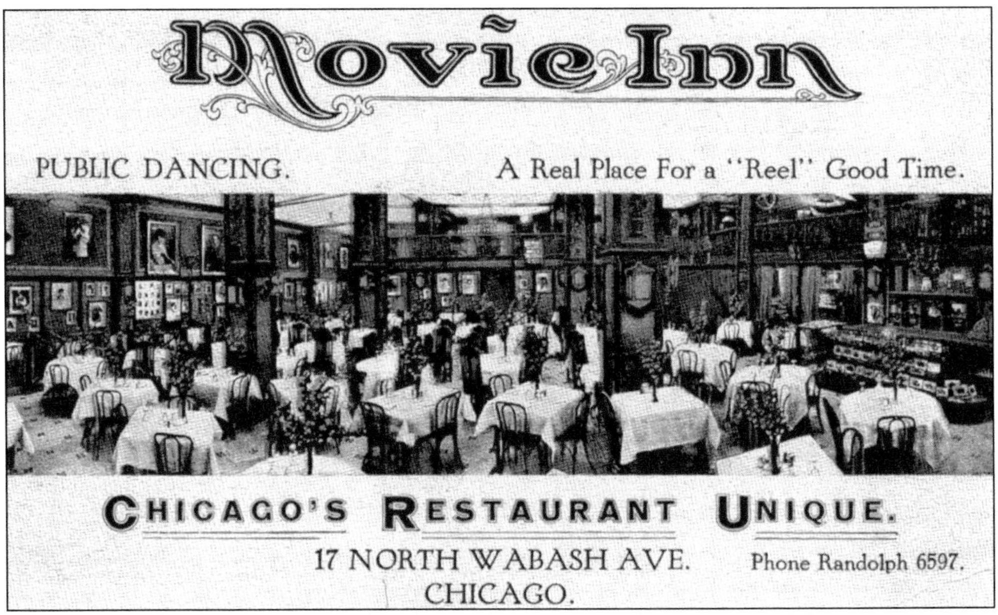

In 1915, A. J. Balaban and his brothers experimented with the concept of showing movies in a restaurant environment. A friend of A. J. and his wife bought out a fancy teahouse named Delvies on the corner of Wabash Avenue and Madison Street. They renamed it the Movie Inn. Here is a promotional announcement for the new venture. Movie posters and pictures decorated the walls. They even installed a theater organ and had musicians to serenade patrons. This concept was ahead of its time and was quite popular with actors. There were many problems with the liquor licenses and other complications. In less than a year, the family decided to close up shop, accept their losses, and retreat to the relative safety of the theater business. (Photograph courtesy of Cherry Robins.)

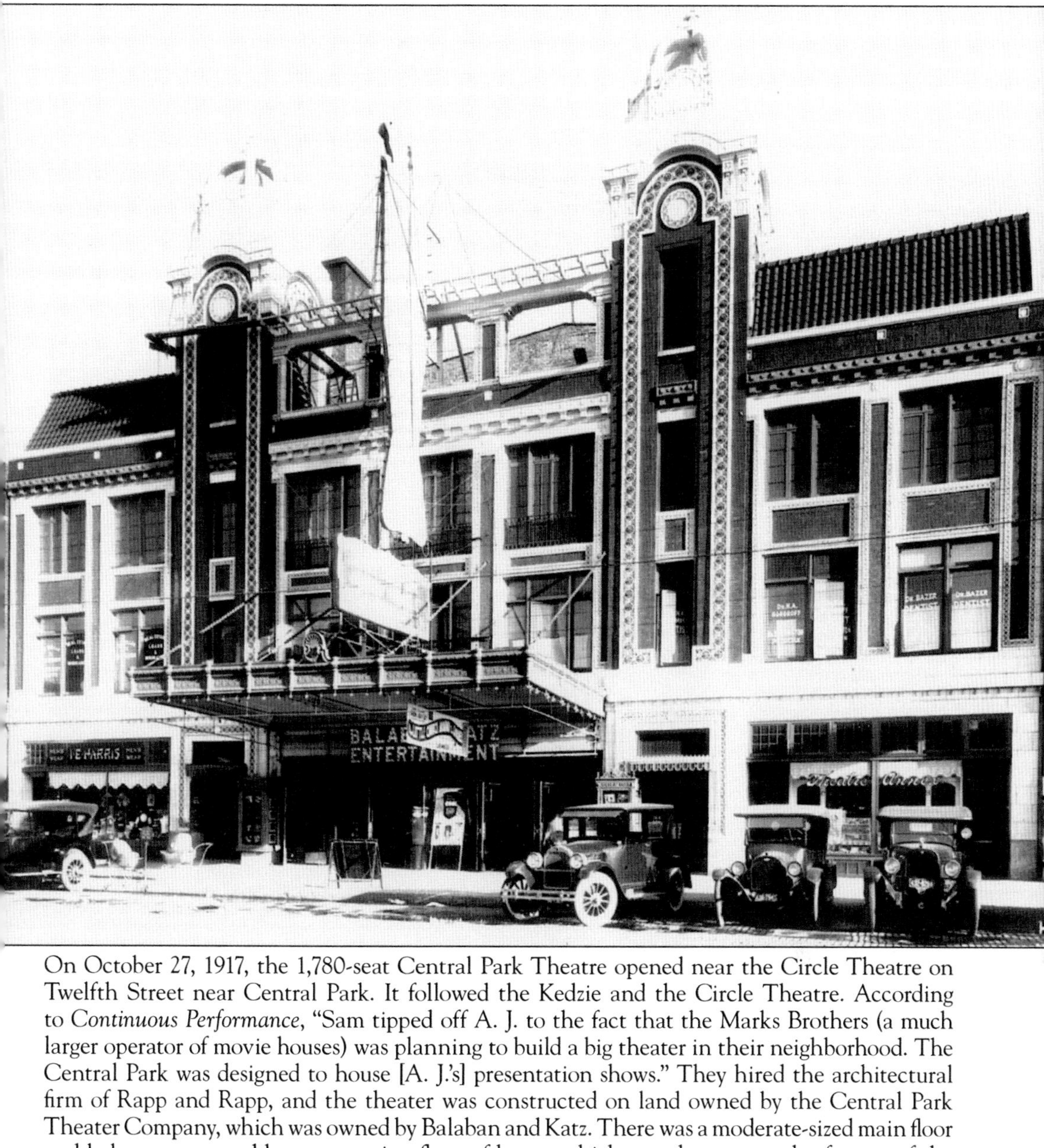

On October 27, 1917, the 1,780-seat Central Park Theatre opened near the Circle Theatre on Twelfth Street near Central Park. It followed the Kedzie and the Circle Theatre. According to *Continuous Performance*, "Sam tipped off A. J. to the fact that the Marks Brothers (a much larger operator of movie houses) was planning to build a big theater in their neighborhood. The Central Park was designed to house [A. J.'s] presentation shows." They hired the architectural firm of Rapp and Rapp, and the theater was constructed on land owned by the Central Park Theater Company, which was owned by Balaban and Katz. There was a moderate-sized main floor and balcony separated by a mezzanine floor of boxes, which was the spectacular feature of the building, giving the audience the feeling of being part of the stage act. Besides the center stage, there were two side stages, decorated like gardens with greens and marble statuary. (Photograph courtesy of Theatre Historical Society of America.)

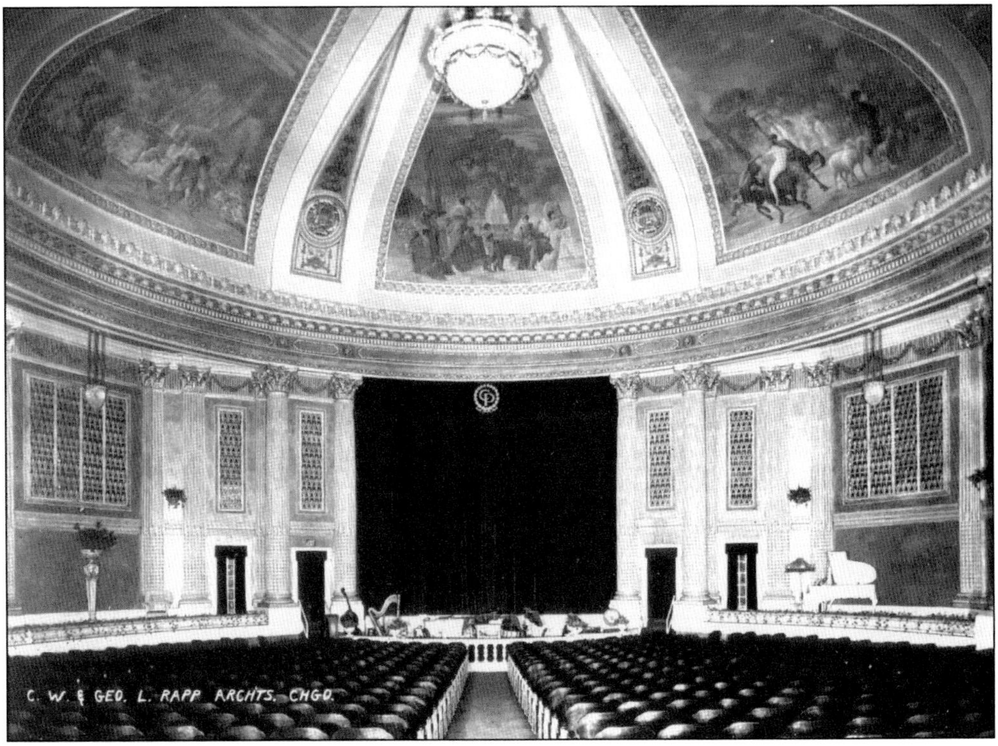

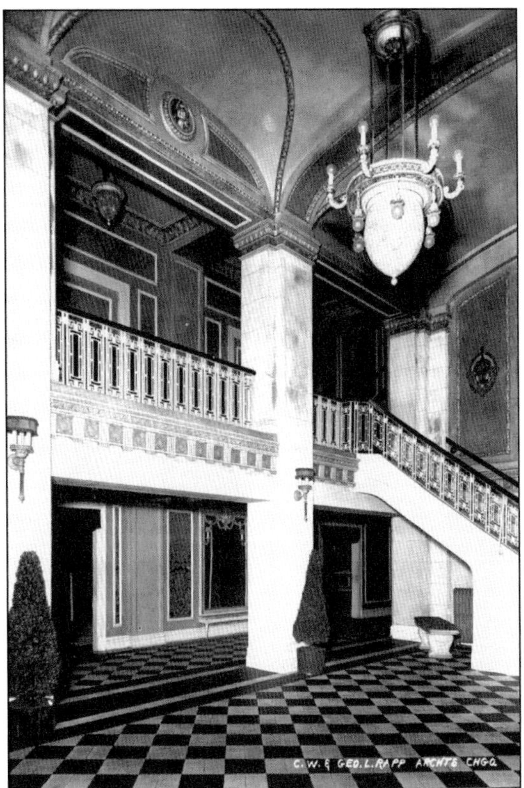

Balaban and Katz experimented with many new innovations with the Central Park Theatre. Most notable was the installation of central air-conditioning. In 1917, virtually no public buildings boasted temperature-controlled environments. According to Ida Scully Balaban (John's daughter), John's future wife Bertha Bruder and Barney both worked at the Western Cold Storage Company. Barney decided to find a way to use the same technology used to cool the food at Western Cold Storage to air-condition all B and K theaters. It was six years before any of their competitors installed air-conditioning. B and K enjoyed an exclusive reputation for providing state-of-the-art comfort to its customers. The Central Park Theatre was an instant hit. A. J. hired Frank Cambria, general manager of Broadway's New York Studios, to manage live shows, and the theater opened at 9:30 a.m. and did not close until midnight, offering its patrons nonstop entertainment for only 10¢! (Photographs courtesy of Theatre Historical Society of America.)

Four

The Chicago Movie Palaces of Balaban and Katz

Admission statistics for the two periods compare as follows:

Theatre	Six months ended June 28, 1925	Six months ended June 29, 1924	Increase or Decrease Amount	Increase or Decrease %
Net admission receipts-				
Chicago	$1,180,158.56	$1,218,112.12	$37,953.56	3.12
Tivoli	612,766.60	616,619.30	3,852.70	.62
Riviera	376,472.35	359,808.50	16,663.85	4.62
Central Park	201,868.70	165,860.35	36,008.35	21.71
Roosevelt	429,567.08	439,362.18	9,795.10	2.23
Total	$2,800,833.29	$2,799,762.45	$ 1,070.84	.04
Number of patrons-				
Chicago	2,208,721	2,262,932	54,211	2.40
Tivoli	1,484,880	1,545,916	61,036	3.95
Riviera	1,005,801	933,544	72,257	7.74
Central Park	545,046	513,806	31,240	6.08
Roosevelt	822,339	824,450	2,111	.26
Total	6,066,787	6,080,648	13,861	.23
Average net admissions-				
Chicago	53.43¢	53.83¢	.40¢	.74
Tivoli	41.27	39.89	1.38	3.46
Riviera	37.43	38.54	1.11	2.88
Central Park	37.04	32.28	4.76	14.74
Roosevelt	52.23	53.29	1.06	1.99
Average of totals	46.17¢	46.05¢	.12¢	.24

Above is a breakdown of admission statistics from the 1924 Balaban and Katz annual report. Notice how the company, while owning only five theaters in Chicago, was already servicing over 12 million patrons a year. Also notice that the average cost of admission was only 46.17¢ per customer. This may seem unbelievably cheap by today's standards, but back then, a whole meal could be purchased for under $1. (Image courtesy of Balaban and Katz Historical Foundation.)

The Chicago Movie Palaces of Balaban and Katz

Theater	Location	Seats	Opening Date
Chicago	175 North State Street	3,861	October 26, 1921
Oriental	20 West Randolph Street	3,217	May 9, 1926
United Artists	35 West Randolph Street	1,696	*April 1, 1929
Roosevelt	110 North State Street	1,535	*July 1, 1922
McVickers	25 West Madison Street	2,264	*February 1, 1926
Regal	4719 South Parkway	2,866	February 4, 1928
Tivoli	6329 Cottage Grove Avenue	3,520	February 16, 1921
Maryland	855 East Sixty-third Street	1,540	September 2, 1928
Tower	1510 East Sixty-third Street	3,015	*September 22, 1928
Southtown	610 West Sixty-third Street	3,206	December 25, 1931
Uptown	4814 Broadway Street	4,320	August 17, 1925
Paradise	231 North Crawford (Pulaski) Avenue	3,612	September 14, 1928
Senate	3128 West Madison Street	3,097	June 1925
Harding	2714 North Milwaukee Avenue	2,962	October 12, 1925
Norshore	1748 North Howard Street	3,017	June 17, 1926
Varsity	1710 Sherman Street, Evanston	1,812	*April 1, 1928
Pantheon	4642 Sheridan Road	2,035	*September 28, 1930
Granada	6427 North Sheridan Road	3,447	*November 1, 1929
Marbro	4124 West Madison Street	3,931	*November 1, 1929
Riviera	4746 North Racine Avenue	1,943	*September 29, 1918
Covent	2653 North Clark Street	1,972	*November 1, 1929
Congress	2135 North Milwaukee Avenue	2,890	*November 1, 1929
Belmont	1632 Belmont Avenue	3,257	*May 9, 1930
Century	2820 North Clark Street	3,056	*February 7, 1930
Alamo	3639 West Chicago Avenue	1,557	*October 1, 1930
Belpark	3231 North Cicero Avenue	2,004	*March 12, 1930
Berwyn	6404 West Twenty-second Street, Berwyn	1,673	*November 1, 1929
Biltmore	2046 West Division Street	1,677	*July 31, 1930
Central Park	3535 West Roosevelt Road	1,780	October 27, 1917
Crystal	2705 West North Avenue	1,860	*September 15, 1929
Gateway	5218 West Lawrence Avenue	2,092	June 27, 1930
LaGrange	80 South LaGrange Road	1,436	*September 20, 1929
Manor	5609 West North Avenue	1,827	*September 1, 1930
Nortown	6320 North Western Avenue	2,105	April 4, 1931
State	5814 West Madison Street	1,895	*November 1, 1929
Alba	4826 North Kedzie Avenue	968	*December 25, 1934

*Date taken over by Balaban and Katz

(Reprinted from the official Balaban and Katz theater manager's manual written in 1934.)

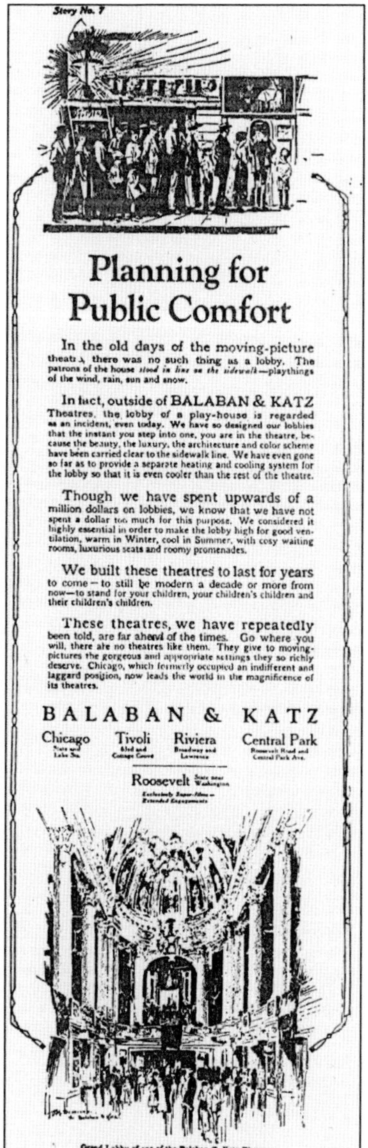

This advertisement for Balaban and Katz appeared in *Balaban & Katz Magazine* and in newspapers. It announced how B and K had spent a million dollars to build beautiful air-conditioned lobbies for the five movie palaces it was operating at the time. For several years, B and K offered the only air-conditioned theaters in Chicago. People would travel for hundreds of miles just to sit and relax in air treated by Balaban and Katz's temperature-control plants. Doctors told their patients to go and sit in B and K theaters to deal with chest congestion and allergies. Previously, theater patrons waited outside in the harsh elements while waiting for a show to begin. Balaban and Katz had realized that the secret to its success was seeing its business from the public point of view. In the hostile Chicago winters, and in the blazing sun, it was a great comfort to the public to know that a Balaban and Katz theater offered a beautiful, clean, comfortable place to see and hear a show. Once the company developed this reputation, many families only sent their kids to shows at Balaban and Katz theaters. They became an institution for family values everywhere. (Image courtesy of Theatre Historical Society of America.)

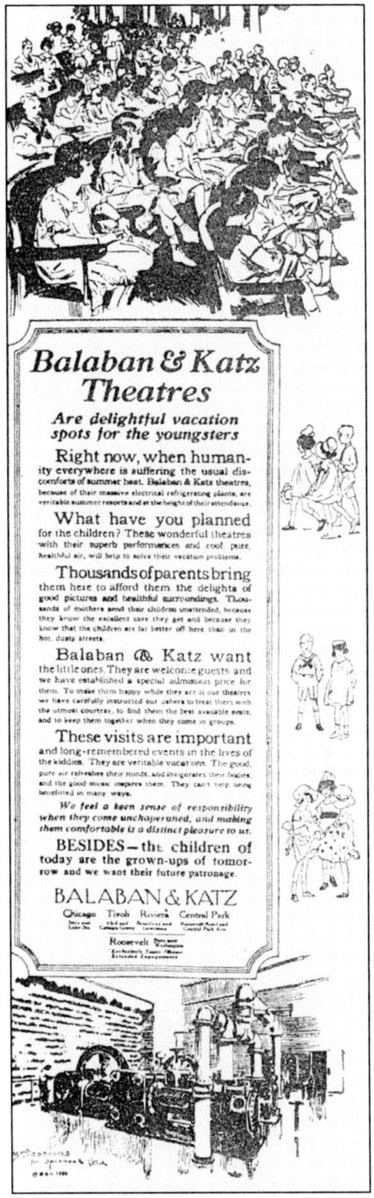

This is another early example of Balaban and Katz developing its family-oriented image. In this message, parents are instructed to send their kids unsupervised to the Balaban and Katz theaters. The movie palaces are referred to here as "delightful vacation spots for the youngsters." At the bottom of the advertisement, one of the massive electrical refrigerating plants (air conditioner) that was installed in each of Balaban and Katz's theaters is shown. Not only did the air-conditioning units cool the theaters, they also filtered out the dust. This was a major concern in the inner-city neighborhoods of Chicago. Today it seems almost ludicrous to ask parents to send their kids downtown alone. Balaban and Katz executives knew that they were training the young theater patrons to be B and K customers from a young age. This type of brand marketing strategy worked. Over the next 20 years, B and K's customers knew what to expect when they visited one of these beautiful theaters. There was a consistency from house to house that was unprecedented previously in the movie industry. (Image courtesy of Theatre Historical Society of America.)

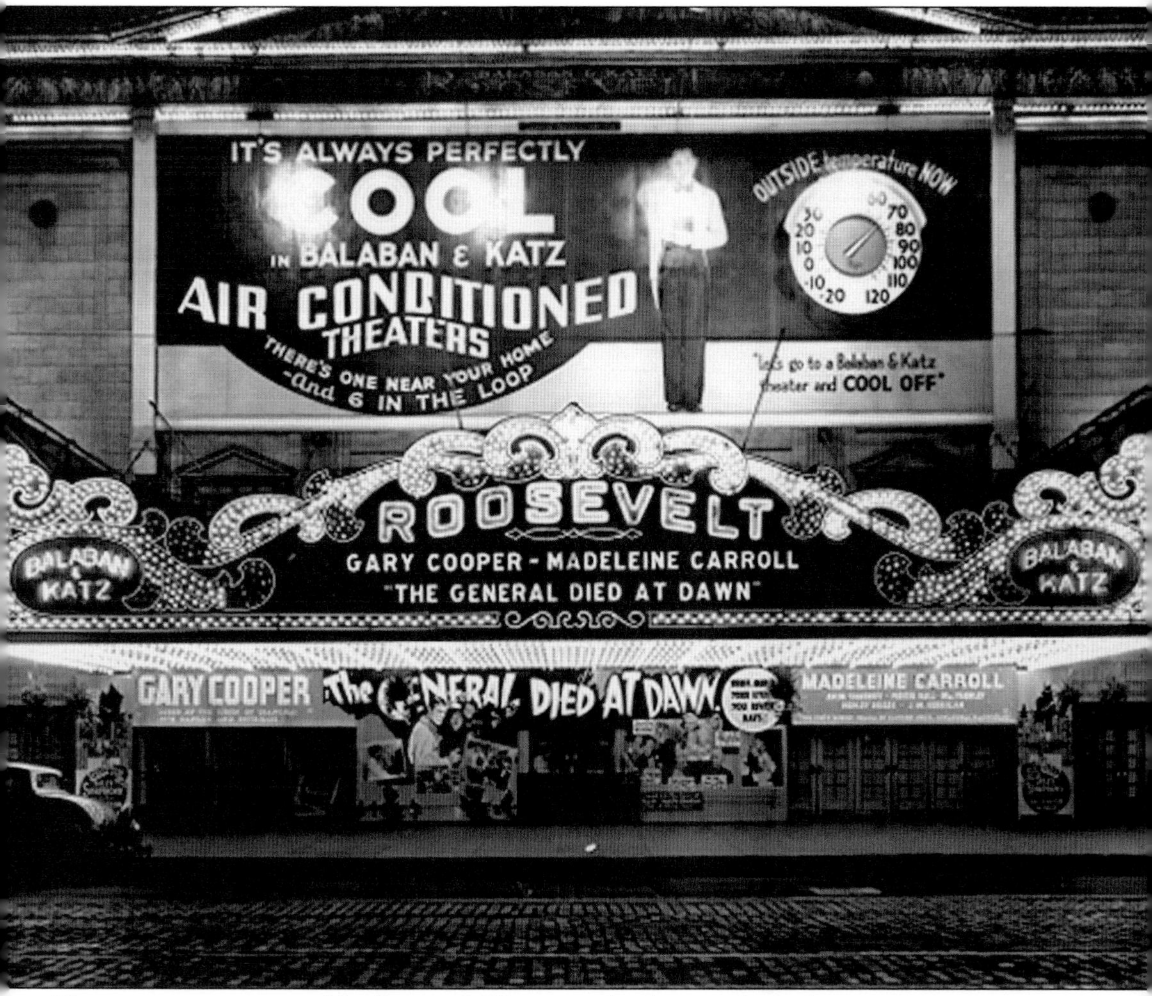

This is an exterior view of the Roosevelt Theatre with a banner above the marquee promoting the air-conditioning system inside the theater. Balaban and Katz was the first theater chain in the United States to offer its customers cooled, filtered air. Barney Balaban worked with Frederick Wittenmeier, chief engineer of the Kroeschell Ice Making Company in Chicago from 1897 to 1917, to install carbon dioxide fan-forced air-cooling systems in all the Balaban and Katz theaters. Previously crude air-conditioning systems had been attempted in public places using ammonia as a refrigerant. Ammonia was a very unstable chemical that posed an explosion hazard. Balaban and Katz revolutionized the theater business by implementing a practical way of filtering and cooling the air economically and safely. Moviegoers could now enjoy movies and live shows year-round. This service gave B and K a distinct advantage over its competitors during a critical early stage of the company's existence. (Photograph courtesy of Balaban and Katz Historical Foundation.)

THE FUNDAMENTAL PRINCIPLES OF

clean-cut appearance, radiant personality, wholesome character, and pleasing voice.

Clean-Cut Appearance

By a clean-cut appearance we have in mind an applicant of normal size and physique and pleasing features. This is very important because of the fact that the first impression received by our patrons is that which is received through the sense of sight. Appearance goes beyond the subject of dress. Many of our employees are required to wear uniforms. In these they may present a very much different appearance than that which they have in clothes of their own choosing.

Radiant Personality

Personality is that quality or those qualities which distinguish one individual from another and is the projecting of those distinguishing qualities in each individual contact with our patrons. This quality is rarely found, but it is one which can be developed through constant effort. It is your duty to correct continuously and call to the attention of each of your employees any acts or expressions which do not measure up to this idea of radiant personality. An organization properly schooled and trained in demonstrating their personality will never become stereotyped, or give the impression that each of your employees is an automaton.

Wholesome Character

By wholesome character we mean a straight-forward, honest, sincerity of purpose, and an earnestness of desire to perform each duty with credit. This is necessary in order to build loyalty which is one of the greatest constructive forces in any organization, without which little is accomplished and many mistakes are made. With loyalty in each of your employees, your organization will be able to meet the most trying circumstances, and solve them

[15]

BALABAN & KATZ THEATRE MANAGEMENT

The Balaban brothers and Sam Katz went to great lengths to micromanage the operations of their 125 theaters, which were spread out in many states throughout the Midwest. This practice followed the general trend in America in the 1920s to build chain store networks in which the customer could count on predictable products offered and services rendered. For example, B and K wanted the air temperature of the Chicago Theatre in Chicago to be the same as the Paramount Theatre in New York. It wanted the ushers at the Uptown Theatre in Chicago to greet its patrons with the same words and tone as those in Balaban and Katz theaters in Indiana. In order to accomplish this, it issued a corporate policy manual called *The Fundamental Principles of Balaban & Katz Theatre Management*. It was a thick, leather-bound manual that was updated frequently and kept in the manager's office of every theater they owned. Above is an example of a page from the manual from 1926. Notice how the company expected the hiring managers to carefully analyze potential applicants for all categories of jobs. Their appearance, education, manners, and wholesome character were all attributes to either qualify or disqualify potential B and K employees. (Image courtesy of Chicago Historical Society.)

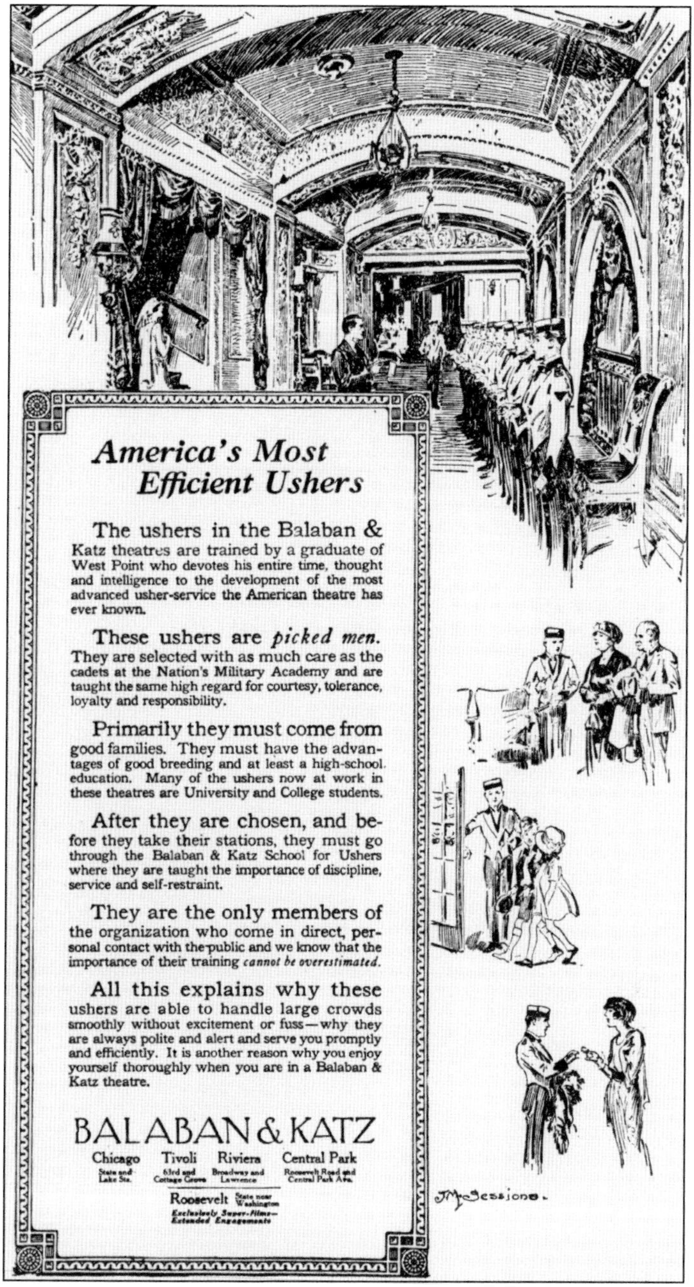

This advertisement appeared in *Balaban & Katz Magazine* and in newspapers. It explains the B and K theory of the importance of training ushers to be the most efficient, polite, well dressed, and disciplined in the world. Knowing that this was a tall order, the company set up an usher training school run by a West Point graduate. The militarist quality of the usher's appearance and movement helped make the patrons of Balaban and Katz theaters feel like royalty. The usher training technique and philosophy was brought to New York by Sam Katz when B and K became part of the Paramount Publix family. After awhile, other companies started to recruit graduates from B and K's usher training school, forcing it to shut down. (Image courtesy of Theatre Historical Society of America.)

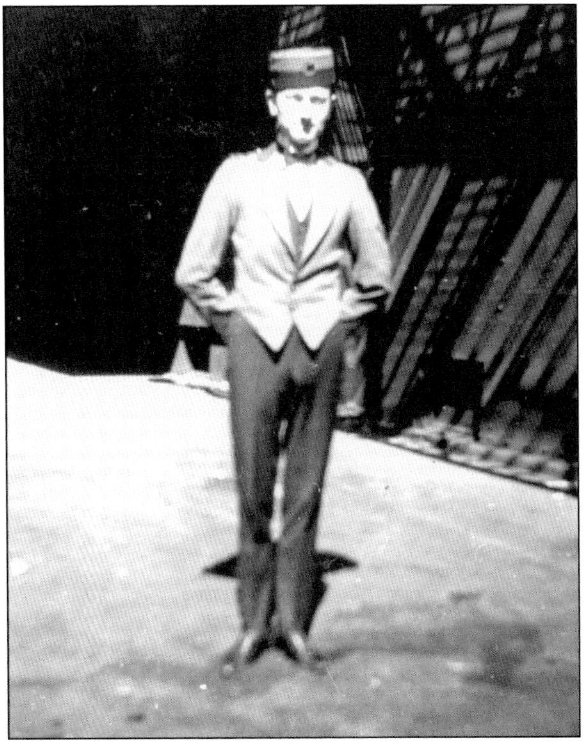

Here are examples of Balaban and Katz ushers' uniforms. The picture to the left shows the winter uniform with woolen pants. The picture below shows a lighter color and material for the warmer months. Employees who failed to wear the appropriate uniform to work were often terminated on the spot. (Photographs courtesy of Theatre Historical Society of America.)

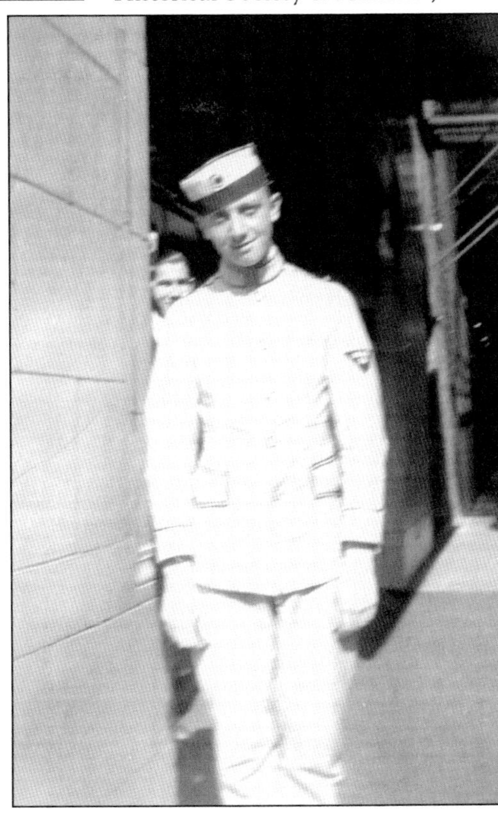

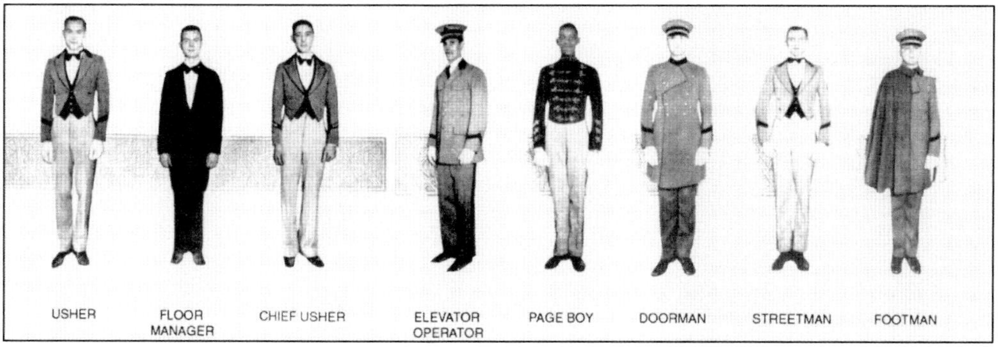

These are uniforms issued to Balaban and Katz service employees. As an employee's rank increased, he was issued a more prestigious uniform and name tag. At the larger movie palaces, such as the Chicago, Tivoli, or Uptown, it was not uncommon for there to be up to 100 employees on duty at any one time. This was dependent on a relatively low hourly wage and large labor pool. As wages went up in later decades, it became impossible to maintain this policy even with the rise of ticket prices. (Photograph courtesy of Theatre Historical Society of America.)

	1			2			3			4		
SHORT	10:00	/	60	1:22	/	/	4.44	/	/	7:59	/	/
TRAILERS	10:07	80	20	1:29	70	/	447	80	/	8:02	130	/
CO-FEATURE	10:10	90	10	1:32	110	40	4:57	120	50	8:12	430	300
	10:20	120	20	1:42	180	70	5:07	190	70	8:22	750	320
	10:30	160	40	1:52	240	60	5:17	250	60	8:32	800	50
	10:40	190	30	2:02	280	40	5:27	250	110	8:42	910	110
	10:50	210	20	2:12	350	70	5:37	450	110	8:52	990	80
	11:00	220	10	2:22	430	80	5:47	550	100	9:02	1120	130
	11:10	230	10	2:32	570	80	5:56	600	50	9:11	1140	20
NEWS	11:19	280	50	2:41	620	110	6:04	720	120	9:19	1240	100
FEATURE	11:27	320	40	2:49	640	60	6:14	880	160			
	11:37	400	80	2:59	830	30	6:24	1080	200			
	11:47	470	70	3:09	860	30	6:34	1200	120			
	11:57	510	40	3:19	940	80	6:44	1310	110			
	12:07	550	40	3:29	990	50	6:54	1400	90			
	12:17	600	50	3:39	1060	70	7:04	1510	110			
	12:27	700	100	3:49	1080	20	7:14	1650	140			
	12:37	780	80	3:59	1180	100	7:24	1750	100			
SATURDAY	12:47	860	80	4:09	1210	30	7:34	1800	50			
MAIN FLOOR	12:57	980	120	4:19	1250	40	7:44	1860	60			
AUGUST 31, 1946	1:07	1080	100	4:29	1310	60	7:54	1890	30			
	1:17	1150	70	4:39	1390	80	7:59	1990	100			
	1:22	1200	50	4:44	1440	50						

This is a "spill card." Key ushers were issued these cards for recording the number of patrons seated in various sections of the theaters and at what time. This information was used to determine how many ushers would be needed to escort patrons out of the theater when the show was over. It also helped identify the number of paying customers versus ones that managed to escape the meager admission cost. (Image courtesy of Theatre Historical Society of America.)

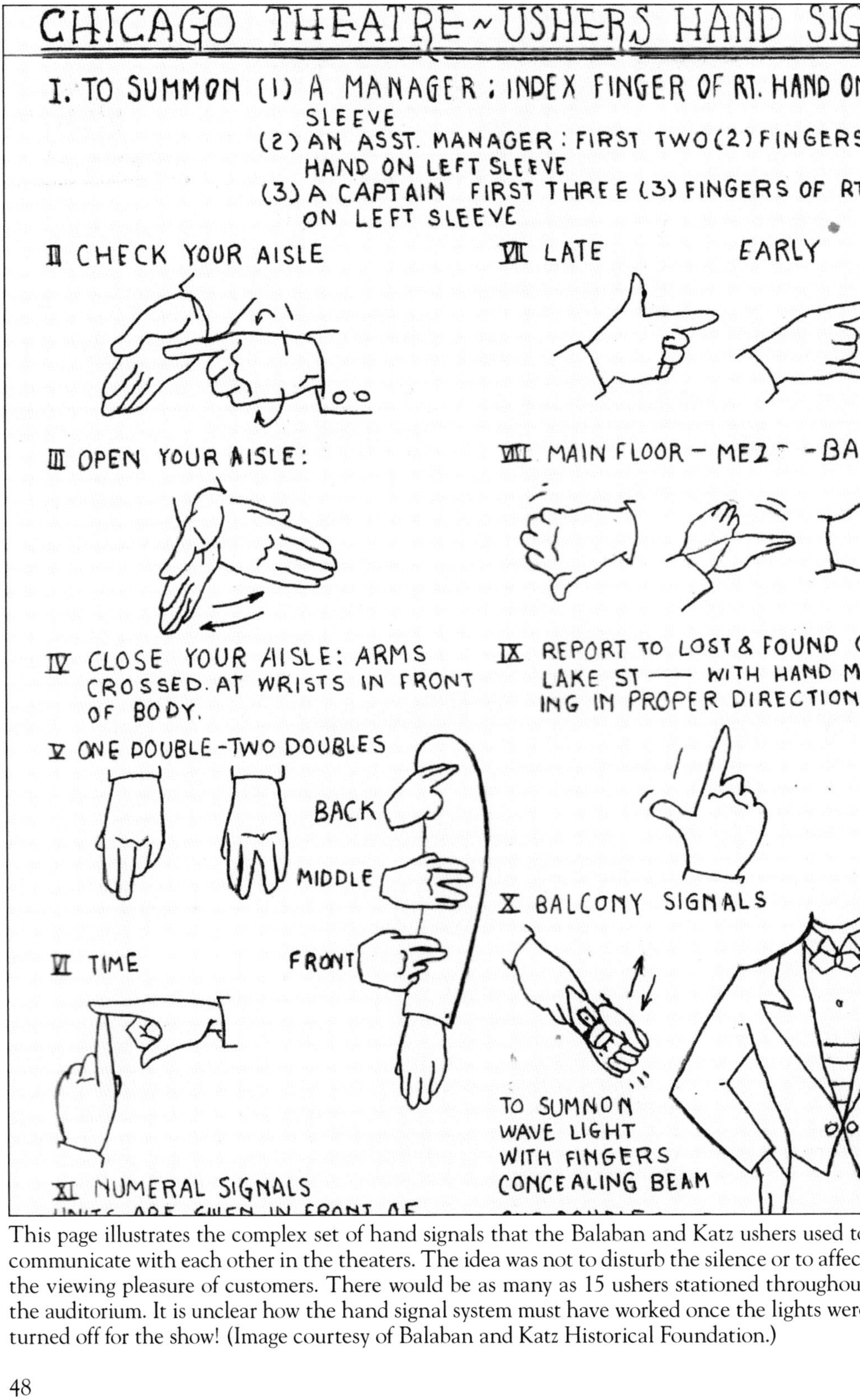

This page illustrates the complex set of hand signals that the Balaban and Katz ushers used to communicate with each other in the theaters. The idea was not to disturb the silence or to affect the viewing pleasure of customers. There would be as many as 15 ushers stationed throughout the auditorium. It is unclear how the hand signal system must have worked once the lights were turned off for the show! (Image courtesy of Balaban and Katz Historical Foundation.)

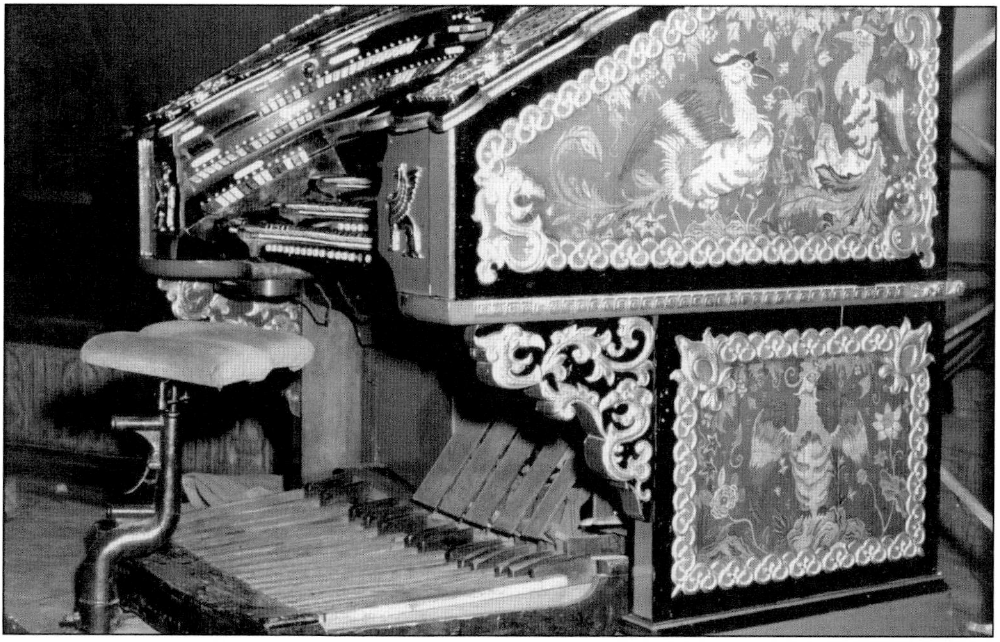

Above is the beautiful organ from the Oriental Theatre. The first ornately decorated Wurlizter organ, it was installed in 1926 when the theater opened. Removed while the theater was closed in the 1970s, it is currently being restored by the Chicago Area Theatre Organ Enthusiasts group to be reinstalled into the Oriental Theatre soon. Below is the Chicago Theatre remote console organ, installed during the 1933 World's Fair. It controlled the main organ, which was located elsewhere in the theater. These organs actually had instruments, such as guitars, drums, and woodwinds, attached to them, and organists could activate each instrument via remote control with pneumatic and mechanical controls. The organ was essential to giving the live orchestras a break from performing. In the smaller theaters, the organist often provided a live sound track for the silent pictures up until the late 1920s. With the arrival of sound in 1927, many of the organs and organists began to disappear from theaters. To this day, the Chicago Theatre contains its grand, meticulously maintained Wurlitzer organ. (Photographs courtesy of John Peters.)

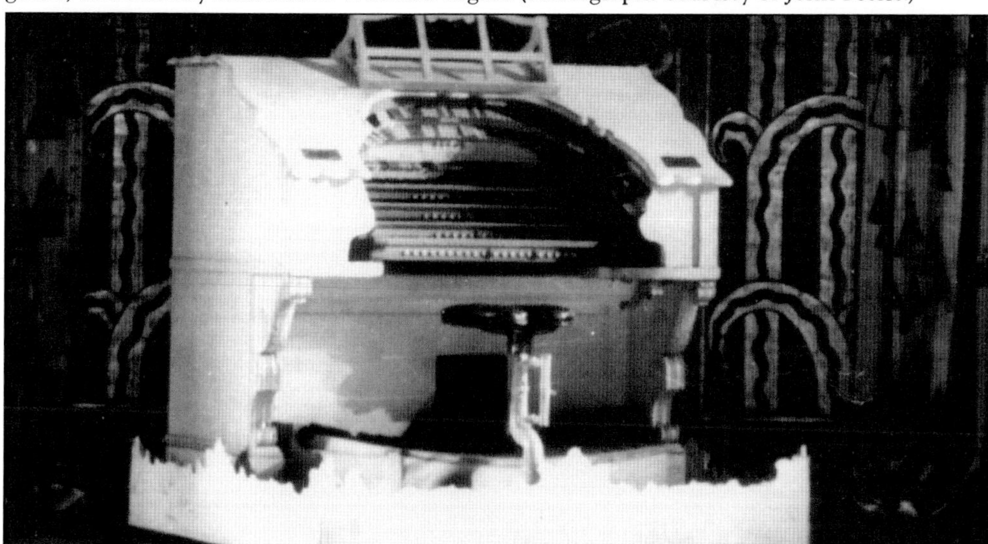

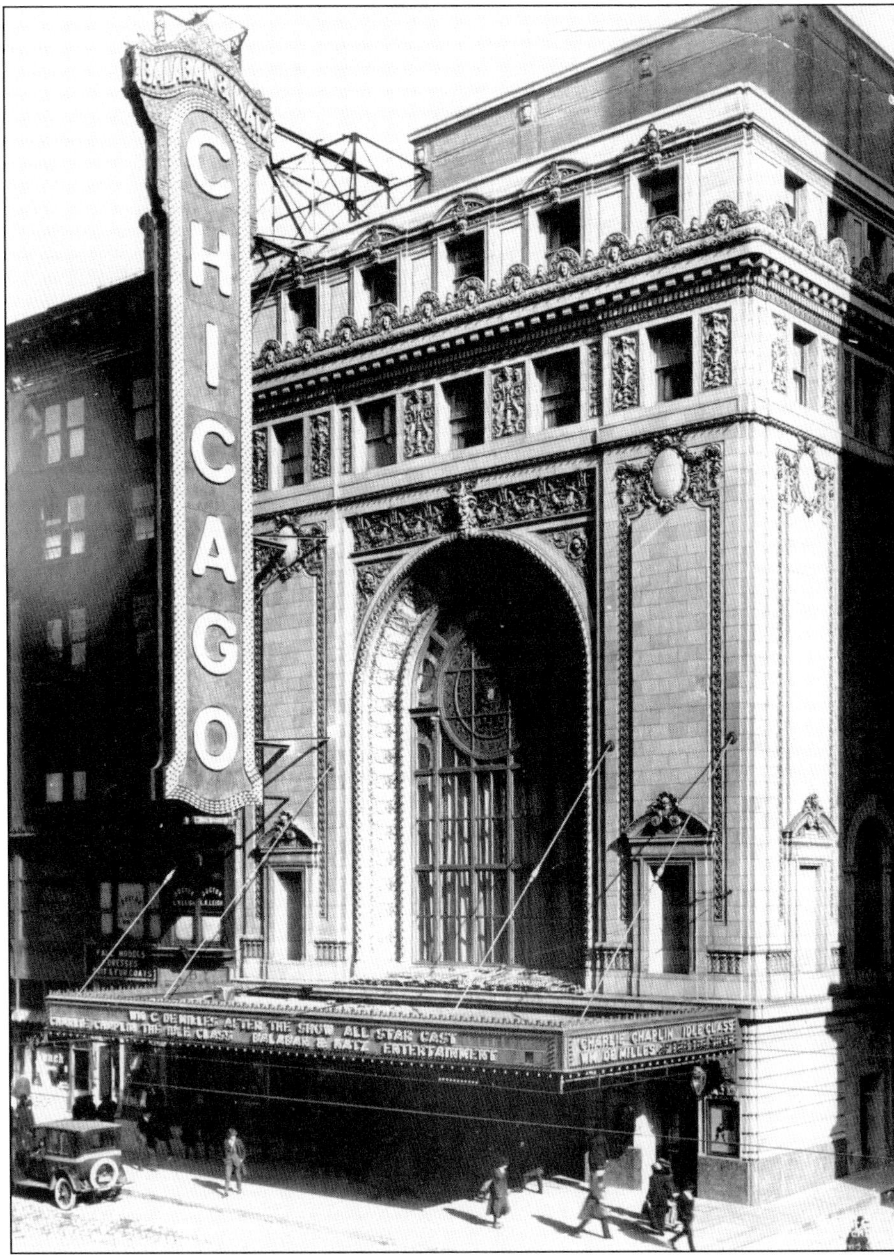

Opened October 26, 1921, the Chicago Theatre, located at 175 North State Street was the flagship of the Balaban and Katz circuit. It housed the corporate offices of the company and an intricate array of other service departments that served the chain. There was another theater in the building, "the Little Chicago," located on the upper floor of the building. The famous movie reviewers Gene Siskel and Roger Ebert met each other while screening films at the Little Chicago. The Chicago had 3,861 seats when it opened and was the first B and K opened in the Loop. The theater was designed by Rapp and Rapp in the French Renaissance mode. B and K spent over $4 million to build the theater. It was the most elegant house imaginable and offered runs of new movies that attracted tourists and upscale clientele from all around Chicago. In 1925, the Chicago Theatre hosted 4.5 million patrons.

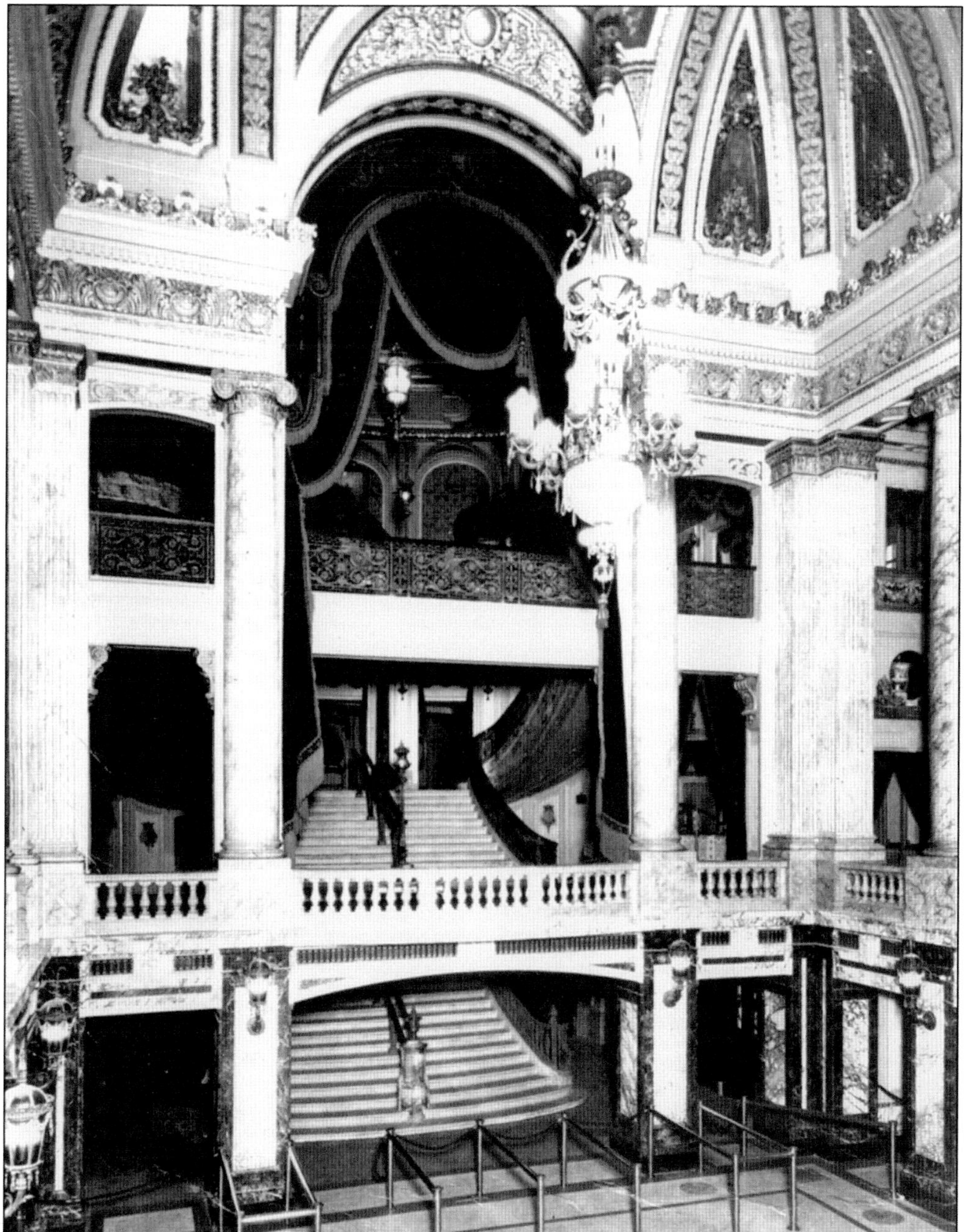

Here is a view of the grand lobby of the Chicago Theatre. Notice the intricately detailed chandelier and staircase railings. Originally called the Ambassador Theatre before its completion, Balaban and Katz raised $1.5 million for the project by issuing bank safeguarded bonds to the public. (Photograph courtesy of Theatre Historical Society of America.)

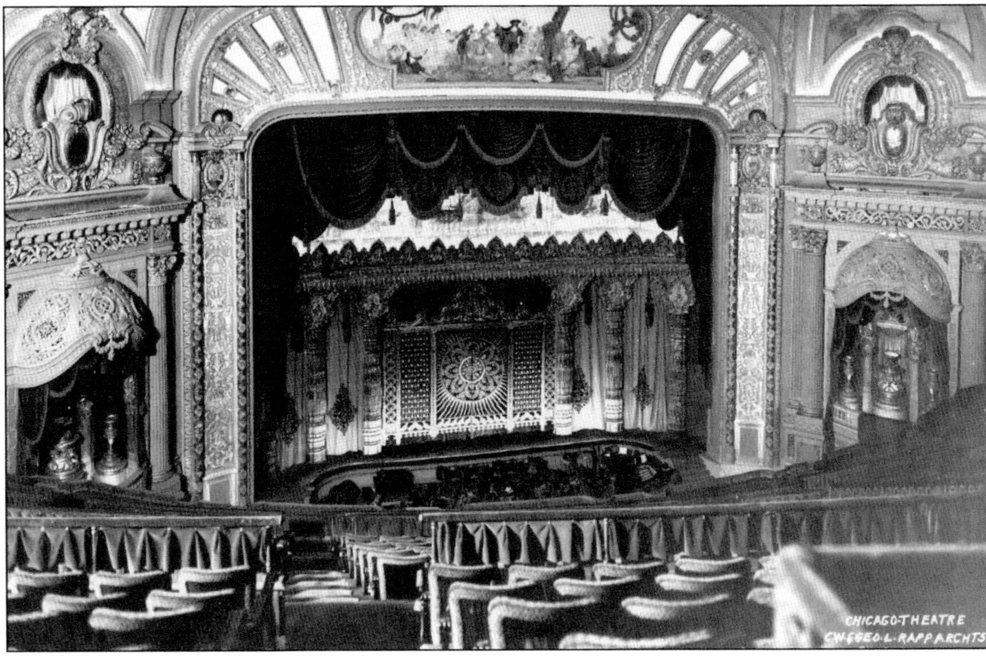

As Balaban and Katz changed hands to United Paramount ABC and then Plitt Theatres, the Chicago gradually lost some of its shine. By the 1970s, it was playing mostly action films and very young urban fare. The city government favored razing the grand movie palace, and a plan was released to build an office tower on the site. A protracted legal battle ensued with many theater preservationists fighting to save the Chicago Theatre. In the end, the city invested millions in the property and helped preserve the "Wonder Theatre of the World." (Photograph courtesy of Theatre Historical Society of America.)

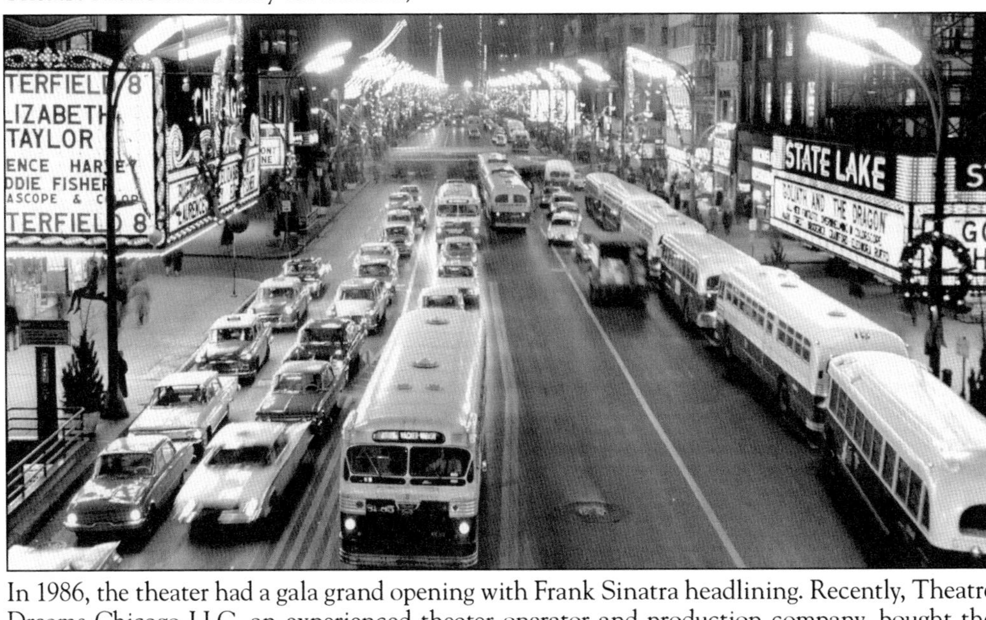

In 1986, the theater had a gala grand opening with Frank Sinatra headlining. Recently, Theatre Dreams Chicago LLC, an experienced theater operator and production company, bought the theater and is improving the structure of the building. It also features a wide variety of high quality entertainment. (Photograph courtesy of Chicago Transit Authority.)

The images here represent some of the fine furnishings that filled the Chicago Theatre's lobby and lounge areas. For half a dollar or less during the day, patrons could feel like royalty. Even the water fountains had constantly circulating water. Other interesting amenities of the Chicago Theatre included a heated sidewalk in front to help keep snow off customers' boots. In the 1950s, it no longer was practical to keep such expensive items in the theater, and many of them were auctioned off. These pictures were taken for insurance purposes. (Photographs courtesy of Theatre Historical Society of America and Joseph R. DuciBella.)

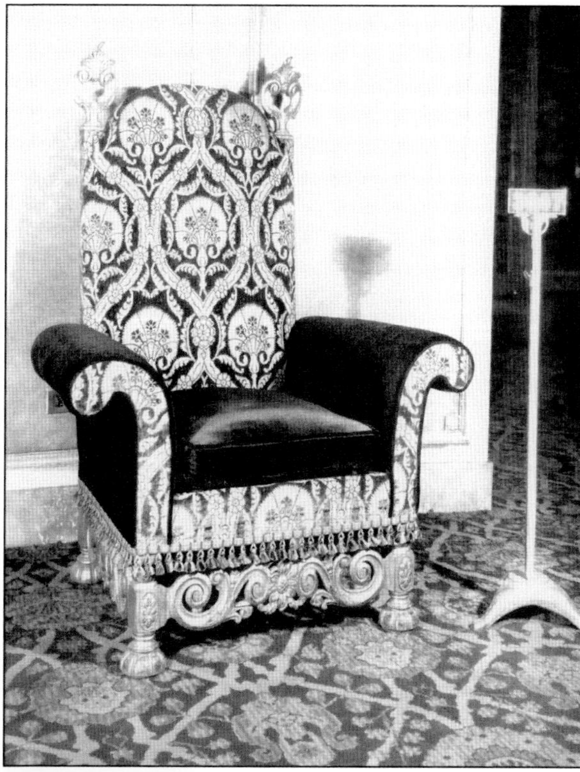

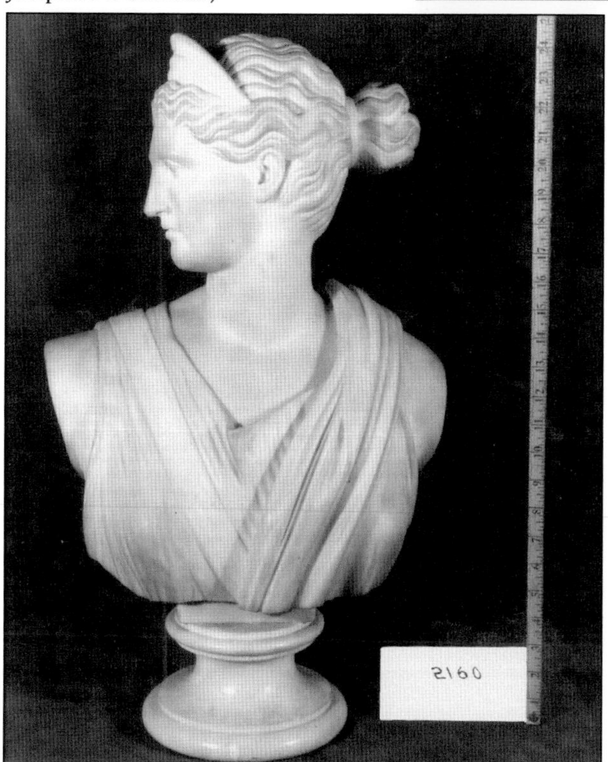

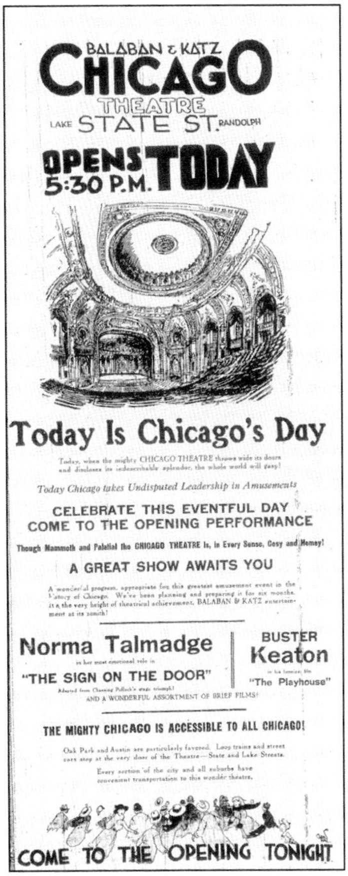

At left is the newspaper advertisement for the Chicago Theatre during its opening week, promoting the theater's proximity to the Oak Park and Austin train stations.
B and K positioned their theaters near train stops whenever possible for easy access by patrons traveling to work and their homes. They anticipated demographic shifts in Chicago's upwardly mobile population and planned theaters in a wider circle of neighborhoods as families moved to the North and West Sides. The theaters in Chicago's bustling Loop business district were not built or acquired until sufficient income was established by the first neighborhood theaters. It allowed for the fixed overhead costs of one theater to be spread amongst a group of properties. This allowed a new, expensive theater to sustain an initial period of lost revenue, as it was subsidized by other theaters in the network. This master plan of building a network of movie palaces that supported each other was a strategy used by later chain store operators. (Advertisement courtesy of Theater Dreams Chicago LLC.)

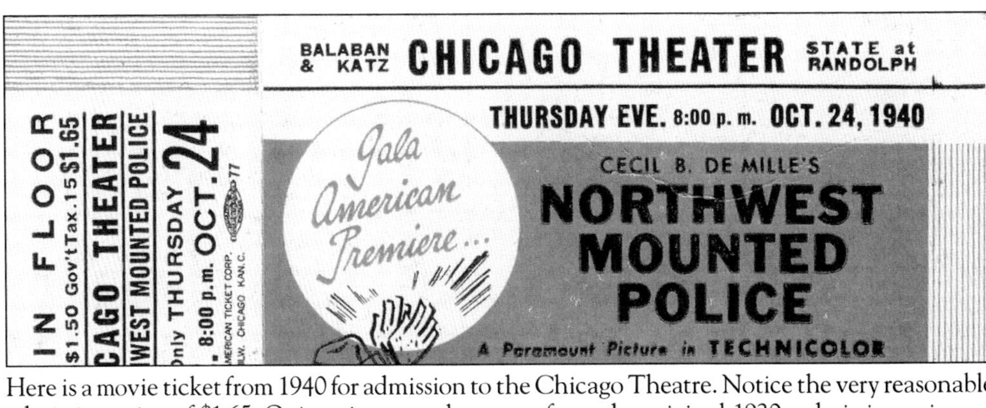

Here is a movie ticket from 1940 for admission to the Chicago Theatre. Notice the very reasonable admission price of \$1.65. Quite a increase, however, from the original 1920s admission prices of 50¢ or less. (Image courtesy of Balaban and Katz Historical Foundation.)

Pictured here is the Balaban and Katz Company coat of arms, which appears in a stained glass window on the second floor of the Chicago Theatre, where the Balaban and Katz Corporation had its corporate offices. The stained glass design consists of a stylized B and K with a looped strand of movie film and a royal looking crown. An interview with Paul Jannusch, former Chicago Theatre chief engineer, revealed that this beautiful window was covered with a heavy curtain for years. This was to reduce the damaging effect on the curtains caused by sunlight refracting through the multicolored glass. It is unknown if the coat of arms was used anywhere else in the company. (Right, photograph courtesy of Chicago Theatre Collection/Theatre Dreams Chicago LLC; below, photograph courtesy of Theatre Historical Society of America.)

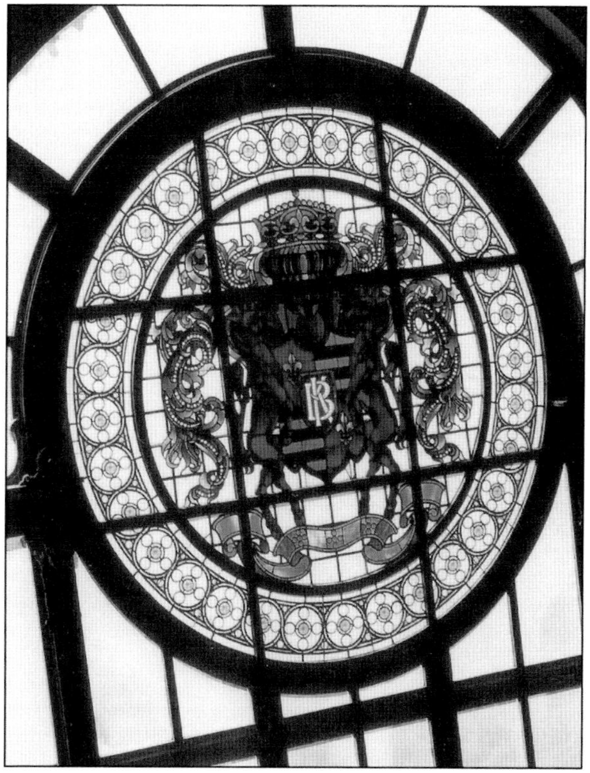

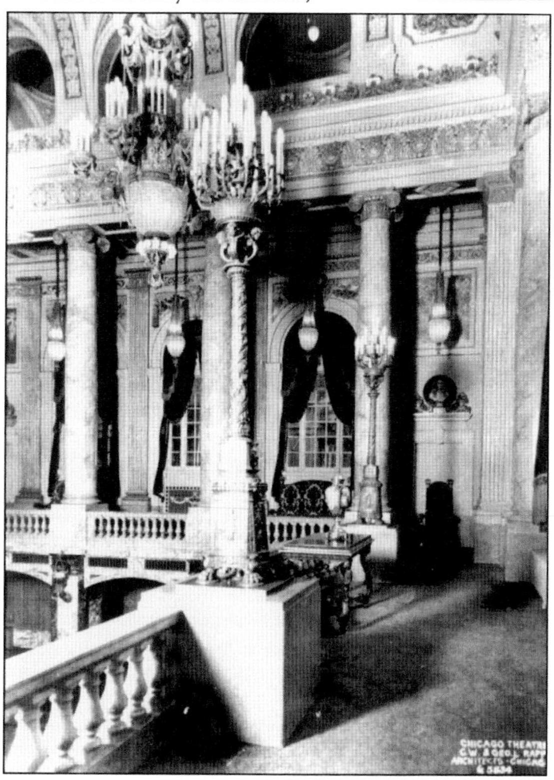

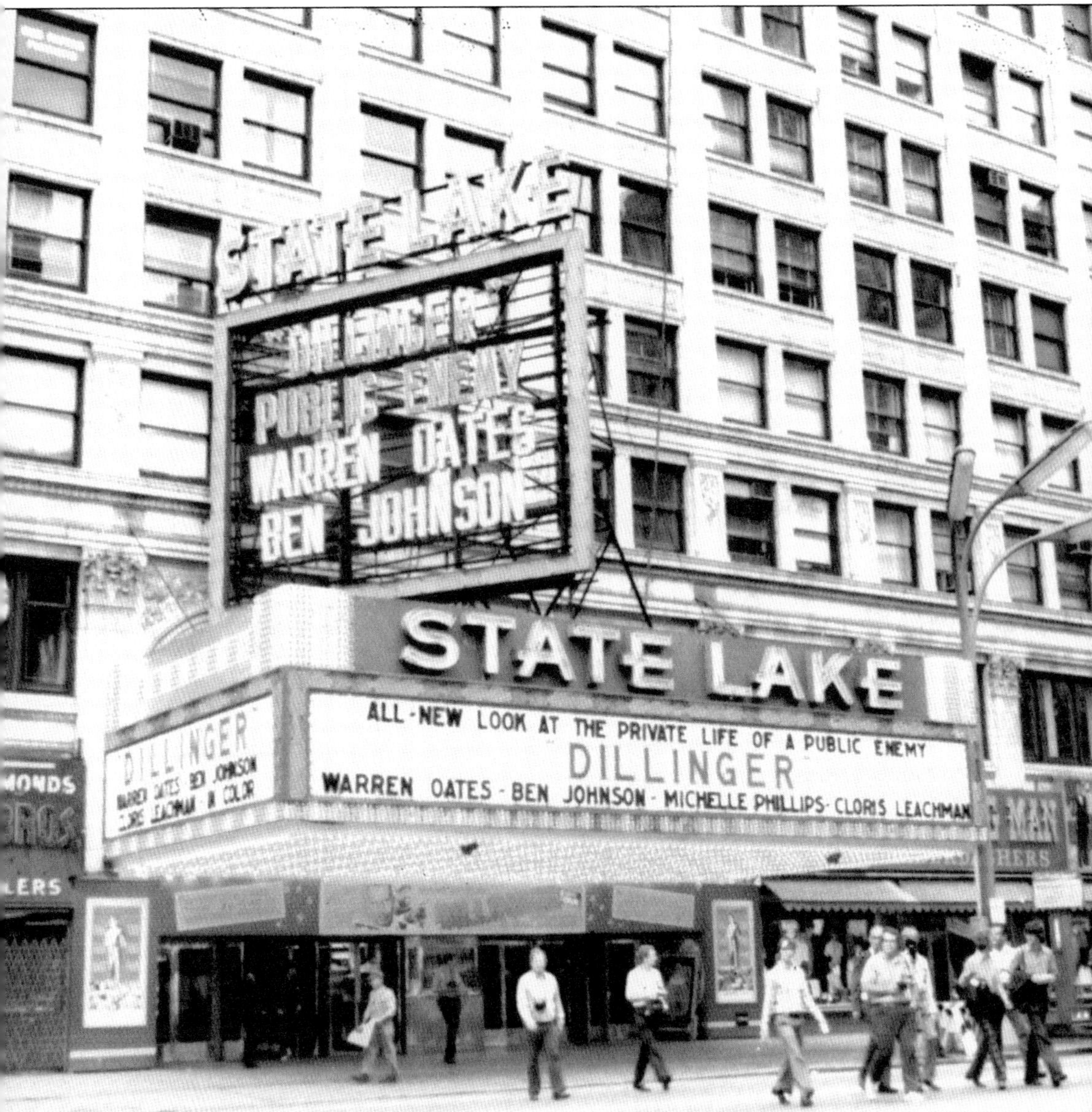

The State Lake Theatre sat on the corner of State and Lake Streets in Chicago's famous Loop district. Built in 1919, it predates Balaban and Katz's arrival to the neighborhood with its Chicago Theatre right across the street in 1921. The State Lake, with about 2,700 seats, was originally a vaudeville theater in the Orpheum circuit and was later integrated into the RKO chain. Many live shows and the best in jazz and swing bands were featured at the State Lake, as well as many first-run pictures. When films with sound came out, the State Lake adapted well and had the reputation of having an advanced sound system. The building eventually housed Balaban and Katz's television station, WBKB, and the offices of the H and E Balaban Corporation. United Paramount ABC Broadcasting, which operated the successor to WBKB along with CBS for a time, took possession of the theater. They eventually gutted the inside and built television studio space there. The exterior façade, minus the marquee, was restored. Recently ABC announced plans to build a ground-level television studio in the location with an on-air window onto State Street. (Photograph courtesy of Theatre Historical Society of America.)

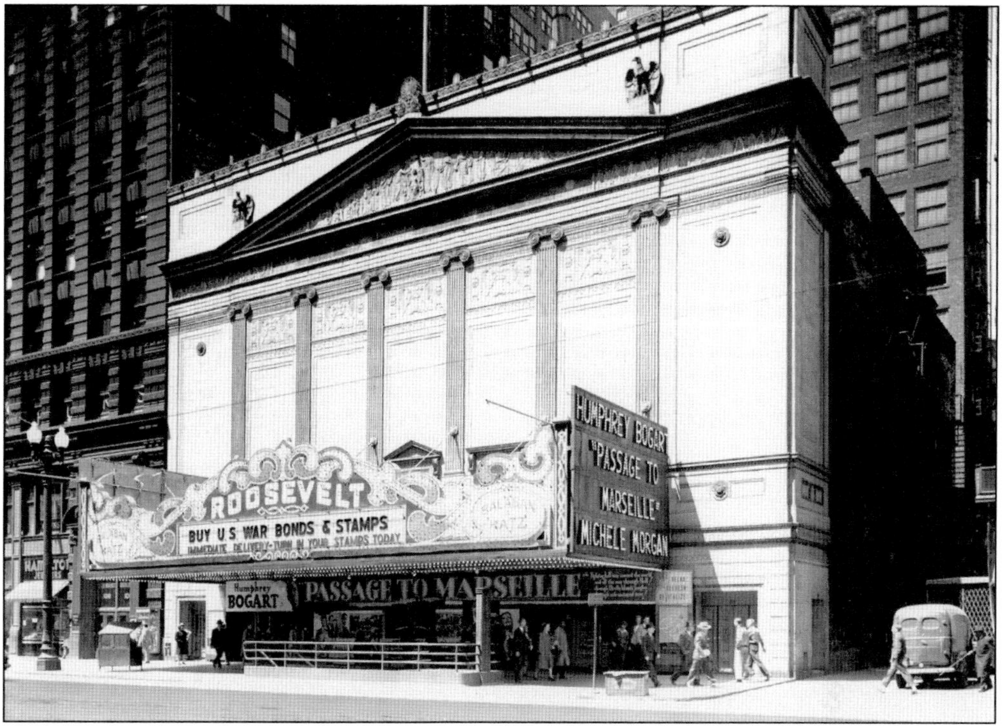

The Roosevelt Theatre opened in 1921. It was built in the Greek Revival style. The Roosevelt was originally owned by the Ascher Roosevelt Theatre Company. The theater had a fairly plain façade until the marquee seen above was added. It was located at 110 North State Street directly across from Marshall Field's, one of the busiest department stores in Chicago. The Roosevelt was leased on May 16, 1922 by the Balaban and Katz Corporation almost two years after opening for $5,000 a week and half of the annual net profits. The Chicago, Oriental, and State Lake Theatres, which were all within one or two blocks of the Roosevelt. Early in 1989, the block that the Roosevelt was on, along with the United Artists Theatre and other historic buildings, was razed to make way for an office building, which was never built. (Above, photograph courtesy of Theatre Historical Society of America; right, advertisement courtesy of Balaban and Katz Historical Foundation.)

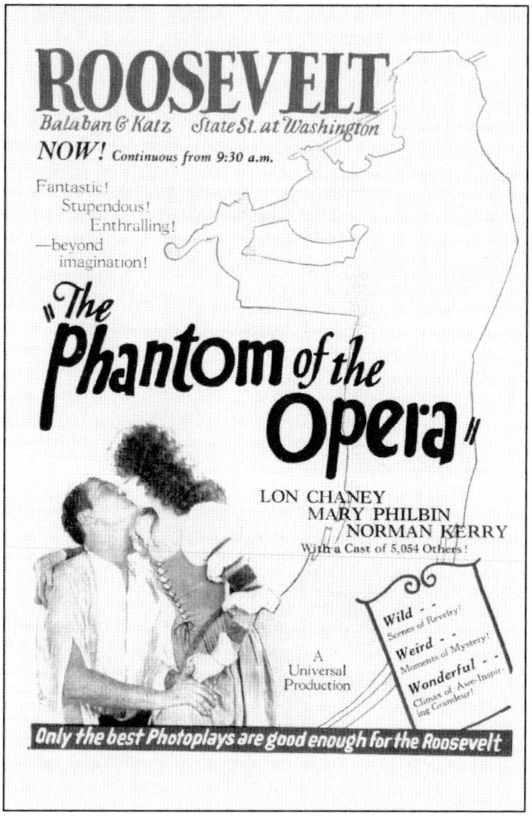

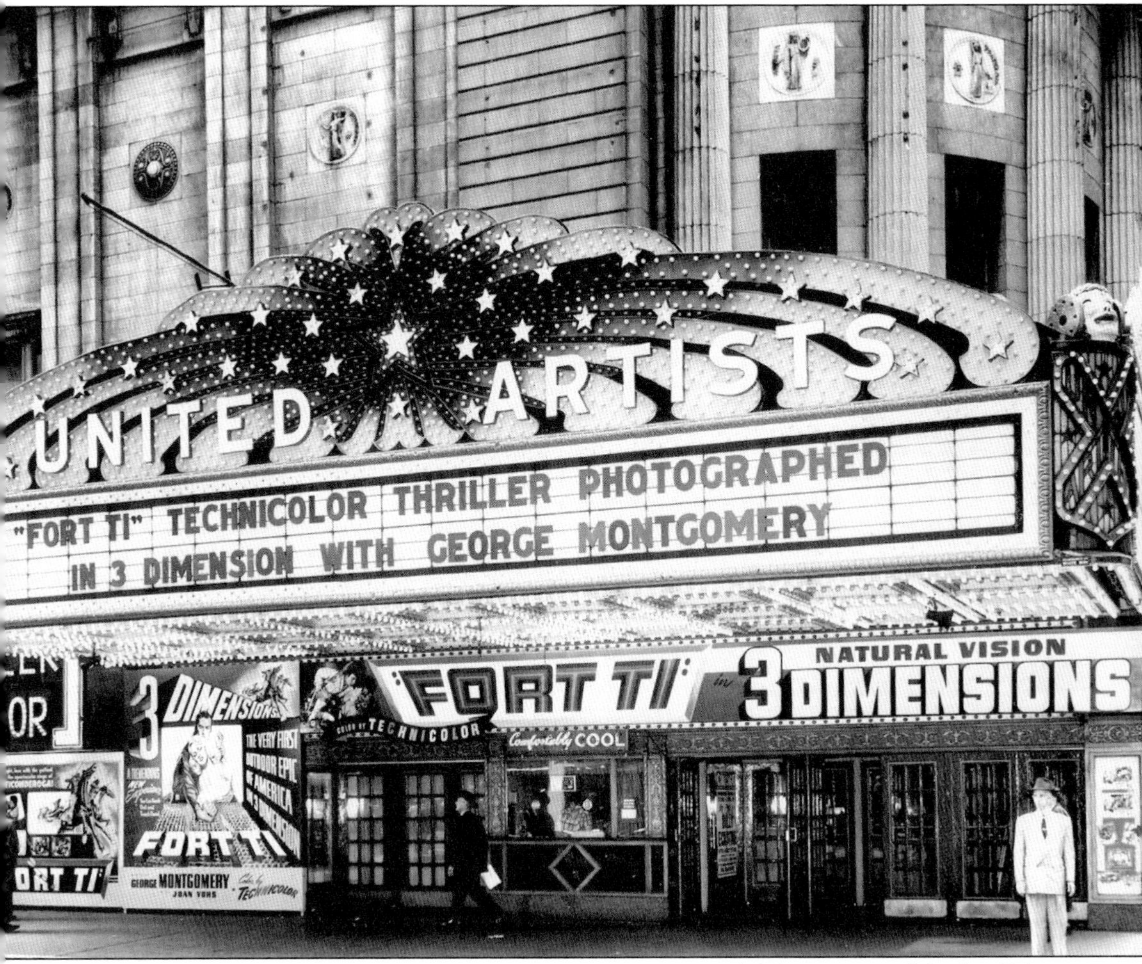

The United Artists Theatre was located at 35 West Randolph Street and had 1,696 seats. Originally called the Apollo Theatre, it was designed by Holabird and Roche in the Greek Revival mode for live stage shows and plays and opened in 1921. The first owner was A. H. Woods, owner of the Woods Theatre a block away. In 1927, the Apollo was purchased by United Artists, an independent movie studio founded by movie stars Mary Pickford, Douglas Fairbanks, Charlie Chaplin, and Gloria Swanson. They drastically changed the interior, removing most of the original decor. The new United Artists Theatre opened on December 26, 1927, featuring *The Dove* with Norma Talmadge. In 1929, the Paramount home office arranged a merger in which 50 percent of the stock went to United Artists and 50 percent to Balaban and Katz. The original deal provided that United Artists book the movies, while B and K operated the theater. This arrangement at first resulted in the exhibition of mostly United Artists-produced pictures. Later, when United Artists merged with MGM, the theater ran mostly MGM pictures. (Photograph courtesy of Balaban and Katz Historical Foundation.)

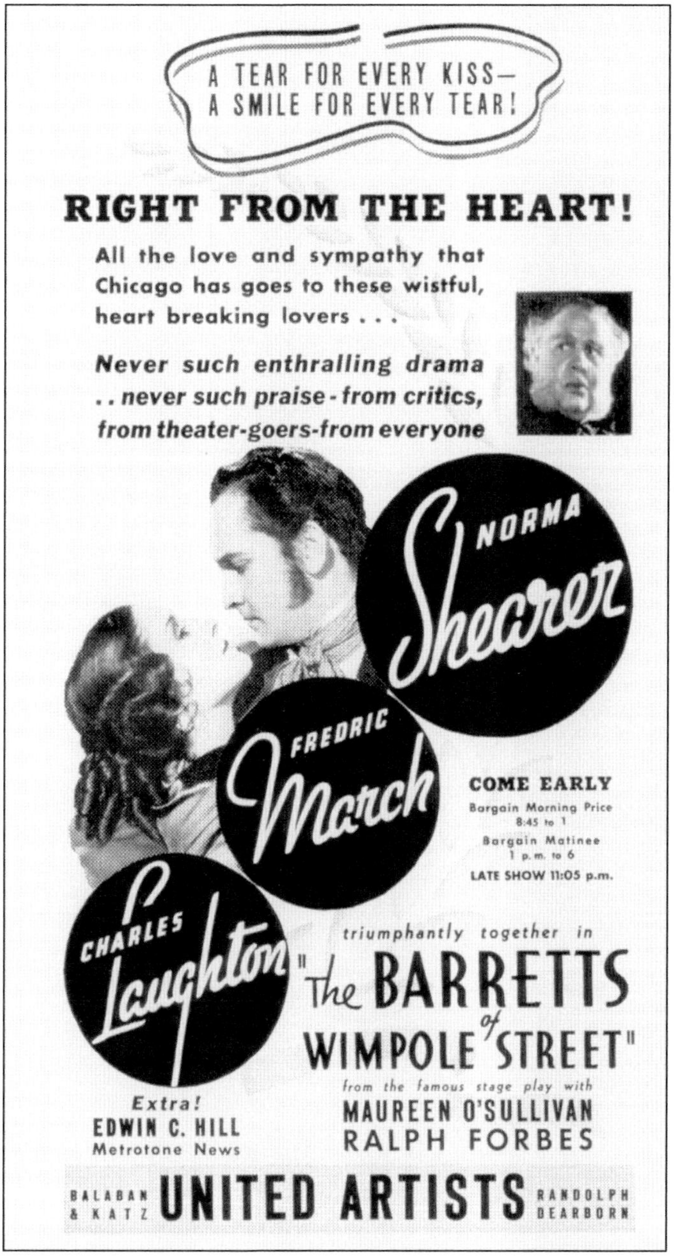

With the onslaught of the Depression in the 1930s, the United Artists Theatre suffered a steep decline in business and never fully recovered. When United Paramount Theatres, of which Balaban and Katz was a subsidiary, merged with ABC in 1950, the theater gradually fell into disrepair. Fewer people were patronizing the Loop theaters. ABC Theatres eventually became Plitt Theatres. The United Artists had to compete with newer theaters that were built near the Loop, and when the plan to raze the block (called block 37) and build an office complex was revealed, Plitt stopped investing any money into maintaining the theater. In 1985, Cineplex Odeon merged with Plitt. The theater closed on November 19, 1987. The United Artists Theatre and most of the surrounding buildings were demolished in 1989. (Advertisement courtesy of Balaban and Katz Historical Foundation.)

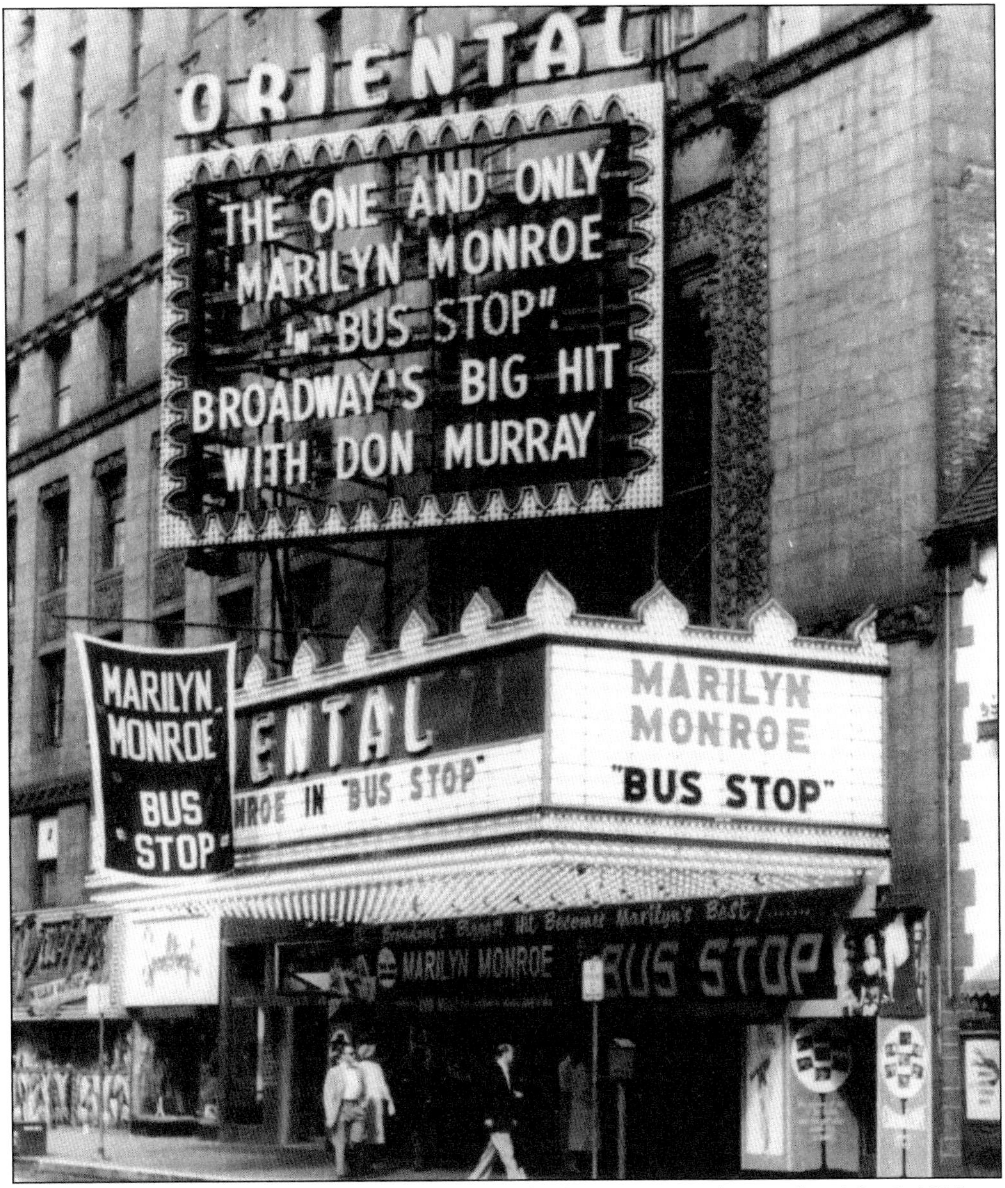

The Oriental Theatre at 20 West Randolph Street had 3,217 seats and opened on May 9, 1926, on the site where the ill-fated Iroquois Theatre had been located. The Iroquois had suffered a tragic fire in which many patrons perished. The Oriental was the second theater in the Loop to be operated by Balaban and Katz, who made sure that proper exit signs were installed and intricate fire procedures utilized to prevent another Iroquois disaster. A. J. Balaban hired Paul Ash to be the house bandleader for the Oriental. Ash had spent some time previously at the McVickers Theatre and was known for making conversation with the audience while the performance was occurring. The decorations in the Oriental were lavish. Special customized chairs were designed and installed to maximize the comfort of the audience. (Photograph courtesy of Theatre Historical Society of America.)

This beautiful photograph from the late 1920s (judging by the cars) shows the wonderful Oriental marquee with the United Artists' marquee clearly visible across the street. This image was taken to document the streetcar schedule as the clock is clearly visible on the left. (Photograph courtesy of Chicago Transit Authority.)

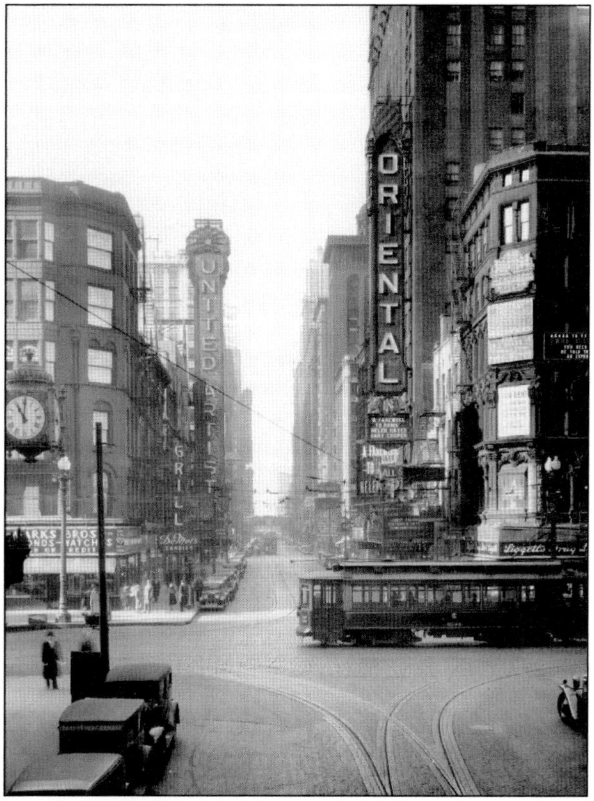

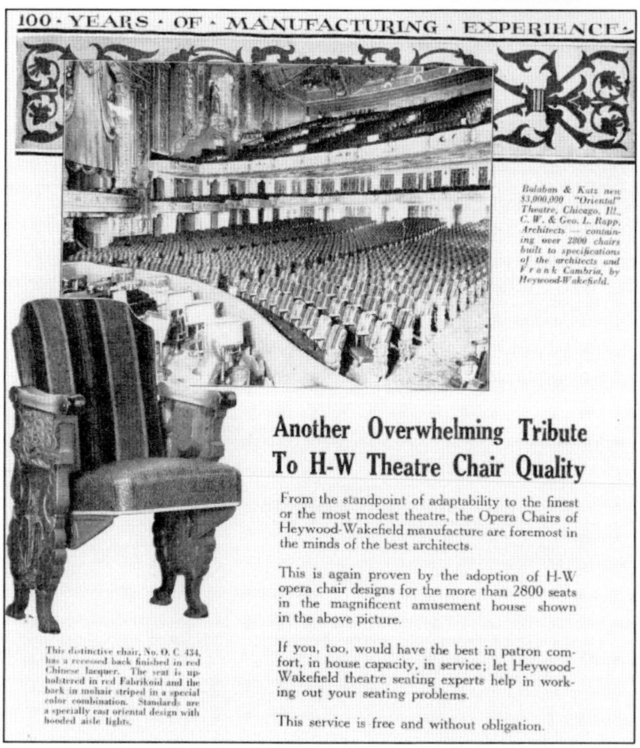

The Oriental Theatre hosted many live jazz shows, including Duke Ellington and his band, which frequently performed there. The Oriental gradually lost business in the 1960s and 1970s and began to showcase second-rate movies. (Photograph courtesy of Theatre Historical Society.)

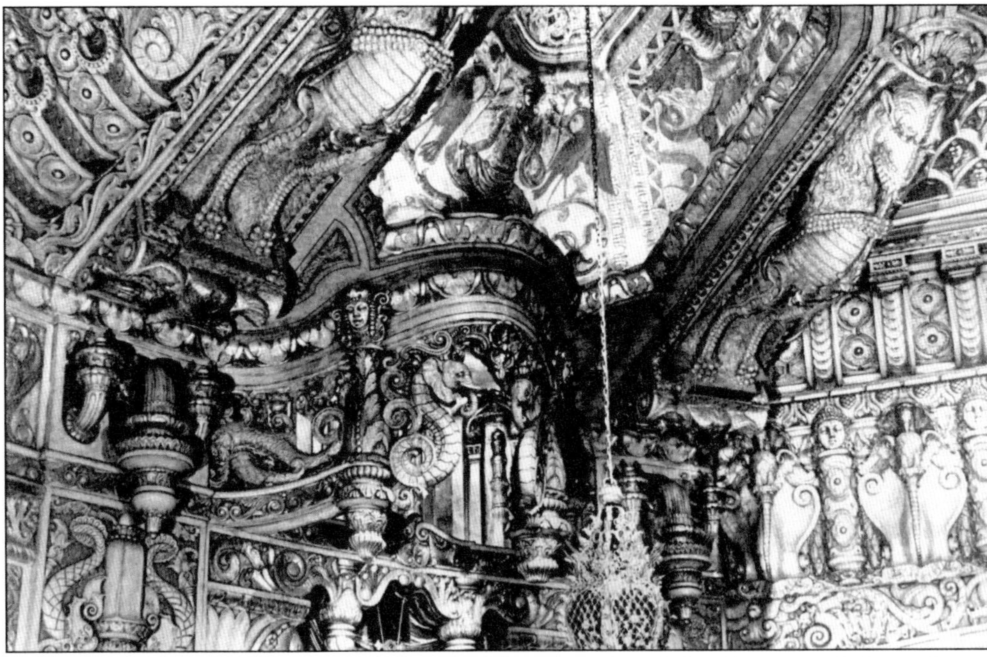

Here we see the ornate interior of the Oriental Theatre with its Indo-Chinese and plaster design. It is rumored that architects Rapp and Rapp designed this palace to please Balaban and Katz but were appalled at the results and refused to visit it once it opened. (Photograph courtesy of Theatre Historical Society of America.)

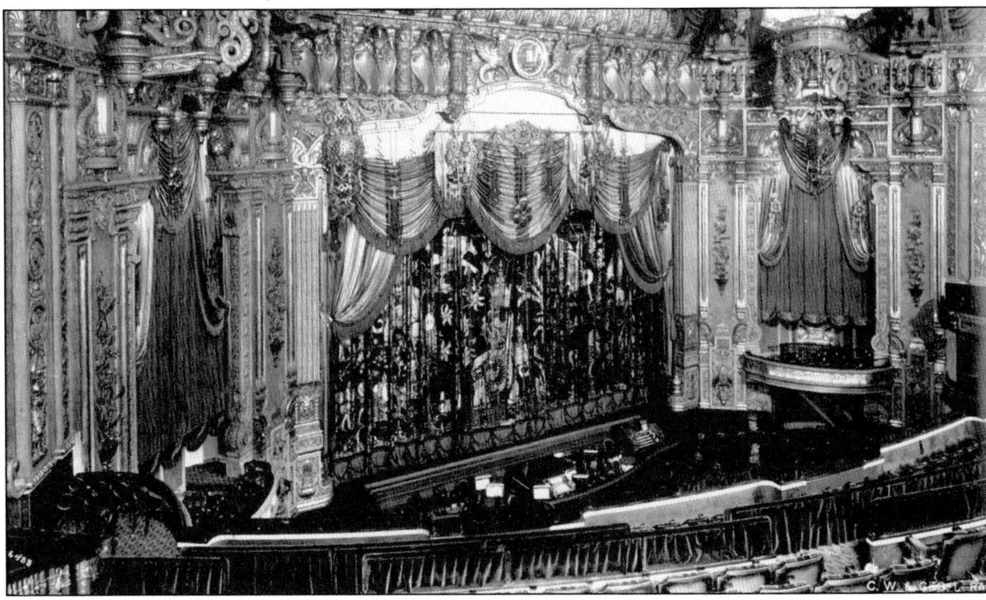

The Loop business district was changing, and the theater tried to adapt to the times. In 1980, the Oriental Theatre finally went vacant and remained so for almost 15 years with an electronic store occupying its lobby. Many people thought it would never reopen. The glorious Oriental was fully restored in 1996 and reopened in 1998 to the delight of fans of live stage shows. It is currently called the Ford Center for the Performing Arts. It is part of a group of theaters that currently features popular Broadway musicals in Chicago. (Photograph courtesy of Theatre Historical Society of America.)

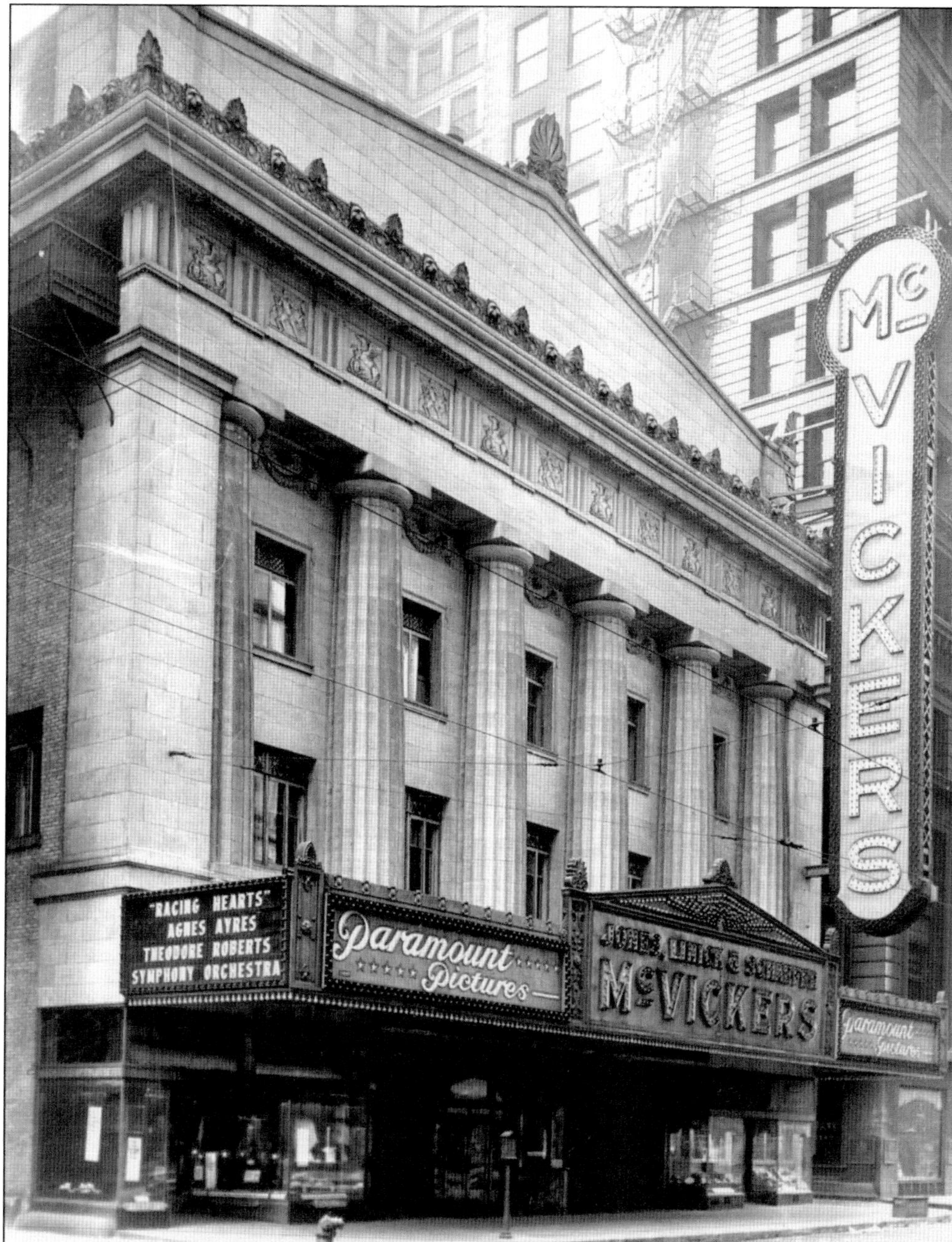

The original McVickers Theatre opened at 25 West Madison Street in 1857. It was destroyed in the Great Chicago Fire in 1871 but was rebuilt right away. In 1922, the theater was demolished and rebuilt again with a distinctive row of columns in the front. Paramount Pictures took control of the theater just before it made arrangements to buy a controlling interest in Balaban and Katz. (Photograph courtesy of Theatre Historical Society of America.)

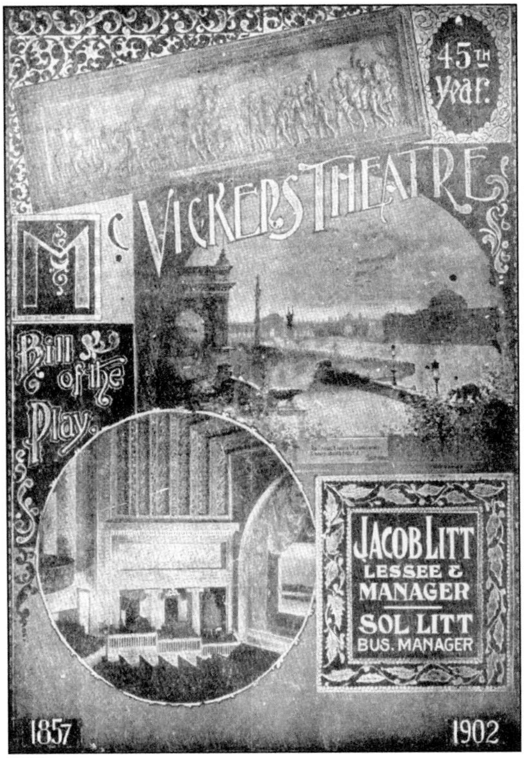

Pictured here is the cover of a rare theater program published long before McVickers Theatre belonged to Balaban and Katz. Notice that in 1902, when this document was printed, the building had already been operating for 45 years. The McVickers reopened as a B and K theater on February 1, 1926, with 2,264 seats. The quality of films shown at the theater decreased during the 1970s, and the theater shut down completely in 1984. It was demolished 1985. One of Chicago's oldest and most famous theaters was gone forever. (Photograph courtesy of Balaban and Katz Historical Foundation.)

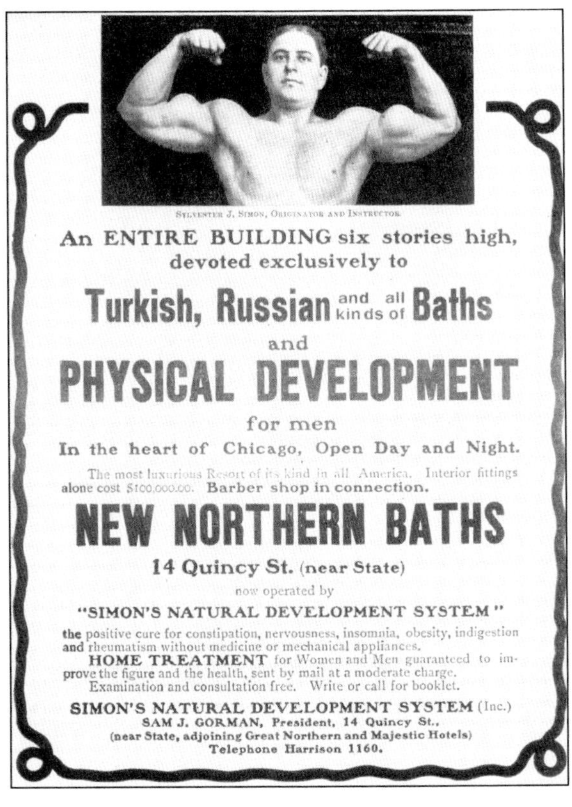

Seen here is one of the many interesting business advertisements featured in the McVickers program above. (Image courtesy of Balaban and Katz Historical Foundation.)

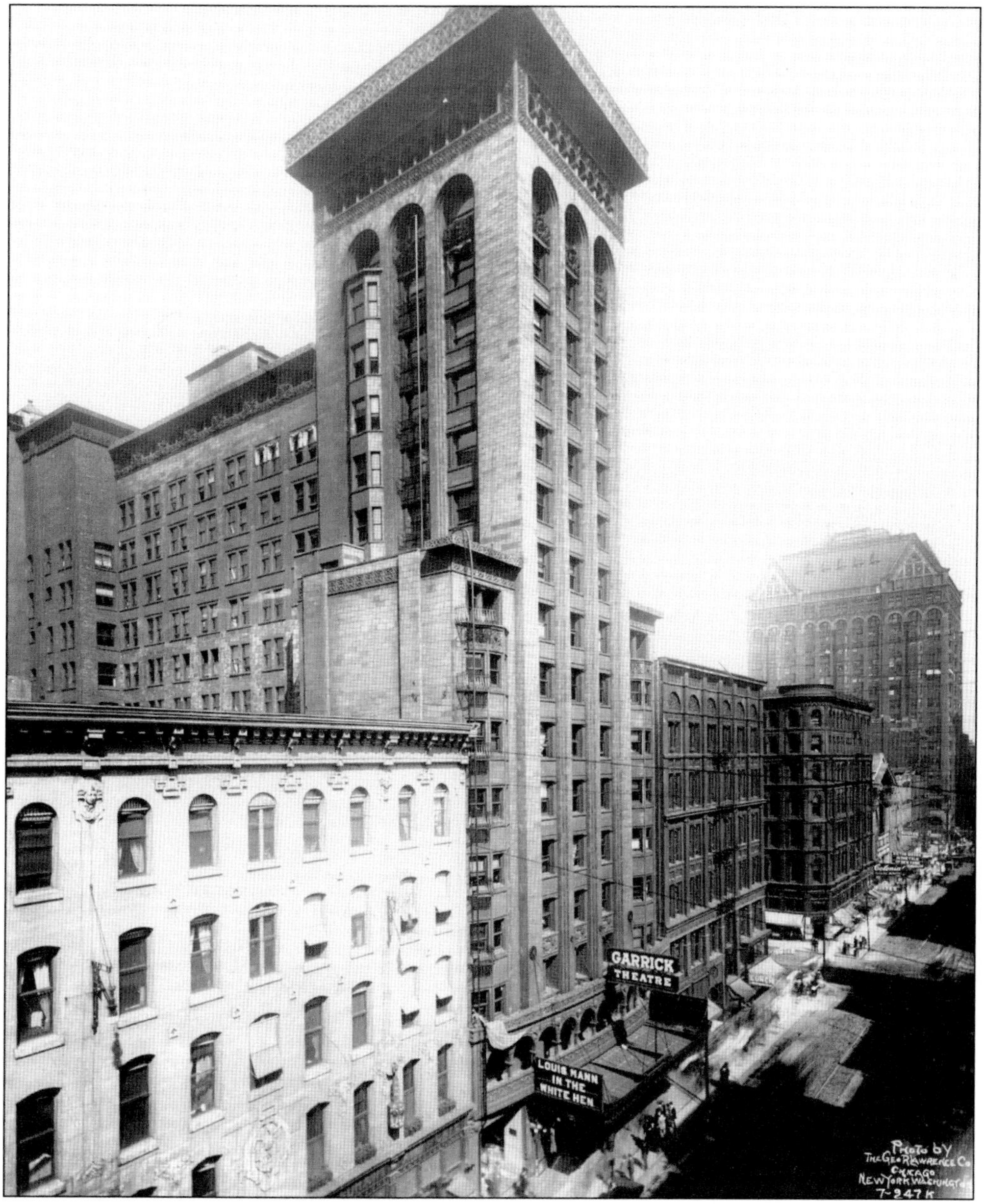

The Garrick Theatre, located at 64 West Randolph Street, was designed by Louis Henri Sullivan and was originally named the Schiller Theatre, as it was part of the Schiller Building. After World War I, it was renamed the Garrick because of negative sentiments in America felt toward Germany. Balaban and Katz leased the Garrick from its owners on March 1, 1934. Once managed by B and K, it was remodeled by the architectural firm of Rapp and Rapp. The theater was decorated in the art deco motif and had 980 seats. The Garrick was used by Balaban and Katz's television station, WBKB television, in the late 1940s and early 1950s. The theater started showing movies again in the mid-1950s. Balaban and Katz made plans to close the theater in 1960. It was going to be replaced by a parking lot, and a passionate attempt to save this historic theater ensued. It was torn down a few months later and replaced with a multilevel parking garage that was demolished in 1990. (Photograph courtesy of Chicago Historical Society.)

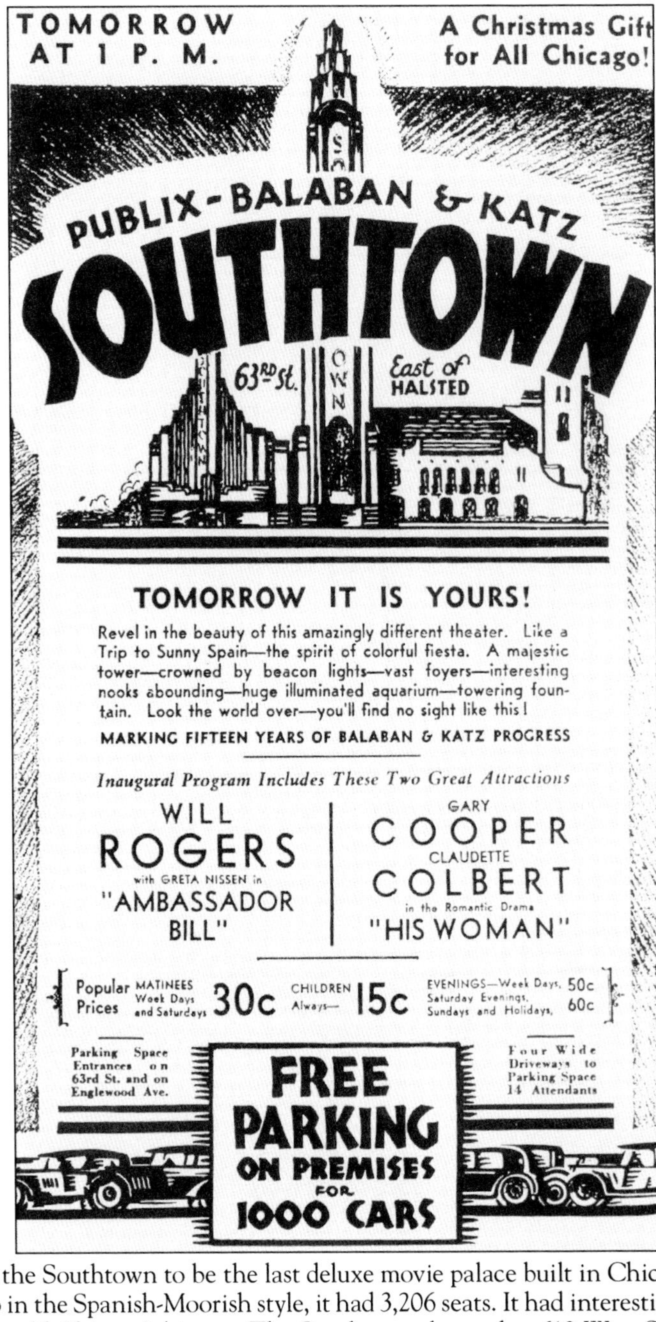

Many consider the Southtown to be the last deluxe movie palace built in Chicago. Designed by Rapp and Rapp in the Spanish-Moorish style, it had 3,206 seats. It had interesting displays in the mezzanine that told Chicago's history. The Southtown, located at 610 West Sixty-third Street, opened on Christmas Day in 1931, and the first movies shown were part of a double feature: *Ambassador Bill* starring Will Rogers and *His Woman* starring Claudette Colbert. Its timing was rather poor, as it was completed just as the Depression set in. The stage was never used for live shows. The Southtown was closed down in 1958 and became a department store. It was torn down in 1991. Notice in the advertisement above the 30¢ bargain matinees and the 14 parking attendants to park 1,000 cars. Accepting tips was strictly forbidden. (Advertisement courtesy of Theatre Historical Society of America.)

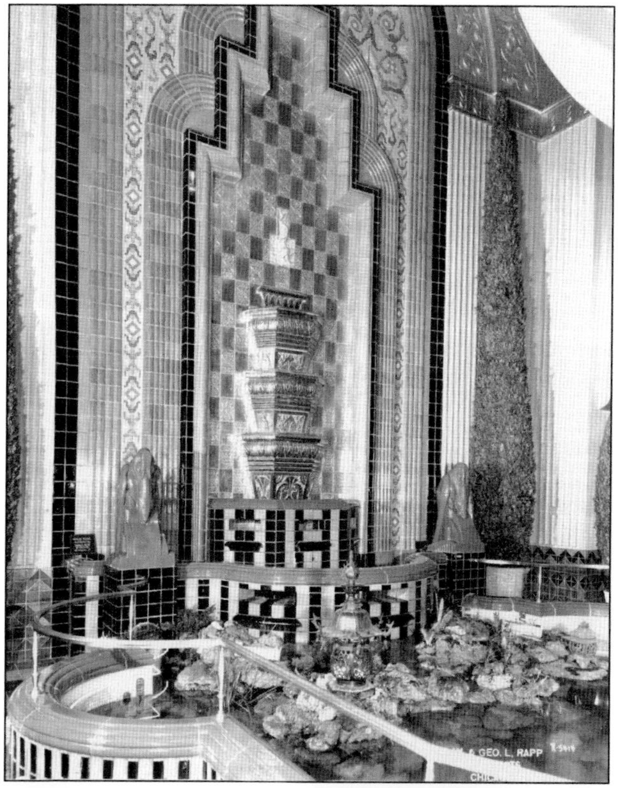

Pictured above is the lobby of the gorgeous Southtown Theatre. John Balaban managed this house for quite a few years. Notice the swans and flamingoes in the center, complete with lily pads. The Southtown was one of the first Balaban and Katz theaters to feature an integrated parking lot in the design. (Photographs courtesy of Theatre Historical Society of America.)

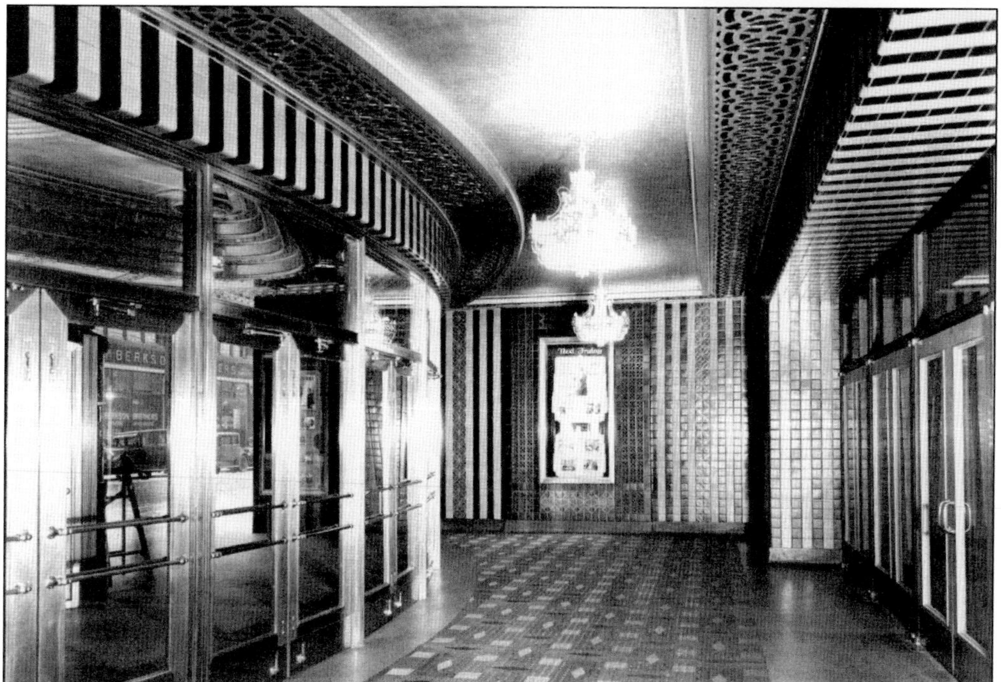

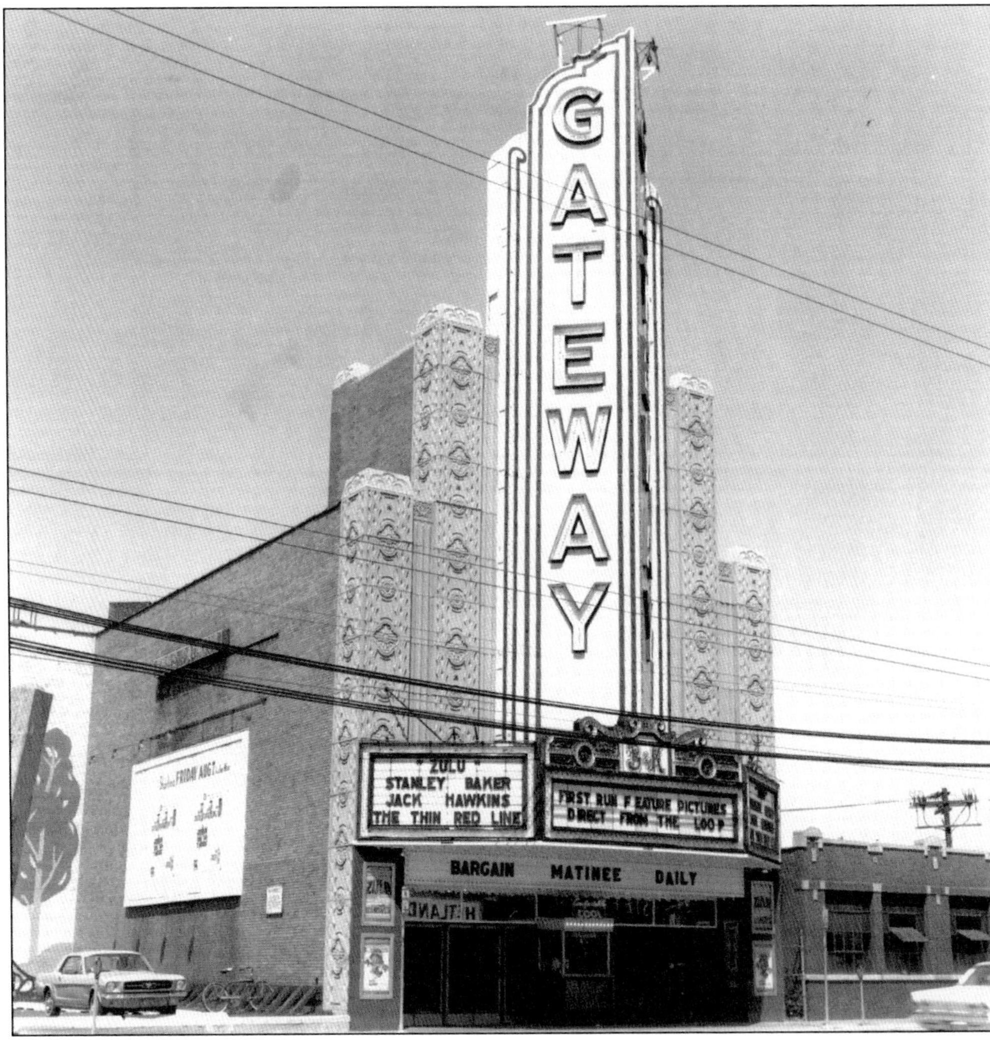

The Gateway Theatre, located at 5218 West Lawrence Avenue, opened on June 27, 1930, and had 2,092 seats. Rapp and Rapp designed the theater in the atmospheric style, which they only used on a few other projects in their careers. Atmospheric design integrated various elements from different eras to create a mood. The Gateway in Chicago and the Paramount in Toledo, Ohio, were the only two atmospherics designed by Rapp and Rapp. (Photograph courtesy of Theatre Historical Society of America.)

The Gateway Theatre did not feature live shows; it did not even have a stage. It was one of the few Balaban and Katz theaters that did not see a huge drop off in business in the 1960s and 1970s. It made money even after B and K and ABC Theatres were sold to the Plitt Company. In the mid-1980s, a Polish American society named the Copernicus Cultural and Civic Center bought the theater. The theater was, until recently, the home to the very active Silent Film Society of Chicago. Recently there has been talk of the theater being torn down to make way for condominiums. (Photograph courtesy of Theatre Historical Society of America.)

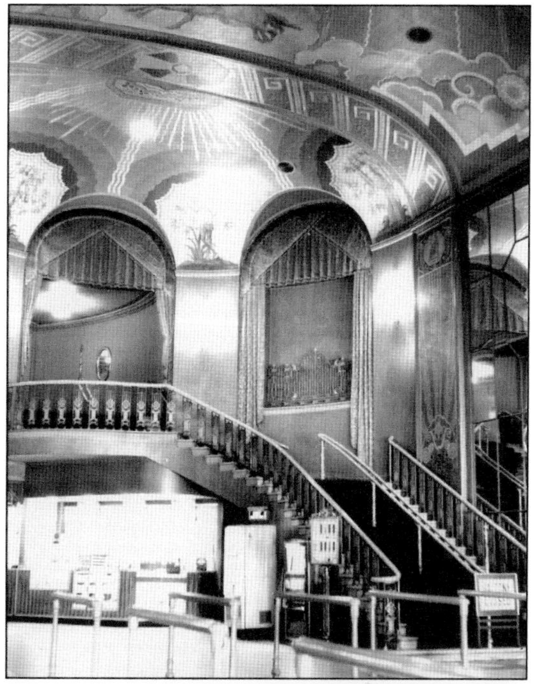

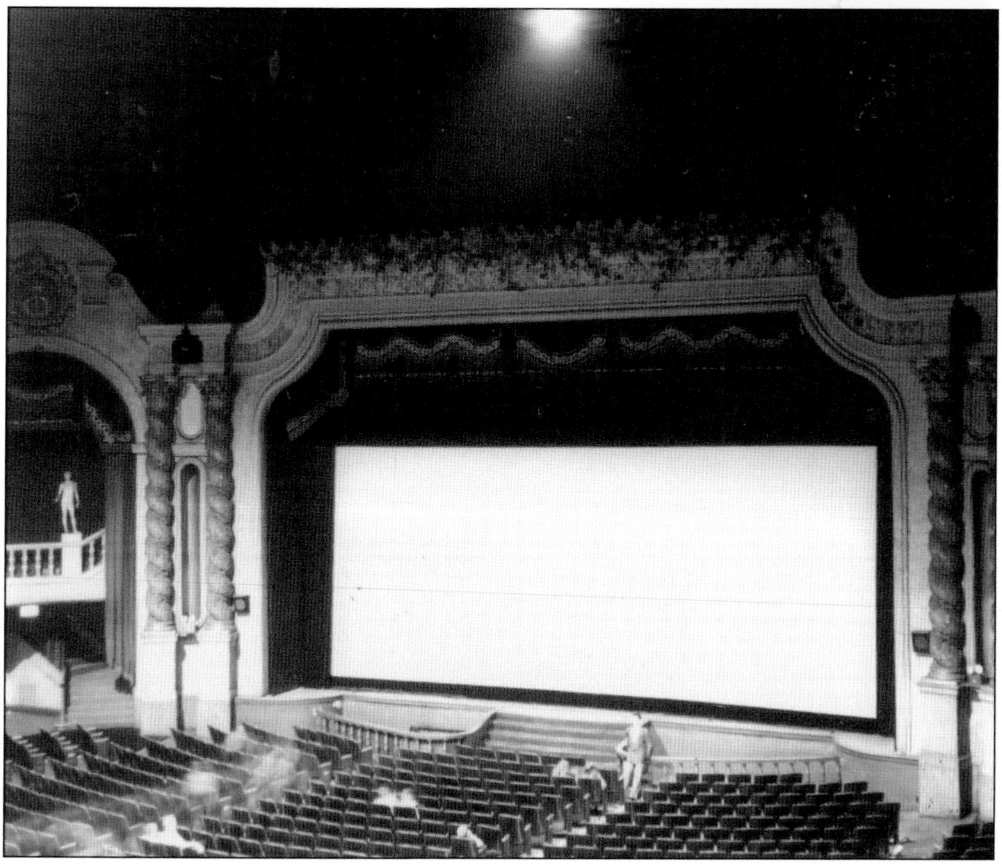

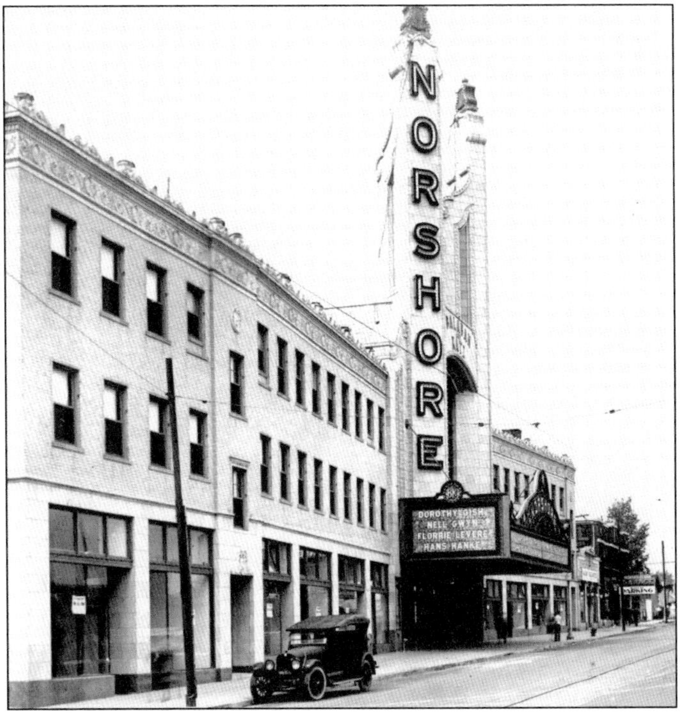

The Norshore Theatre located at 1748 North Howard Street was designed by Rapp and Rapp and was constructed in 1926. It opened on June 17, 1926. It was leased to a corporation in which Balaban and Katz had a 50 percent interest and the Orpheum circuit had a 50 percent interest. Balaban and Katz took over the full operation soon after it opened. (Photographs courtesy of Theatre Historical Society of America.)

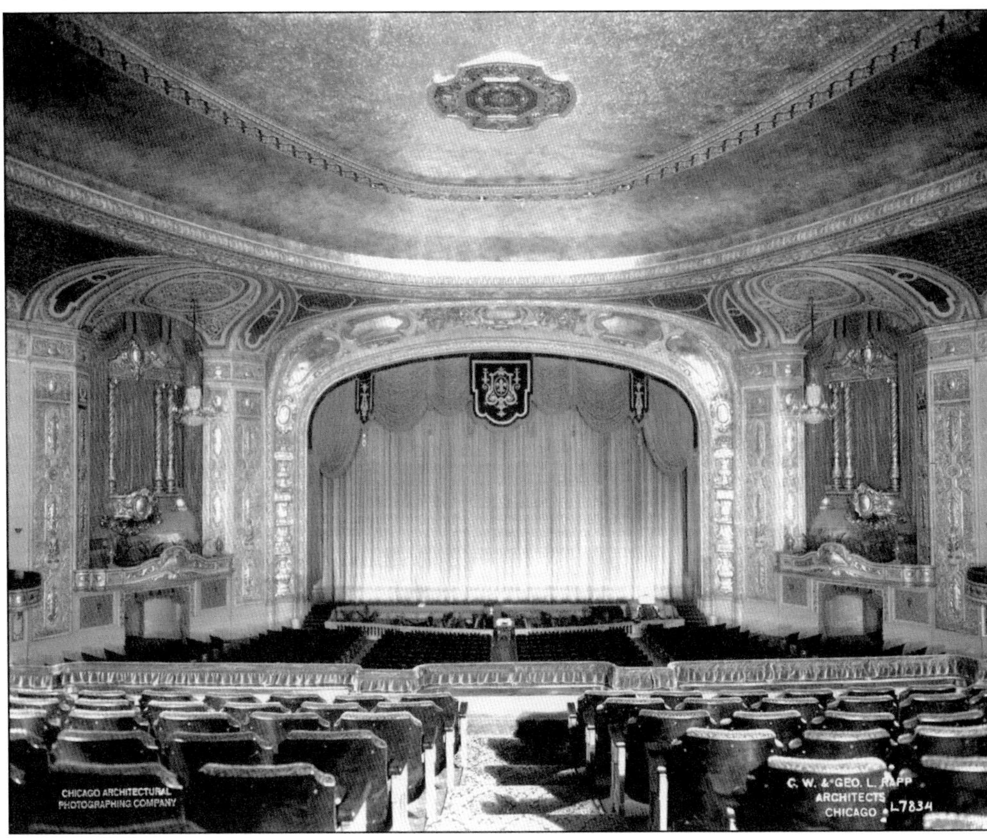

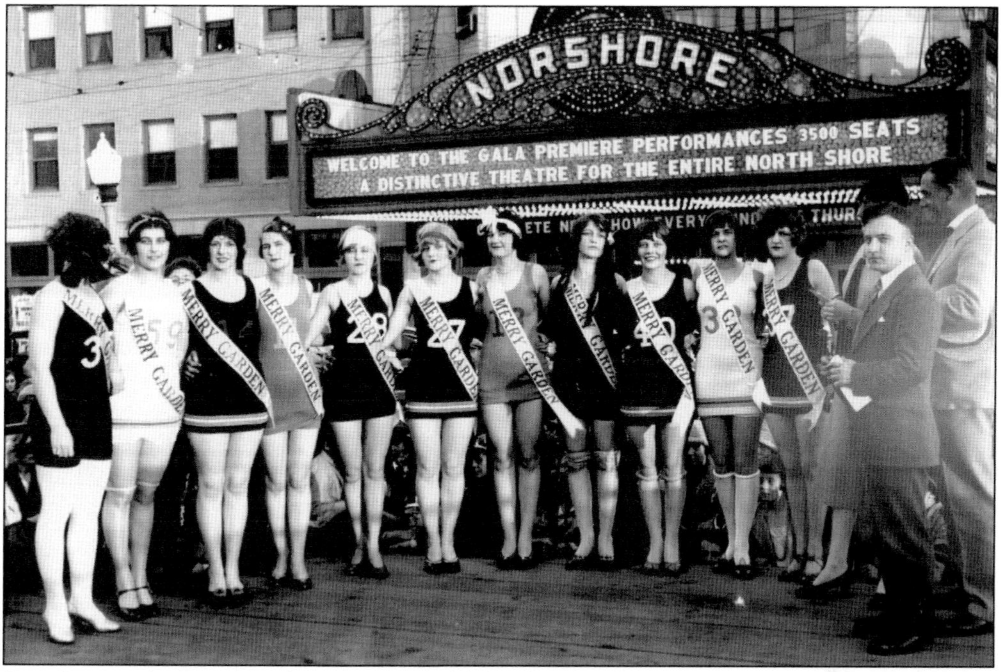

Seen here is the Miss Norshore contest held the day the theater opened in 1926. (Photograph courtesy of John Peters.)

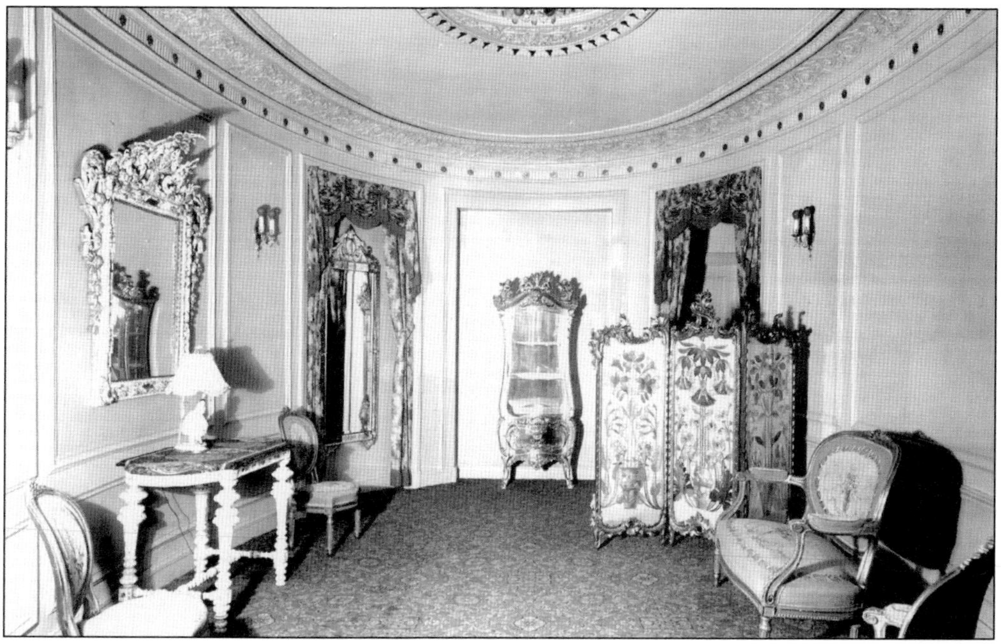

Pictured here is the ornate Norshore ladies' room. B and K spared no expense to keep the customers happy. Here ladies of all socioeconomic status could powder their noses, chat, and enjoy being pampered. The building was filled with fine antiques imported from all over the world. David Balaban managed the 3,017-seat theater for the first few years it was open. The Norshore closed in 1957 and was torn down in 1960 to make room for a financial company. (Photograph courtesy of Theatre Historical Society of America.)

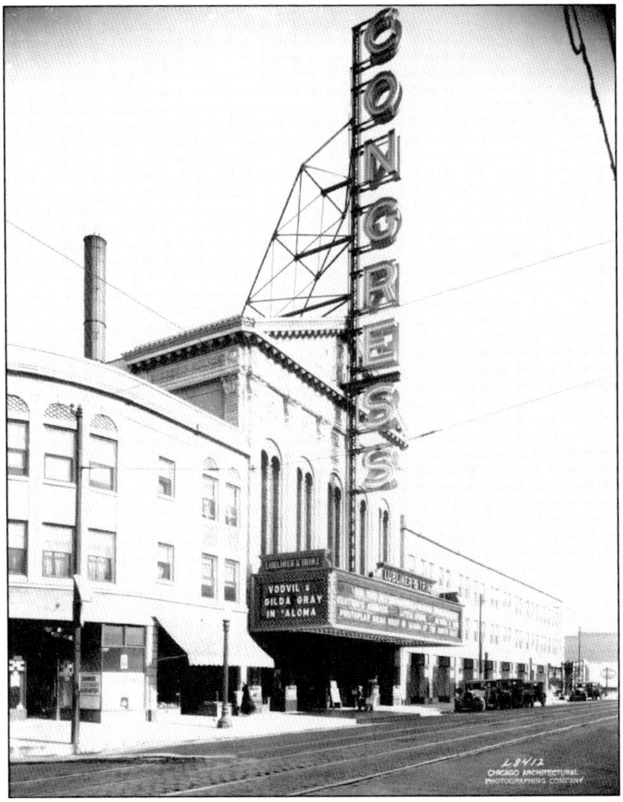

The Congress Theater is located at 2135 North Milwaukee Avenue and opened on September 5, 1926. The theater features a fancy dome-covered seating area and plaster decorations. It is one of the few surviving movie palaces in Chicago from the 1920s. It was built by Lubliner and Trinz Theatres Incorporated, which was a partnership between the former Lubliner and Trinz Company and Balaban and Katz Corporation. (Photograph courtesy of the Theatre Historical Society of America.)

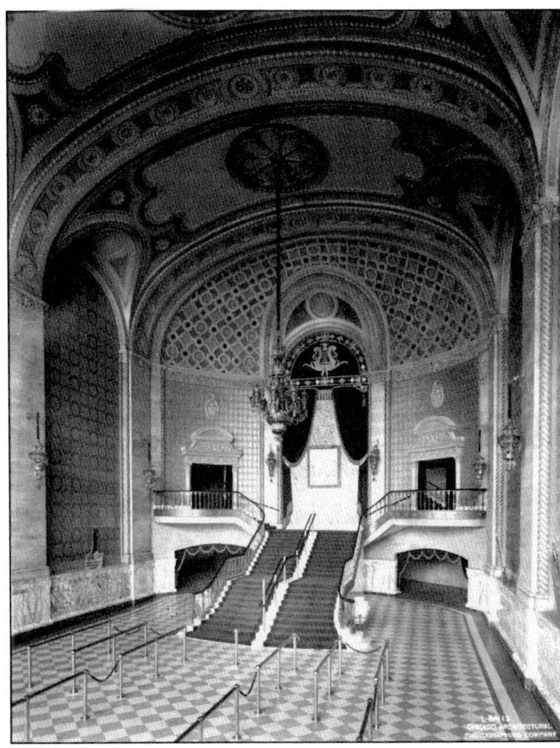

On July 15, 1925, Lubliner and Trinz merged with B and K. A new corporation was formed, with 50 percent of the stock owned by Balaban and Katz and 50 percent owned by Lubliner and Trinz. Balaban and Katz paid almost $500,000 for half the company. Lubliner and Trinz contributed the fixtures and equipment, which it held in the 26 theaters it previously owned, including the Congress. Lubliner and Trinz received 50 percent of the profits of all theaters it owned jointly with Balaban and Katz. It is speculated that this merging of forces help prevent an "overseating" of Chicago. It is amazing that in the mid-1920s there were about 600 theaters in Chicago. Many of these houses were 200- or 300-seat converted stores. (Photograph courtesy of the Theatre Historical Society of America.)

The opening movie at the Congress Theater was *Rolling Home*, complimented by a selection of vaudeville acts. The Congress eventually carried a variety of new names reflecting its Latino clientele. During the 1970s, it was known as Teatro Azteca, which featured Spanish films and live entertainment. (Photograph courtesy of Theatre Historical Society of America.)

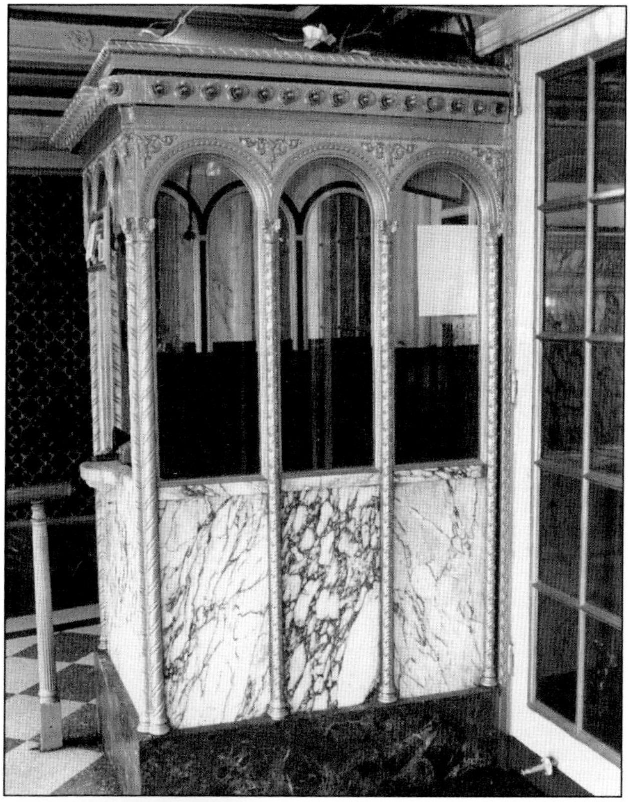

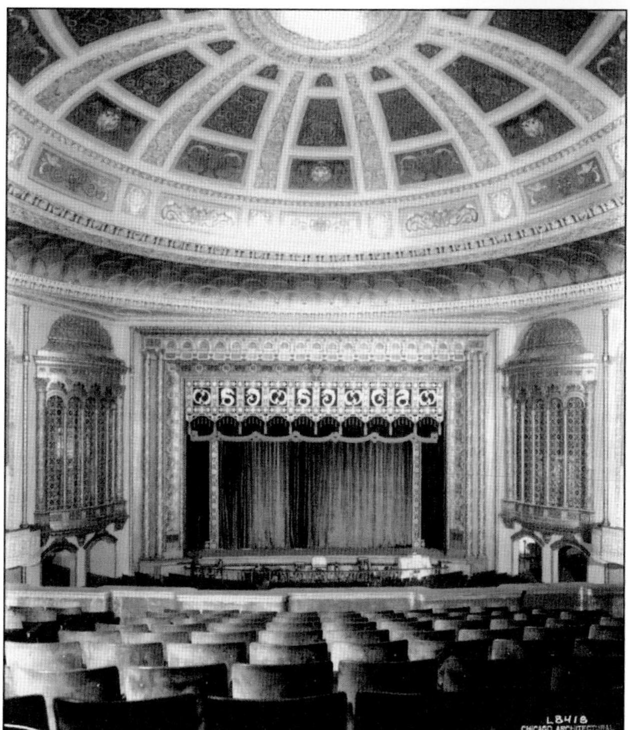

The Congress thankfully escaped the wrecking ball when, in 2000, it was threatened with demolition. Its supporters successfully fought off a proposed condominium project. It stands as a symbol of positive community activism in action. It is a successful concert venue today. (Photograph courtesy of Theatre Historical Society of America.)

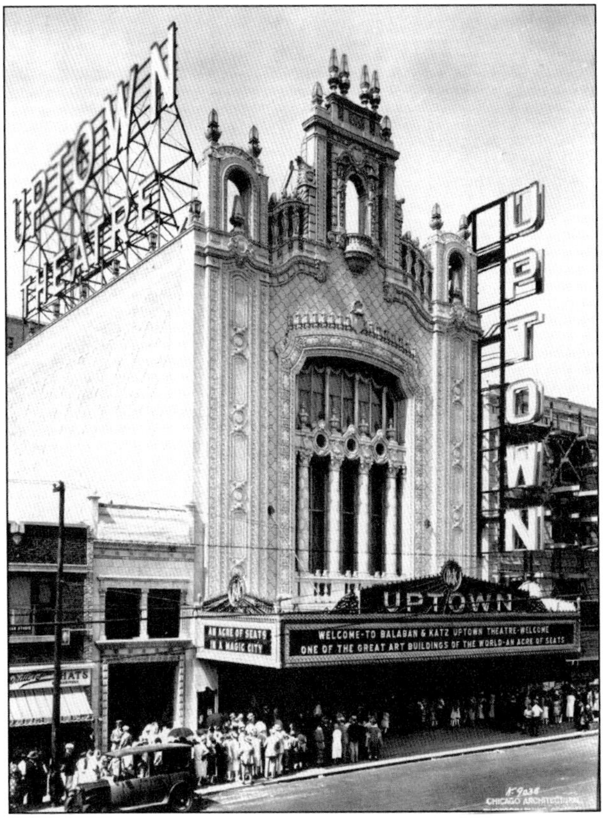

The Uptown Theatre, located at 4814 Broadway Street, was completed in the French baroque style on August 17, 1925. It was fabulously huge, boasting almost an acre of seats, with a total of 4,320! The theater has an unusual shape to it. When Balaban and Katz Theatres acquired the property, it was unable to buy out the building next door. So, the lobby runs perpendicular to the auditorium. Many people thought that the Uptown was too large a theater for the neighborhood when it opened. Although the theater created quite a lot of excitement early on, it had a lot of trouble drawing ample crowds to keep the theater filled consistently. The theater survived the transition between ownership changes at Balaban and Katz until Plitt sold it to the Rabiela family in 1976. (Photographs courtesy of Theatre Historical Society of America.)

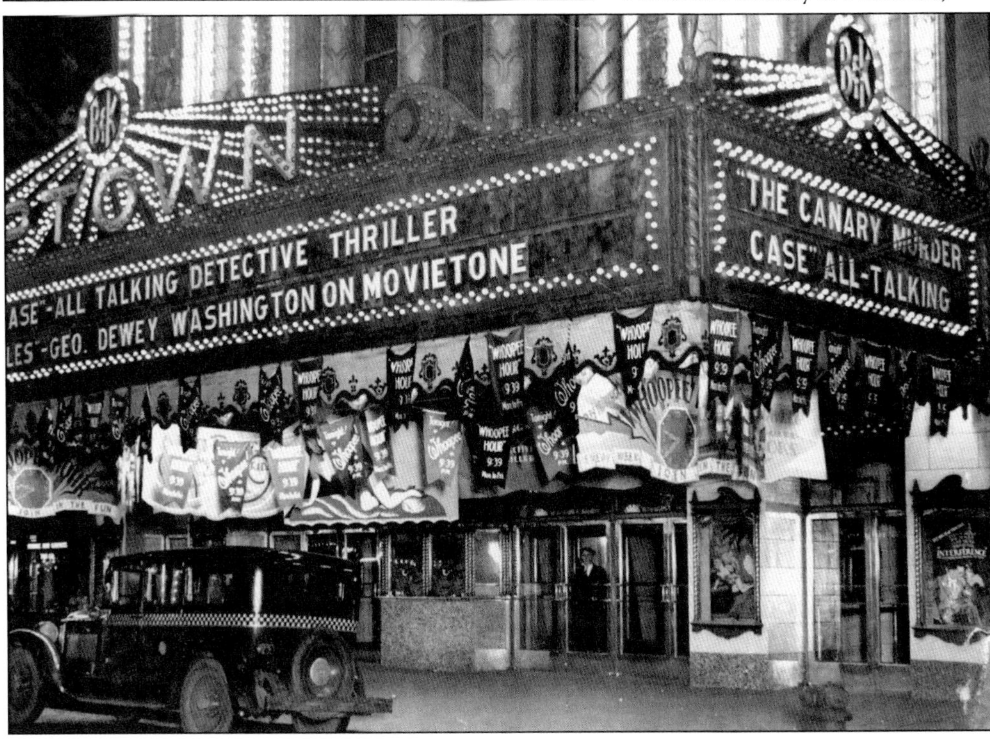

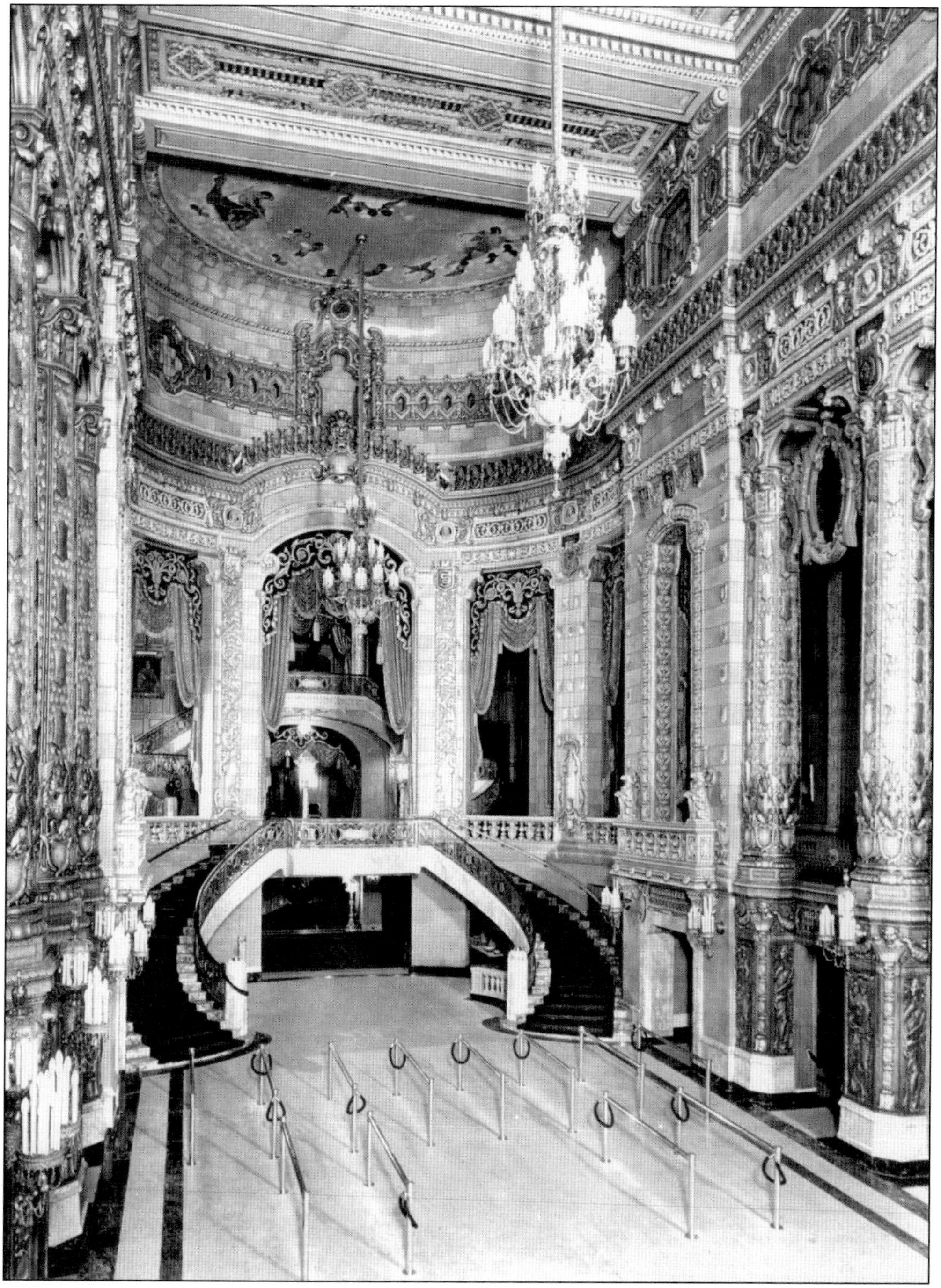

The Uptown Theatre featured one of the most ornately decorated lobbies of any theater in the world. It was the second-largest movie theater in the United Sates, second only in size to Radio City Music Hall in New York City, when it was built. David Balaban managed this movie palace for a time. His son Max has fond memories of raiding the concession stand as his dad conferred with the many staff members. At opening, the Uptown had more than 100 employees. (Photograph courtesy of Theatre Historical Society of America.)

Balaban & Katz

Uptown Theatre

Week of Dec. 7, 1925

OVERTURE
"IL GUARANY"
By GOMEZ
UPTOWN THEATRE ORCHESTRA
Direction JOSEF KOESTNER

SCREEN NOVELTY

Balaban & Katz Present
MISS RUTH BREWER
in a remarkable demonstration of musical versatility

WEEKLY NEWS VIEWS

MILTON CHARLES
at the
UPTOWN THEATRE
MIGHTY GRANDE ORGAN
playing
"The Thanksgiving Spirit"

Balaban & Katz Production
"THE FOAM SPRITE"
Miss Marie Herron, *Soprano*
Marie Yurieva, Veceslav Svobode, *Dancers*

First National Pictures Present
"THE DARK ANGEL"
CAST

Hilary Trent	*RONALD COLMAN*
Kitty Vane	*VILMA BANKY*
Gerald Shannon	*Wyndham Standing*
Lord Beaumont	*Frank Elliott*
Miss Pindle	*Helen Jerome Eddy*
Roma	*Florence Turner*
Sir Evelyn Vane	*Charles Lane*

SELECTED KOMIC-KARTOON

STARTING MONDAY
The story that has all New York abuzz

"The Grand Duchess and the Waiter"

with the most graceful lover on the screen
ADOLPHE MENJOU
FLORENCE VIDOR

At Other Balaban & Katz Theatres this Week

CHICAGO STATE ST. between RANDOLPH and LAKE STS.
RAMON NOVARRO
"THE MIDSHIPMAN"

ROOSEVELT STATE STREET near WASHINGTON ST.
Wild Revels! Weird Scenes!
"The Phantom of the Opera"

TIVOLI COTTAGE GROVE AVE. and 63d STREET
Ronald COLMAN, Vilma BANKY
"THE DARK ANGEL"

CENTRAL PARK Roosevelt Road & Central Park Ave.
WORLD'S PREMIER VAUDEVILLE AND SCREEN MASTERPIECES

(Program subject to change)

This is an advertisement from *Balaban & Katz Magazine* announcing the opening of the Uptown Theatre. Notice the wide variety of entertainment options the theater had to offer. The Uptown enjoyed many years of successful shows and became famous in Chicago's North Broadway neighborhood. The eventual demise of the economy with the onset of the Depression and the disappearance of most of the live shows did not help the Uptown. In effect, there were too many entertainment options on the North Side. Gradually the area began to change. Many of the single-family homes were replaced with housing projects. Almost miraculously, the Uptown was not torn down as were many of the North Side venues, such as the Granada. (Advertisement courtesy of Balaban and Katz Historical Foundation.)

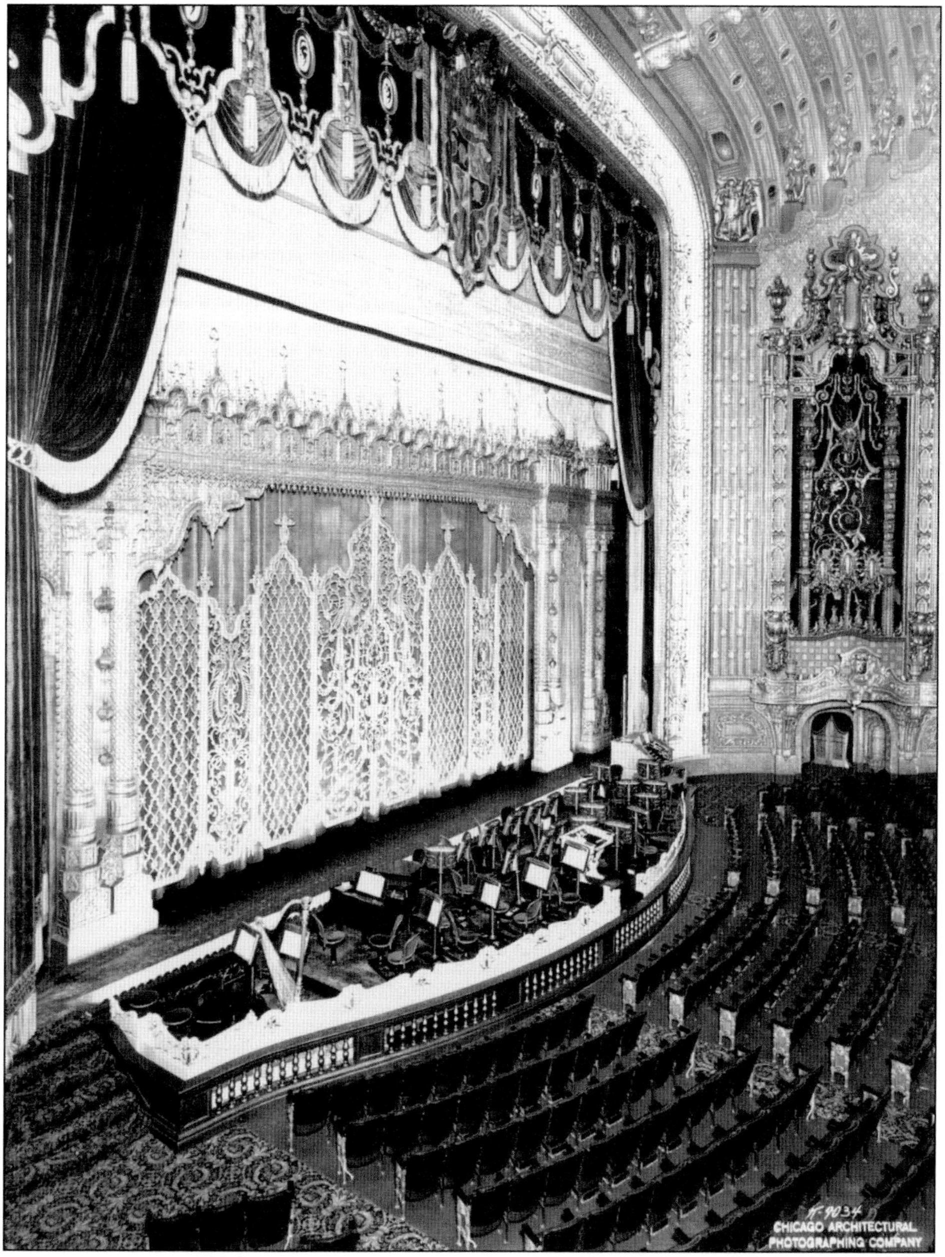

From 1976 to 1981, the Uptown hosted many big-name rock and roll bands and showed Spanish language films in between. Groups like the Grateful Dead and Genesis and Rod Stewart all got a chance to play at the Uptown before sold-out crowds. The Rabielas unfortunately lost the building, and the fate of this magnificent theater became complicated in legal battles, foreclosures, and so forth. Several different attempts to save the building have fallen through. Meanwhile, the building's integrity has been affected from water damage, vandalism, and neglect. A few organizations meet regularly to discuss the fate of this unique movie palace and to celebrate its past. Hopefully, the City of Chicago and the parties who actually hold title to the Uptown will eventually decide to save it before it is too late. Too many of these irreplaceable movie palaces have already been lost. (Photograph courtesy of Theatre Historical Society of America.)

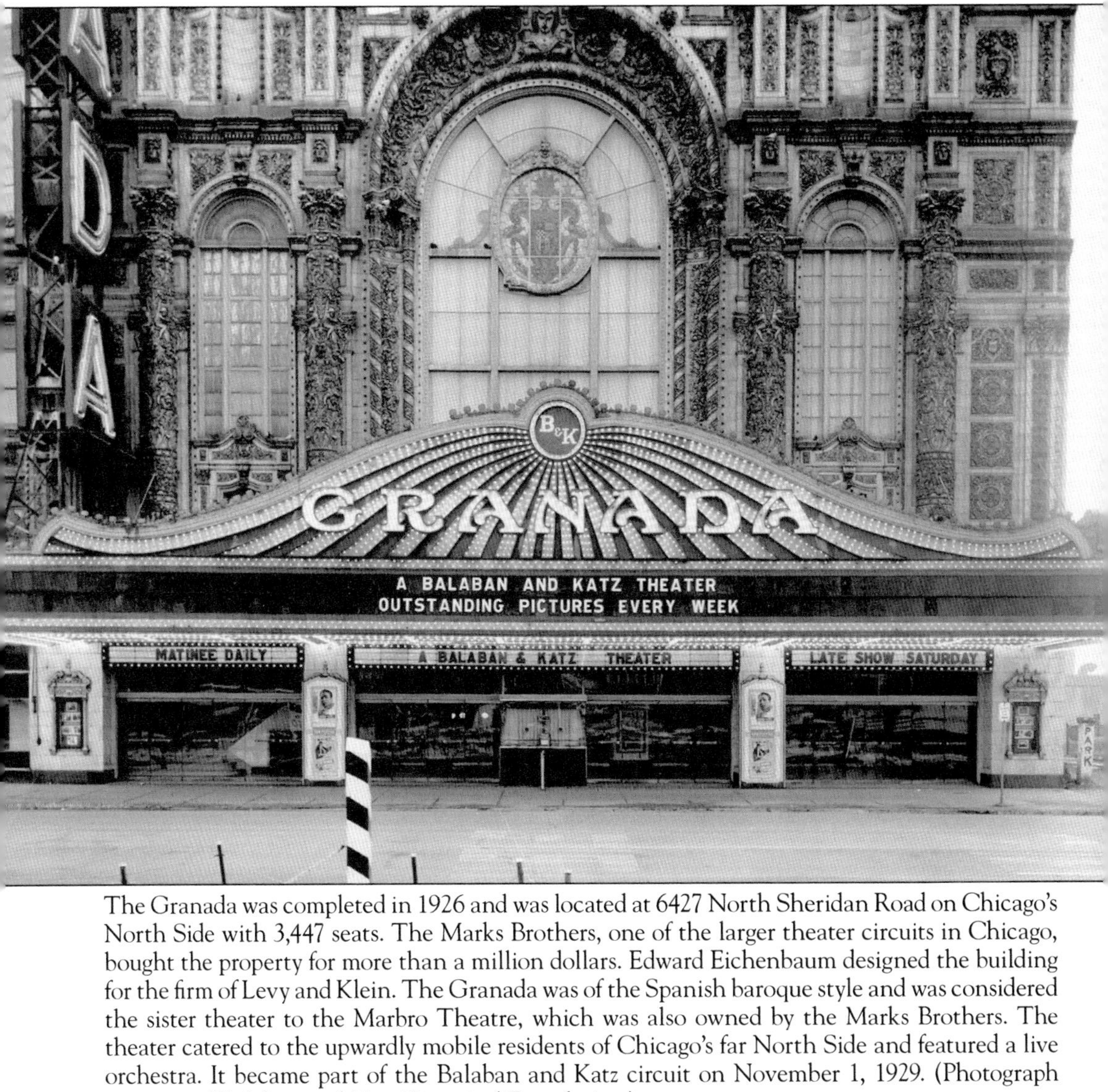

The Granada was completed in 1926 and was located at 6427 North Sheridan Road on Chicago's North Side with 3,447 seats. The Marks Brothers, one of the larger theater circuits in Chicago, bought the property for more than a million dollars. Edward Eichenbaum designed the building for the firm of Levy and Klein. The Granada was of the Spanish baroque style and was considered the sister theater to the Marbro Theatre, which was also owned by the Marks Brothers. The theater catered to the upwardly mobile residents of Chicago's far North Side and featured a live orchestra. It became part of the Balaban and Katz circuit on November 1, 1929. (Photograph courtesy of Balaban and Katz Historical Foundation.)

This advertisement is for the Granada Theatre when the Marks Brothers owned it. From the 1940s to the 1970s, the theater enjoyed modest success. It survived the transition through three owners: Balaban and Katz, United Paramount ABC, and Plitt Theatres. It became a second-run house with bargain matinees. The rent was raised drastically in the early 1970s; the Plitt organization refused to pay since the theater was barely profitable. The theater closed in 1975. A concert promotions company rented the theater in 1979 and produced rock shows there. Complaints from neighbors relating to rowdy kids and a lack of parking eventually doomed the theater. An offer close to $1 million was made for the property. Demolition began in the spring of 1990. An apartment complex named the Granada Centre is on the property now. (Image courtesy of Theatre Historical Society of America.)

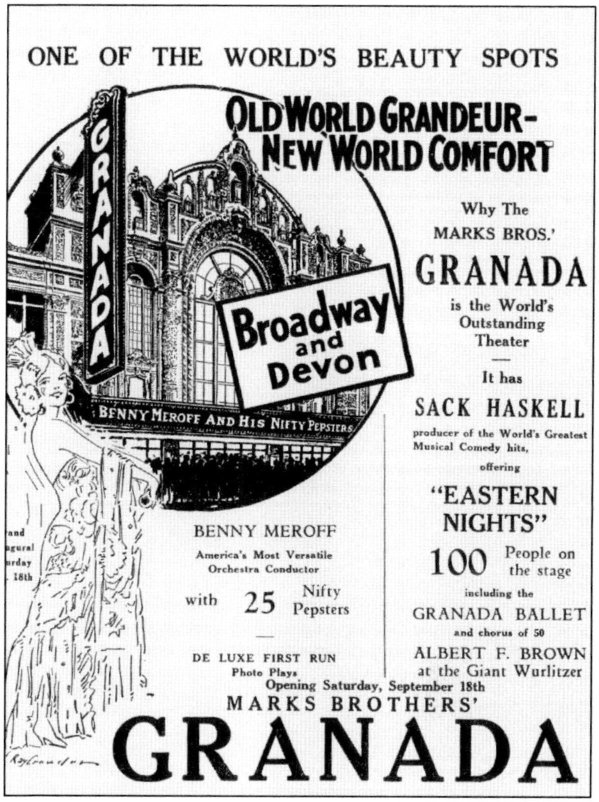

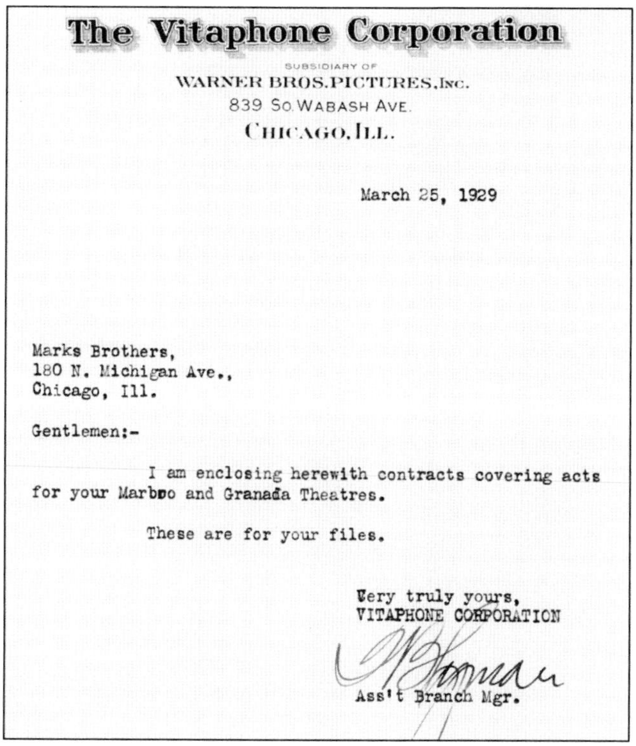

The Vitaphone Corporation

SUBSIDIARY OF
WARNER BROS. PICTURES, INC.
839 SO. WABASH AVE.
CHICAGO, ILL.

March 25, 1929

Marks Brothers,
180 N. Michigan Ave.,
Chicago, Ill.

Gentlemen:-

I am enclosing herewith contracts covering acts for your Marbro and Granada Theatres.

These are for your files.

Very truly yours,
VITAPHONE CORPORATION

Ass't Branch Mgr.

Here is a letter from the Vitaphone Corporation in 1929 regarding the Granada's and Marbro's sound equipment. Each month, every theater in the country that used the Vitaphone system for sound reproduction was obligated to pay Vitaphone (a division of Warner Brothers) a fee. (Image courtesy of Balaban and Katz Historical Foundation.)

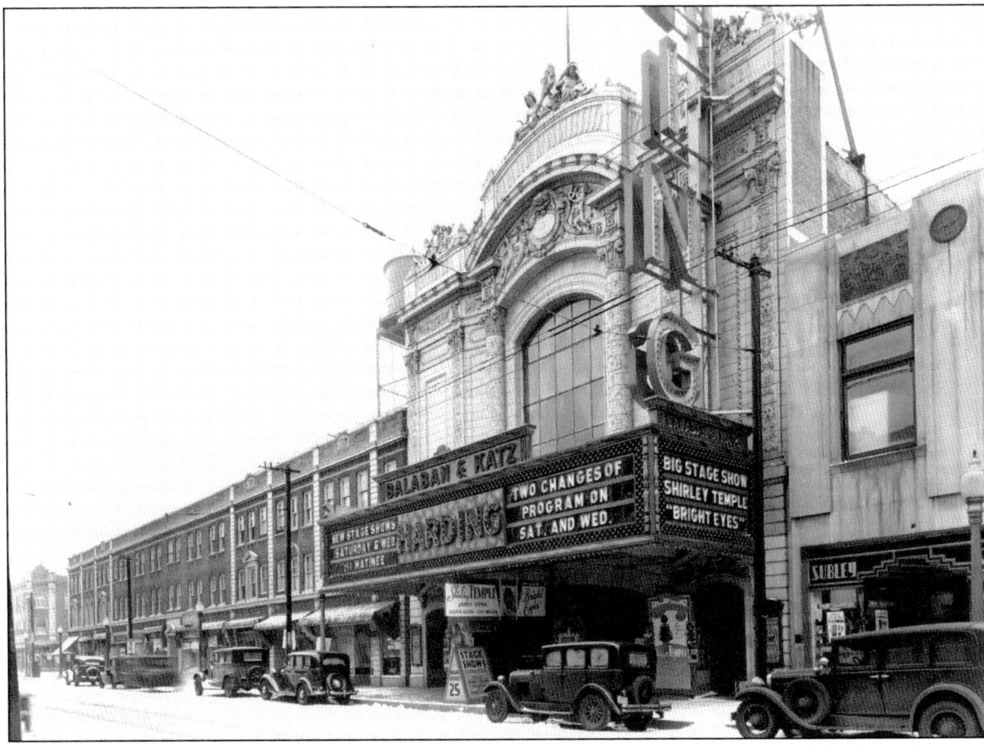

The Harding Theatre was located at 2714 North Milwaukee Avenue and had 2,962 seats. Freidstein and Company designed it in the Italian Renaissance and neoclassical style, and Lubliner and Trinz began construction of the theater before it entered into a partnership with Balaban and Katz in 1925. (Photographs courtesy of Theatre Historical Society of America.)

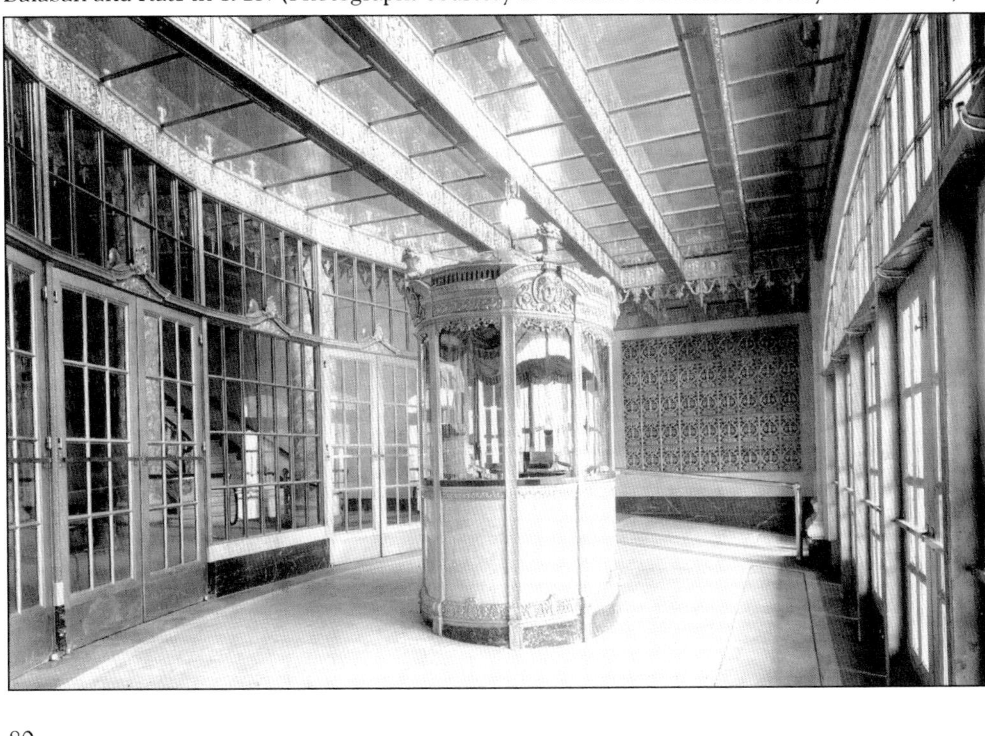

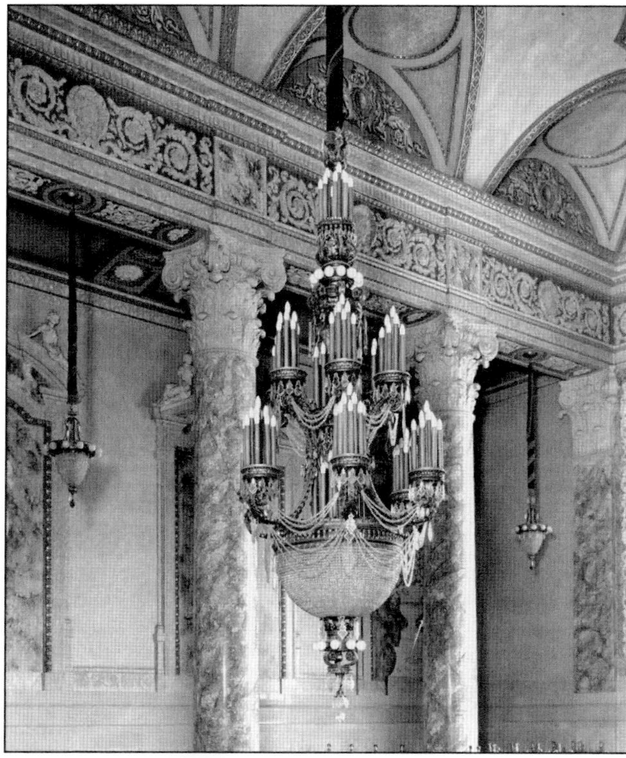

By the time the Harding Theatre was finished, Lubliner and Trinz and B and K shared responsibility for it. It was part of a trio of similar theaters, which included the Congress and the Tower Theatres. The Harding was shuttered in 1963 and was demolished soon thereafter. (Photographs courtesy of Theatre Historical Society of America.)

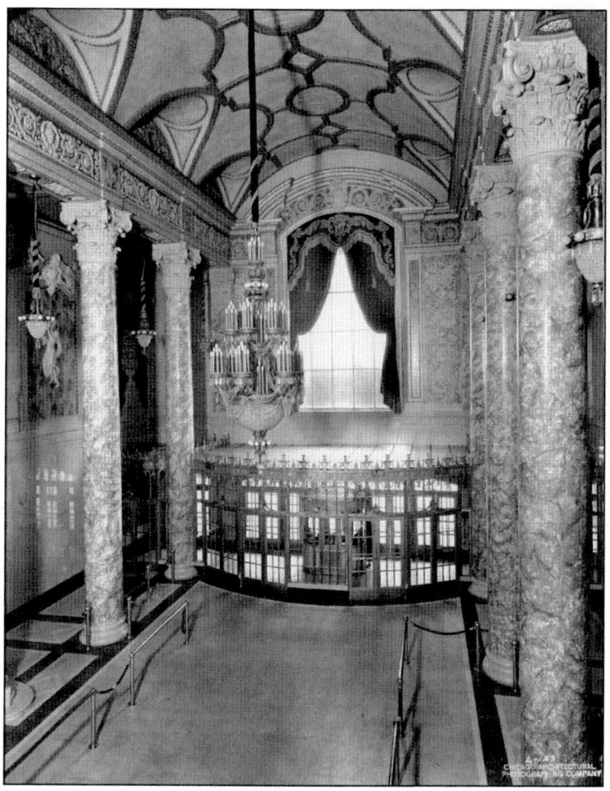

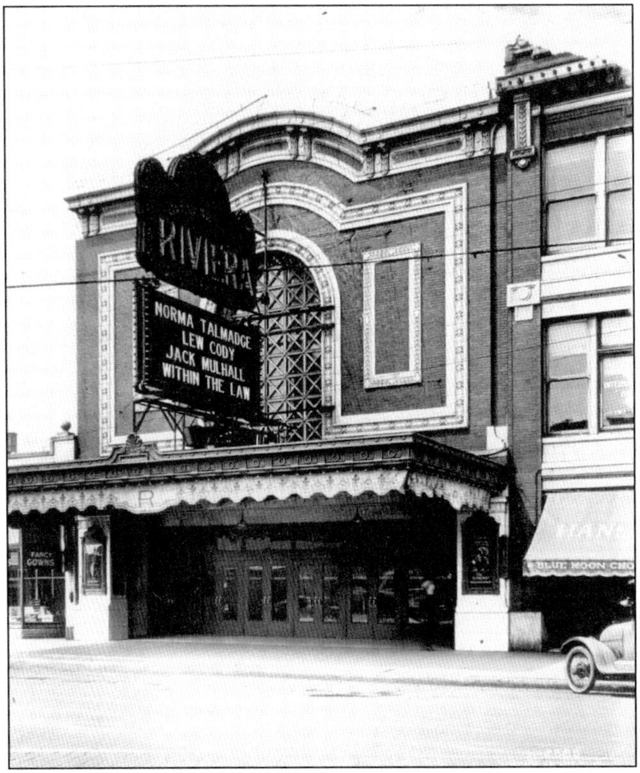

On September 29, 1918, the Riviera Theatre opened at 4746 North Racine Avenue. Balaban and Katz took over the project after another company called Jones, Linick and Schaefer had run out of money before it was finished. When the Riviera opened, Lubliner and Trinz and Ascher Brothers circuits were operating in the North Side of Chicago and had a great deal more influence in offering first-run movies than did Balaban and Katz. So, B and K drew large crowds to the Riviera through the production of wonderful stage shows and by offering live orchestral accompaniment of silent films. (Photographs courtesy of Theatre Historical Society of America.)

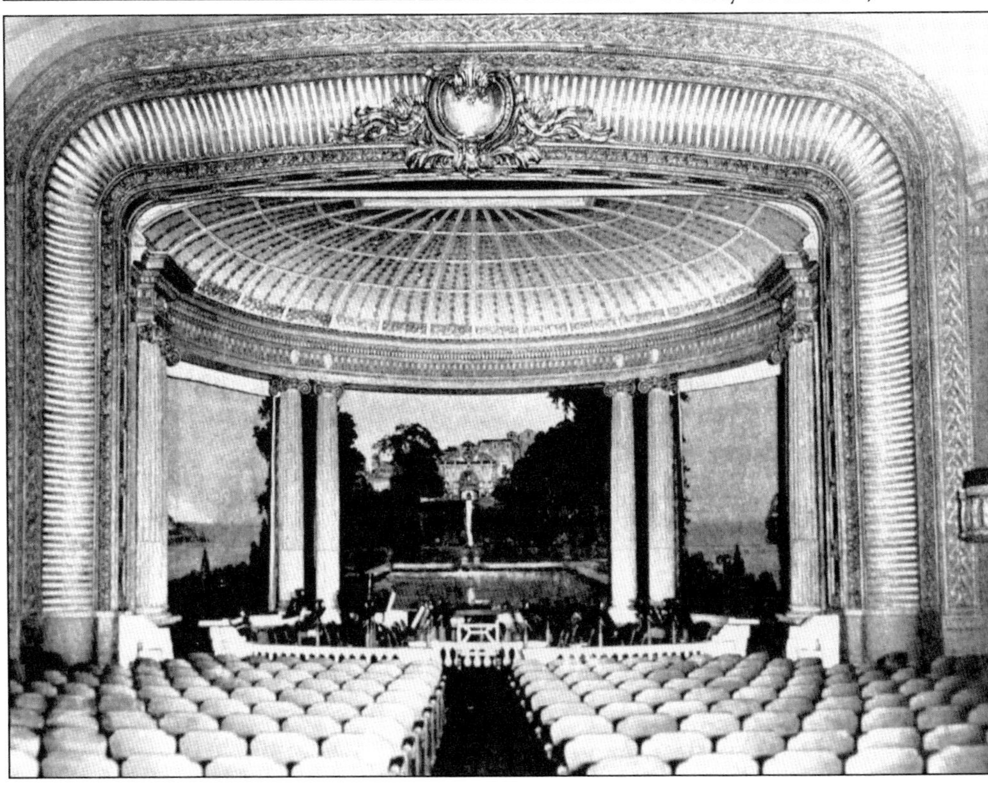

Balaban & Katz

Riviera Theatre

Week of Aug. 10, 1925

OVERTURE

"BEAUTIFUL GALATHEA"

By Suppe

RIVIERA THEATRE ORCHESTRA

ADOLPH DUMONT, *Conductor*

"LIFE'S GREATEST THRILLS"

A Newsweekly Review

Balaban & Katz Present

BOYD SENTER

Assisted by Jack Russell

"THE LOITERER"

A WONDER SCENIC

Balaban & Katz Present

"HARMONIOUS MOMENTS"

introducing

MARIO and LAZARIN

Metro Goldwyn Pictures Present

"THE SPORTING VENUS"

THE CAST

Lady Gwendolyn	*BLANCHE SWEET*
Donald McAllen	*RONALD COLMAN*
Prince Carlos	*LEW CODY*
Countess Van Alstyne	*Josephine Crowell*
Donald's Father	*George Fawcett*
Sir Alfred Grayle	*Edward Martindel*
Housekeeper	*Kate Price*
Carlos' Valet	*Hank Mann*
Detective	*Arthur Hoyt*

SELECTED COMEDY

Starting Monday

IT OPENS NEXT WEEK

The Theatre of a Thousand and One Wonders

Balaban & Katz

UPTOWN

BROADWAY AND LAWRENCE

UPTOWN SQUARE

ATTEND THE OPENING

A WHOLE ACRE OF SEATS

At Other Balaban & Katz Theatres this Week

CHICAGO STATE STREET between RANDOLPH and LAKE STS.

LEWIS STONE, ANNA Q. NILSSON

in **"THE TALKERS"**

ROOSEVELT STATE STREET Near WASHINGTON ST.

DOUGLAS FAIRBANKS in

"DON Q, SON OF ZORRO"

TIVOLI COTTAGE GROVE AVE. and 63d STREET

Fourth Annual Million Dollar FUR FASHION SHOW

CENTRAL PARK Roosevelt Road & Central Park Ave.

WORLD'S PREMIER VAUDEVILLE AND SCREEN MASTERPIECES

WURLITZER ORGANS AND MUSICAL INSTRUMENTS ARE USED IN BALABAN & KATZ THEATRES

(Program subject to change)

2

Here is an advertisement for the Riviera Theatre as it appeared in *Balaban & Katz Magazine*. The theater had opened seven years earlier. To compete quickly with other new theaters in the neighborhood, Balaban and Katz opened this movie palace before the paint was even dry. Note that the promotion of the Riviera Orchestra has more emphasis than the MGM movie playing. The Balaban and Katz live shows carved out a unique niche in Chicago's entertainment scene. According to the program, the Uptown Theatre, which was within walking distance to the Riviera, was set to open the following week. (Right, advertisement courtesy of Balaban and Katz Historical Foundation; below, photograph courtesy Theatre Historical Society of America.)

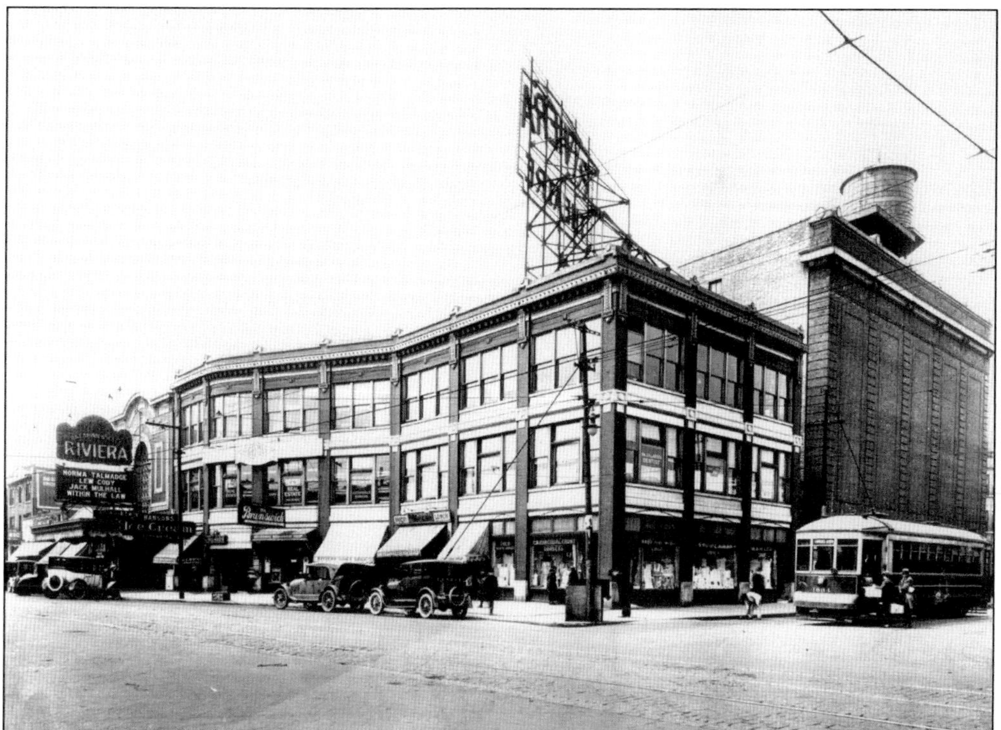

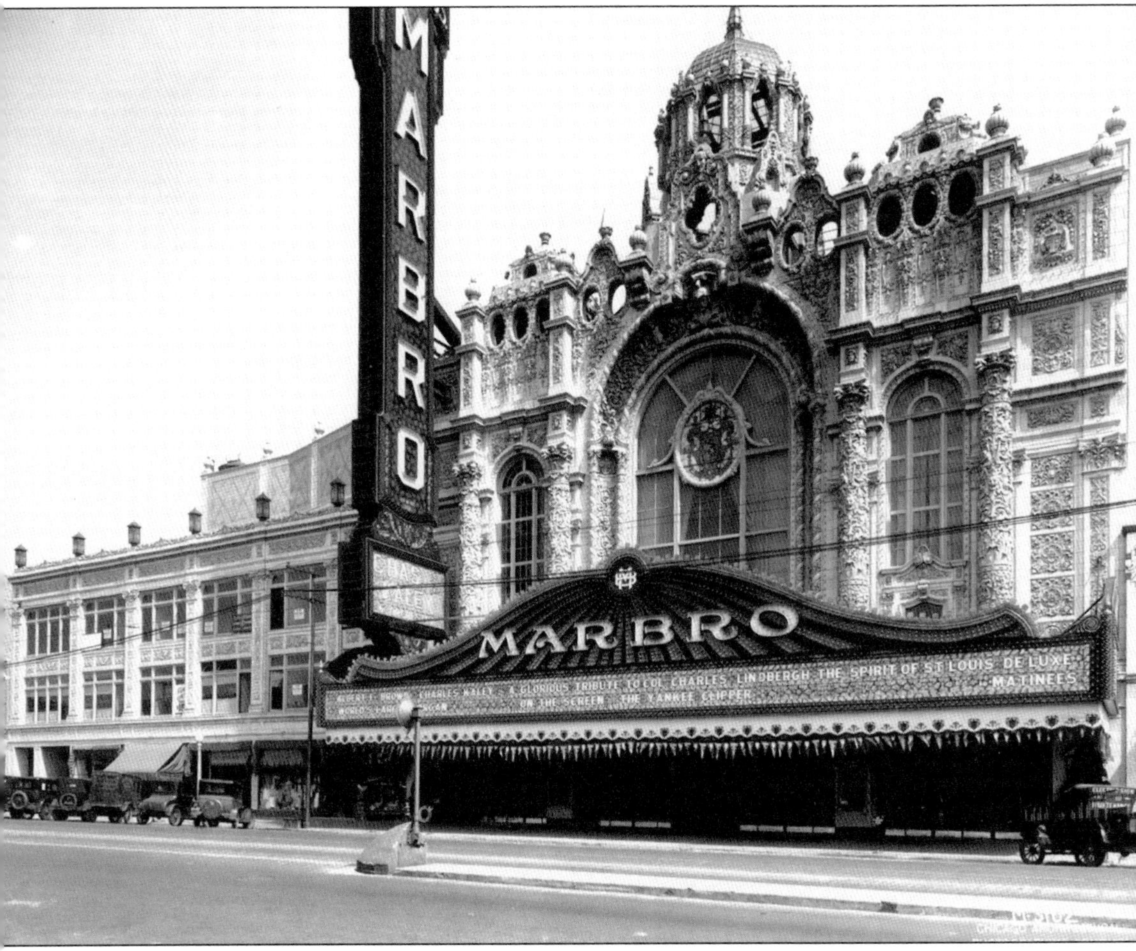

The Marbro Theatre was located at 4124 West Madison Street. It was built by the Marks Brothers circuit, hence the name. Edward Eichenbaum designed it in the Spanish baroque style for the firm of Levy and Klein. It was the sister to the Granada Theatre and the Diversey Theatre (also known as the Century) and opened for business in 1927. On opening day, it featured the Gloria Swanson film *The Loves of Sunya* and performances by Benny Meroff and organist Albert Brown. The Marks Brothers sued Balaban and Katz, claiming antitrust violations and unfair competition. The suit was settled with Paramount Publix buying the Marks Brothers out and obtaining ownership of the Granada, Marbro, and all Marks Brothers properties. (Photograph courtesy of Theatre Historical Society of America.)

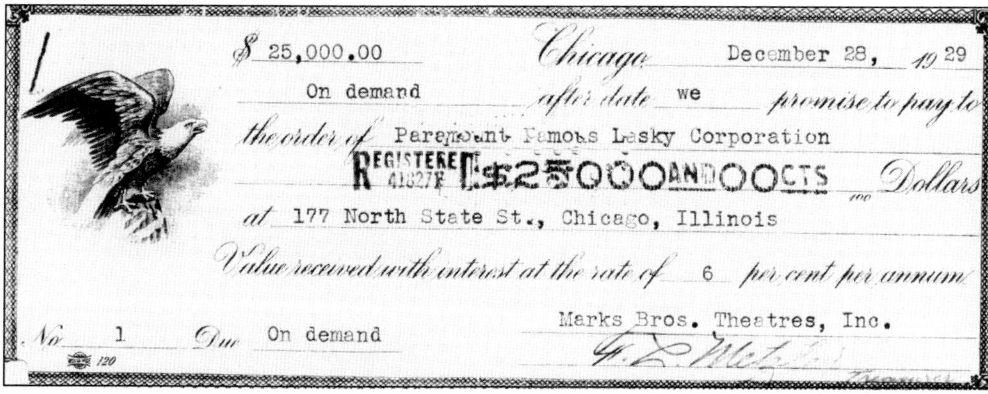

$ 25,000.00 Chicago December 28, 1929

On demand after date we promise to pay to the order of Paramount Famous Lasky Corporation

REGISTERED 41327F $25000 AND 00 CTS Dollars

at 177 North State St., Chicago, Illinois

Value received with interest at the rate of 6 per cent per annum

No. 1 Due On demand

Marks Bros. Theatres, Inc.

Late in 1929, Paramount Famous Lasky Corporation took over the assets and financial obligations of Marks Brothers Theatres Incorporated. (Photograph courtesy of Balaban and Katz Historical Foundation.)

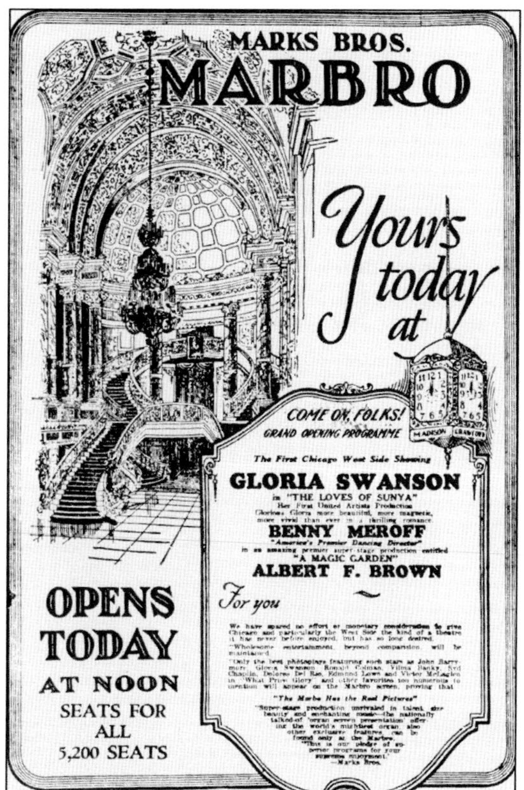

To the right is the opening day newspaper advertisement for the Marbro Theatre, taken over by Balaban and Katz on November 1, 1929. It was located very close to the Paradise Theatre and had 3,931 seats. The Marbro was one of the largest theaters in Chicago and was beautiful inside with its unusual two-story marble staircase in the lobby and huge stairs to the mezzanine. Balaban and Katz had trouble profiting with the Marbro, due in part to its huge size, and in 1963, it was closed. Unfortunately, it was torn down in 1964. (Advertisement courtesy of Theatre Historical Society of America.)

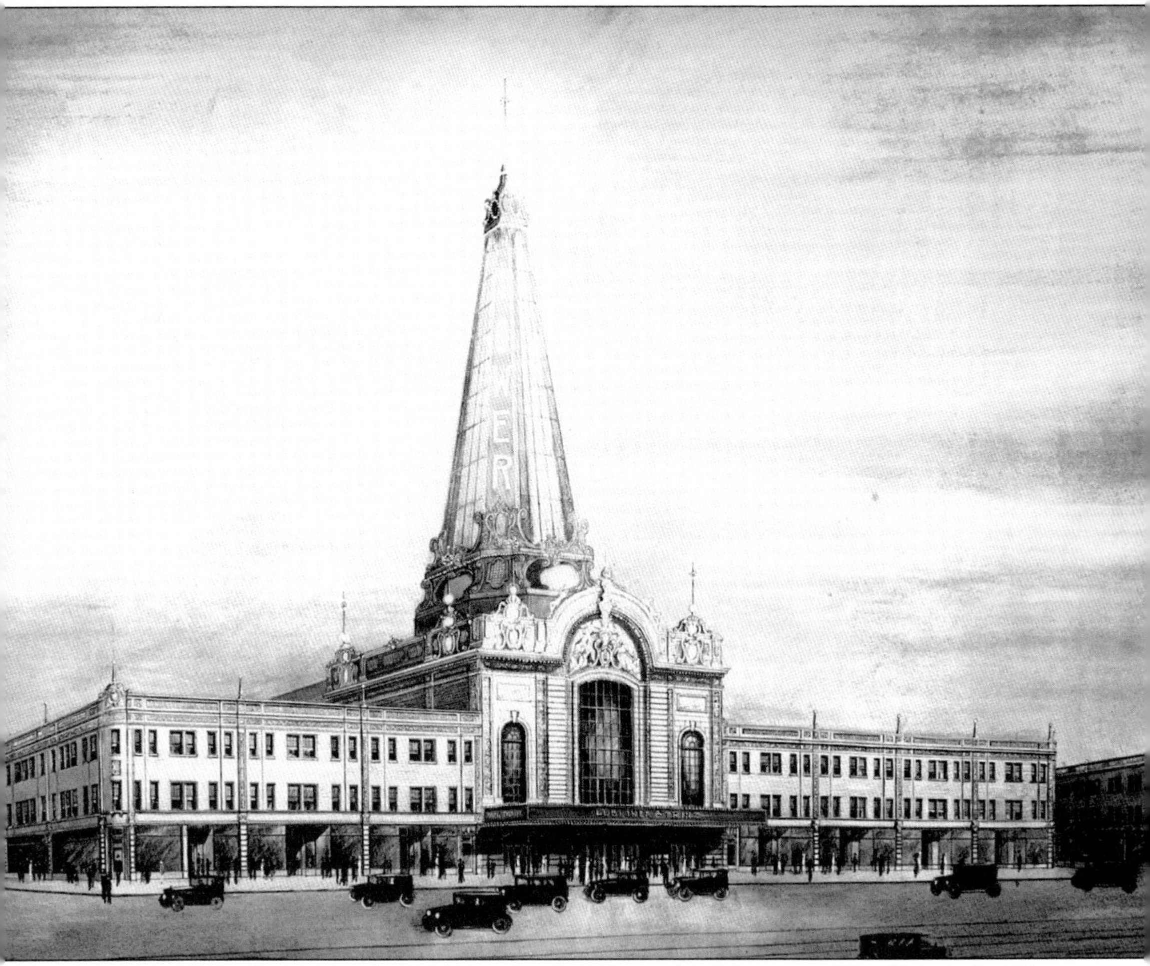

The Tower Theatre was located at 1510 East Sixty-third Street in Woodlawn, the Chicago neighborhood south of Hyde Park. It had 3,015 seats and was opened in early 1926 by Lubliner and Trinz. After the merger of Lubliner and Trinz with Balaban and Katz, it was reopened on September 22, 1928, as a B and K theater. Freidstein and Company built the Tower Theatre in the Italian Renaissance and neoclassical style, as well as its two sister theaters, the Harding and the Congress. (Illustration courtesy of Theatre Historical Society of America.)

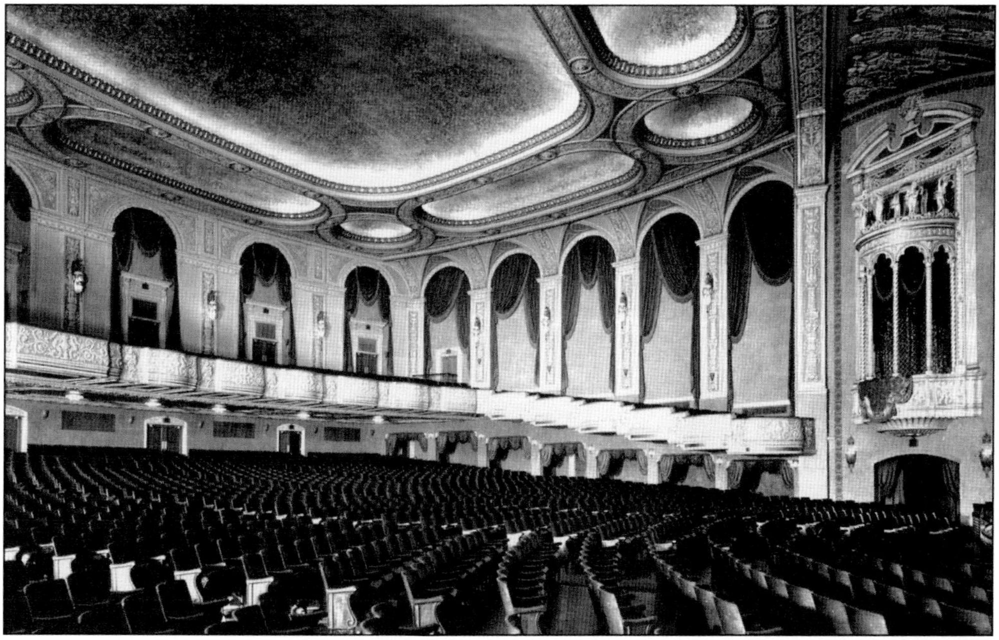

Notice in the picture below how close the elevated train was to the Tower Theatre building. The Tower was the least ornate of the three sister theaters, which also included the Harding and the Congress. It featured vaudeville as well as motion pictures during its first decade of operation. The Tower was designated as a b-level movie house as opposed to the nearby Tivoli Theatre, also owned by Balaban and Katz. This meant that it had to wait weeks before the newest films could be shown there. This caused considerable friction with Balaban and Katz's lease partner, who felt they were being purposely put at a disadvantage and sued Balaban and Katz. The suit ended peacefully. Balaban and Katz occupied the Tower Theatre for many years. (Photographs courtesy of Theatre Historical Society of America.)

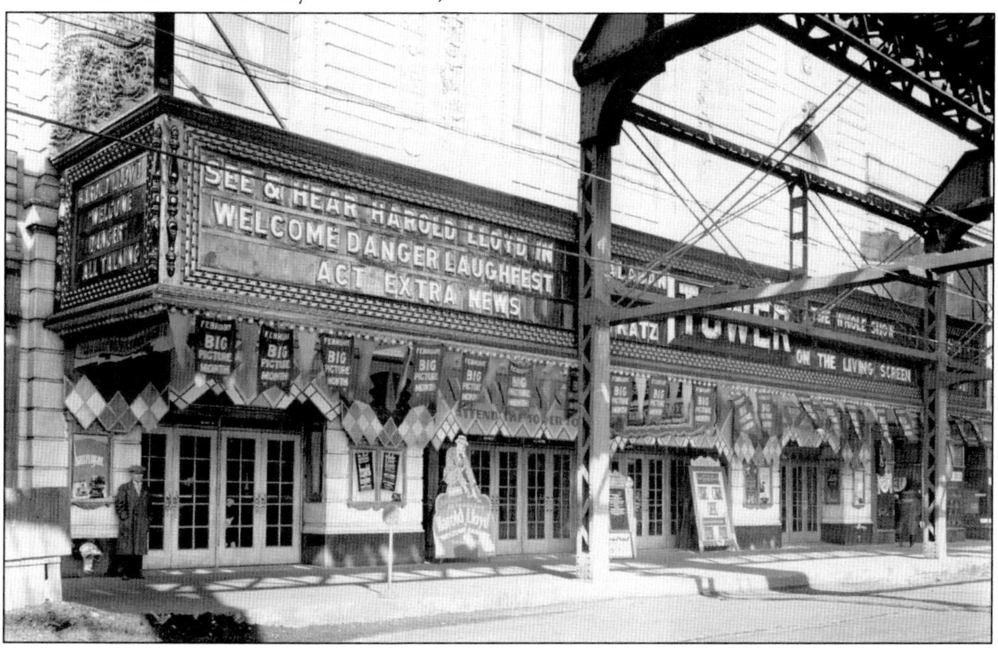

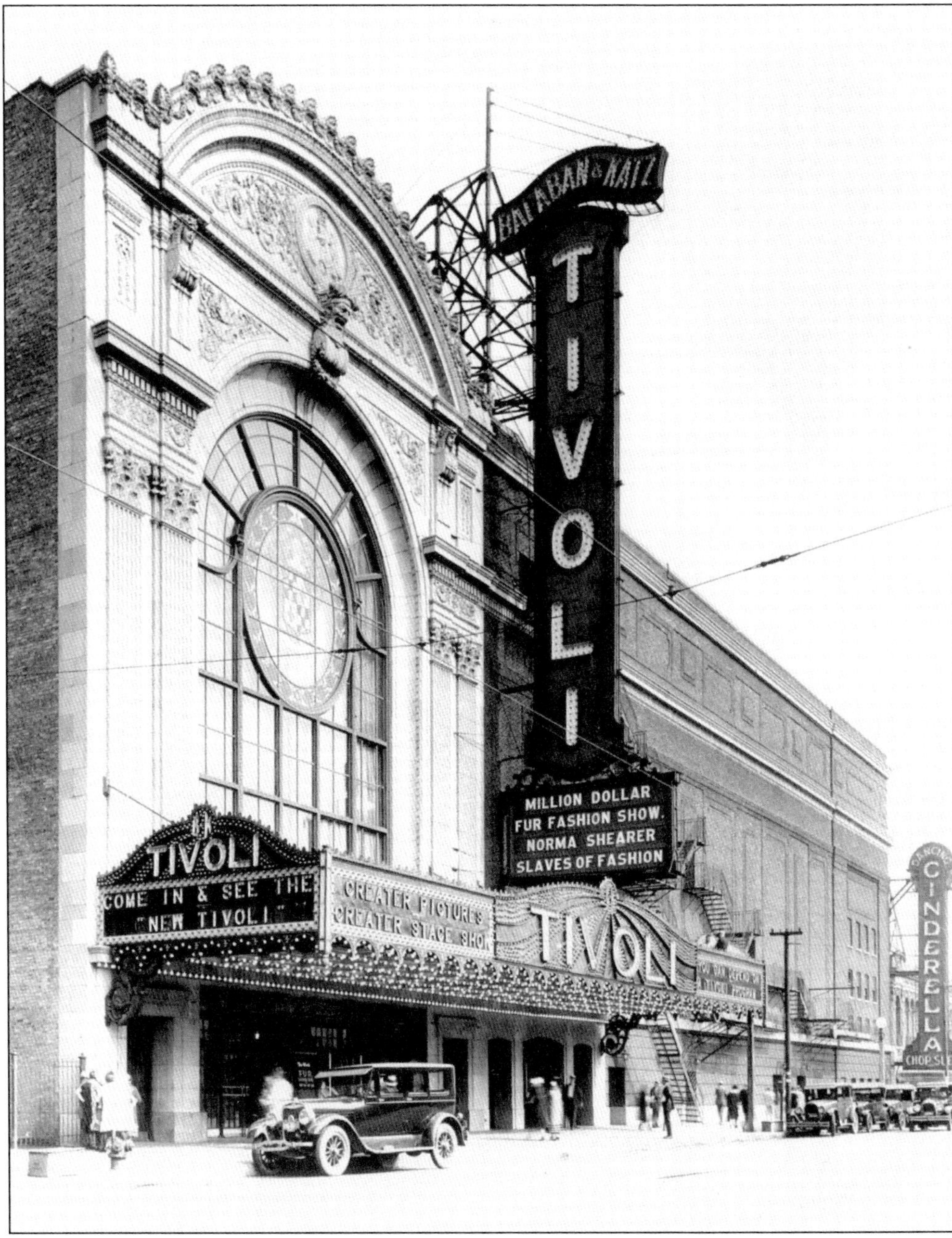

The Tivoli Theatre opened on February 16, 1921, with 3,520 seats. It was located at 6329 Cottage Grove Avenue on Chicago's South Side. It was designed by Rapp and Rapp in the French Renaissance motif. John Balaban managed it in the beginning in its early years. It was extremely fancy and featured many new services to attract the affluent theater patron: ushers in white gloves to greet customers, a children's playroom, and an advanced air-conditioning system with zone-controlled thermostats and fans. The Tivoli even had a built-in eavesdropping system, which allowed the theater mangers to listen in on how the employees were treating the customers. Rudeness was a cause for immediate dismissal. (Photograph courtesy of Theatre Historical Society of America.)

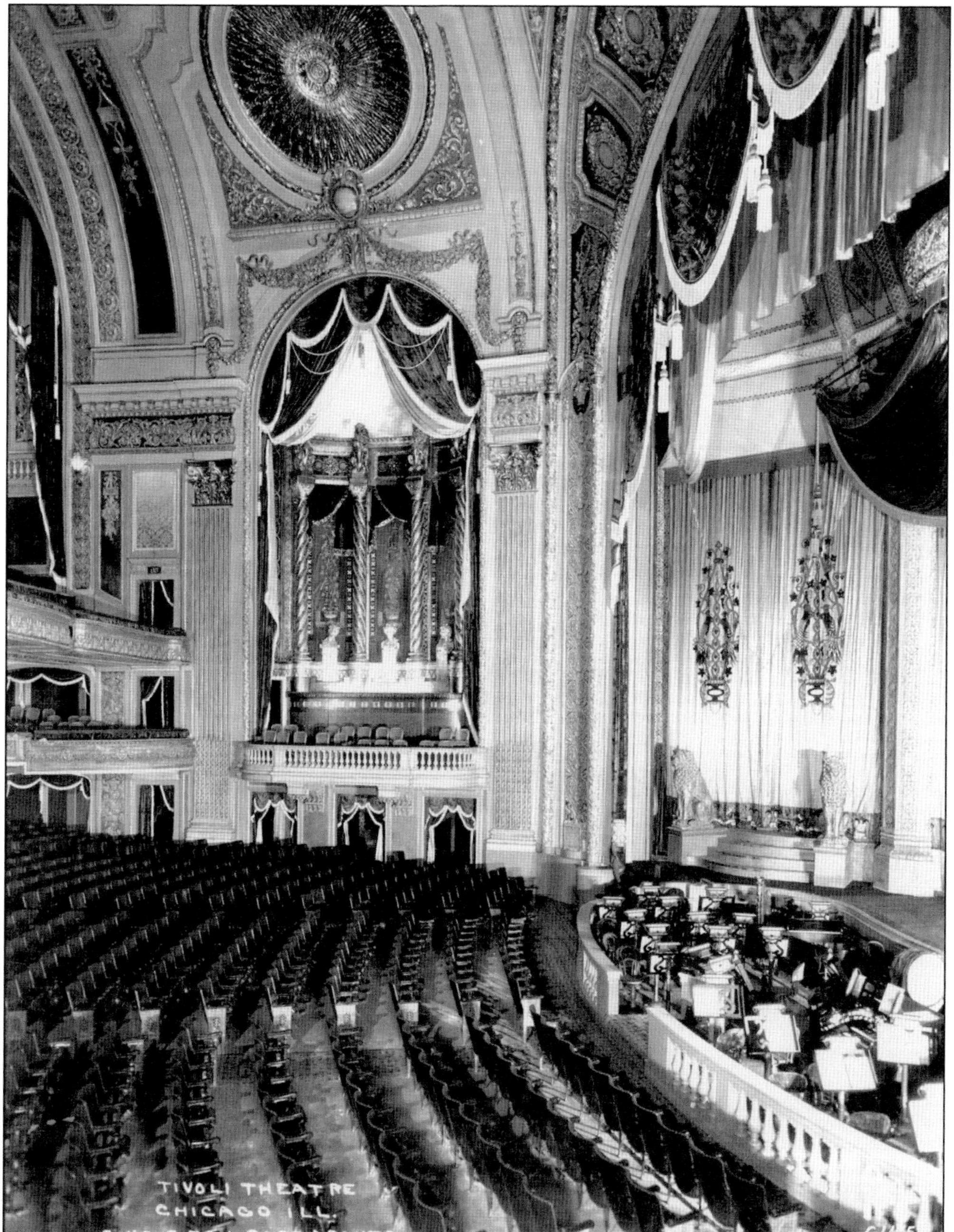

The Tivoli's lobby was full of antiques and valuable artwork collected from all over the world, including China. It was the movie palace that all others where judged against. The Tivoli was a first-run movie house. The neighborhood surrounding the theater began going down hill, and, unfortunately, so did the theater. In 1958, B and K instituted an ill-fated modernization program in which they covered the original decor with plaster board and contact paper. Nothing helped, and this glorious movie palace was closed in 1963 and demolished soon after. A parking lot marks the spot where the Tivoli once stood. (Photograph courtesy of Theatre Historical Society of America.)

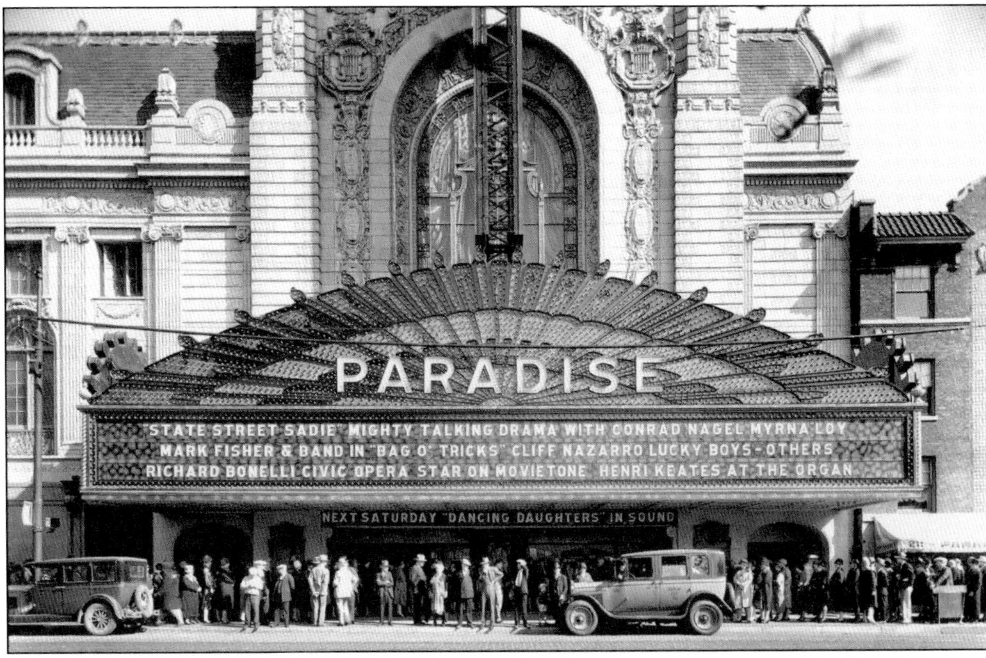

The Paradise Theatre had 3,612 seats and was located at 231 North Crawford (Pulaski) Avenue. It was designed by John Eberson and was intricately decorated. The Paradise Theatre opened on September 14, 1928. The first film featured was *The Fleet's In*, starring Clara Bow. (Photographs courtesy of Theatre Historical Society of America.)

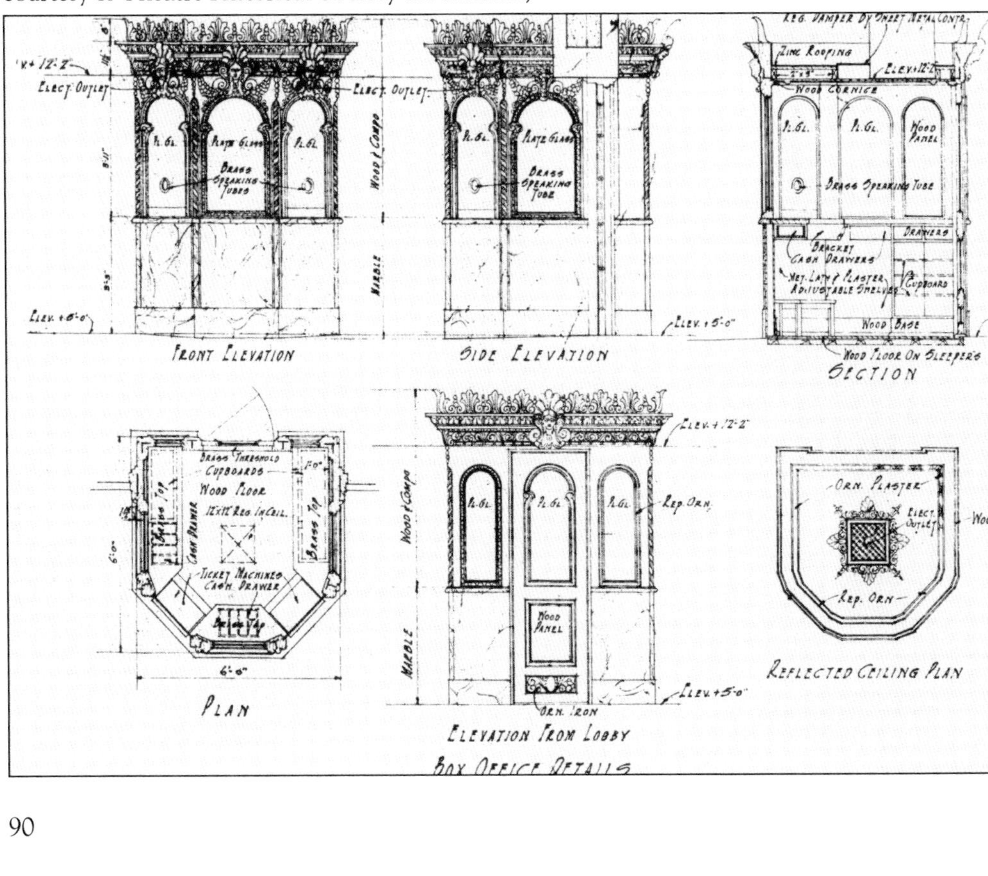

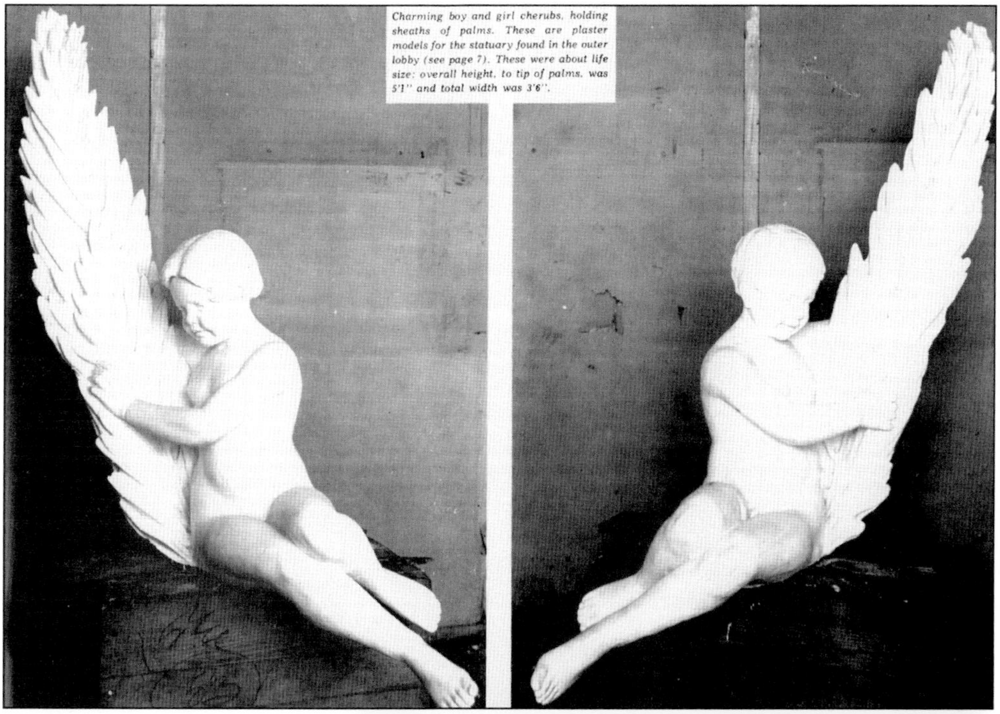

Pictured to the right is the domed ceiling of the Paradise that caused an echo during movie sound tracks. This negatively affected its attendance figures once sound pictures replaced silent pictures. The Paradise was never profitable, and in 1956, Balaban and Katz closed the theater. Pictured above are close-up views of the beautiful statues that adorned the Paradise's interior. (Photographs courtesy of Theatre Historical Society of America.)

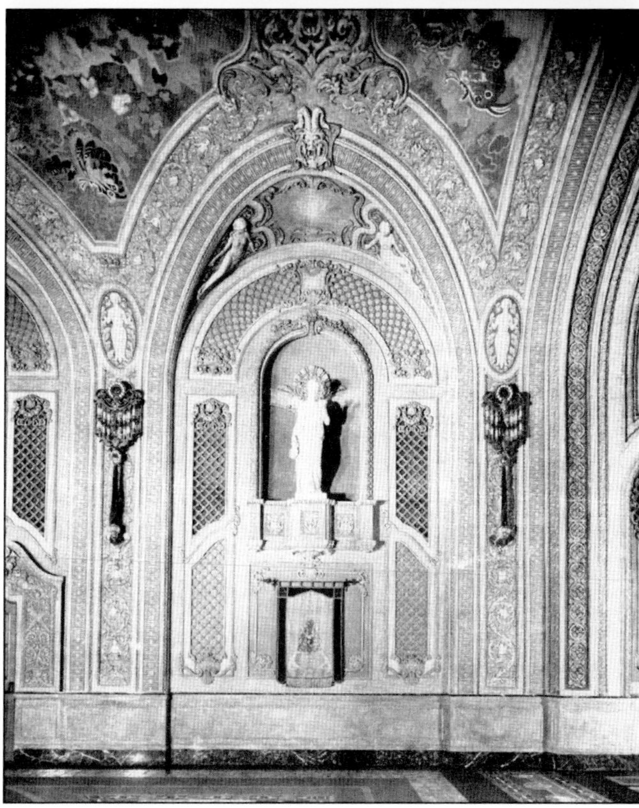

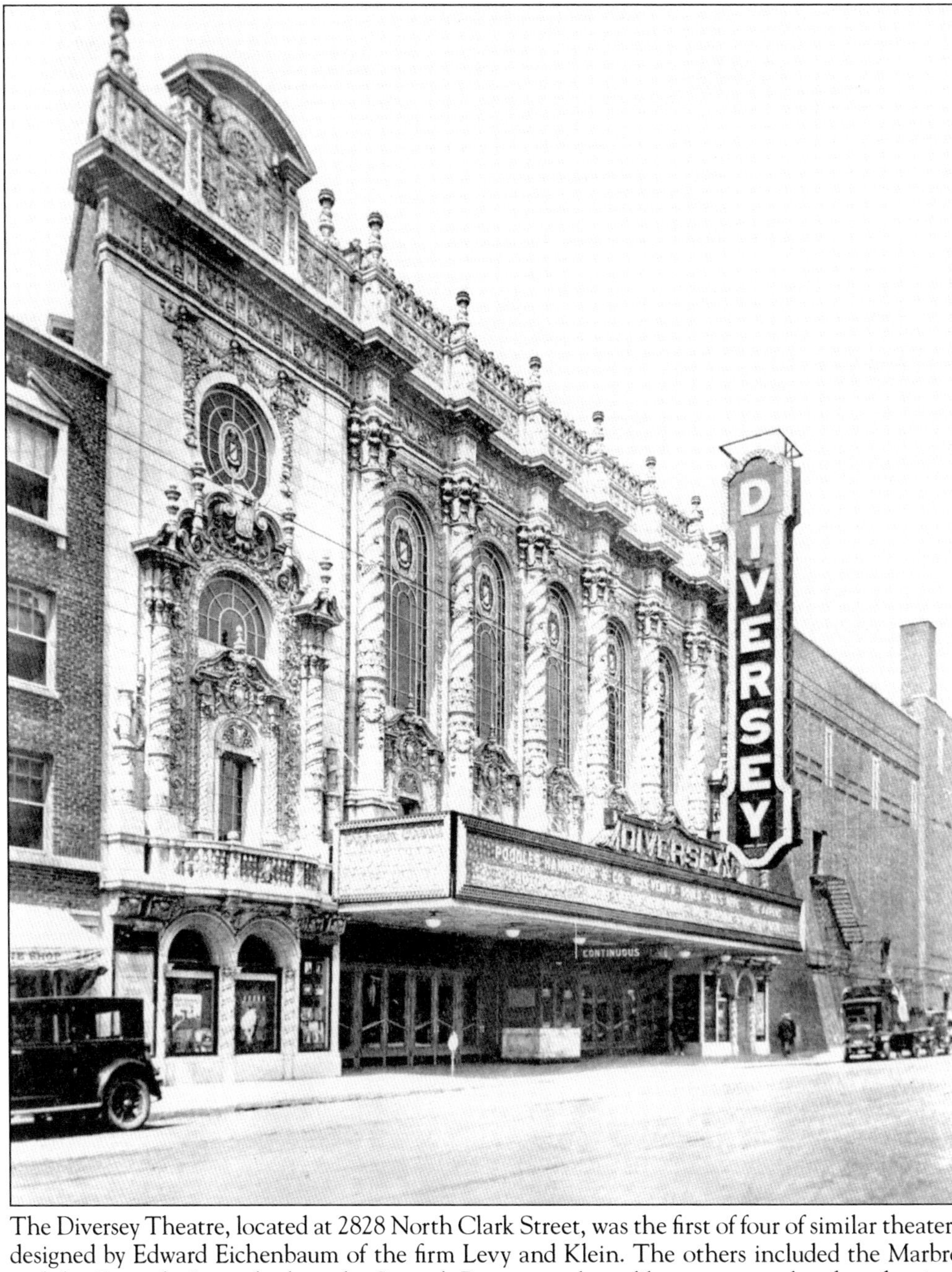

The Diversey Theatre, located at 2828 North Clark Street, was the first of four of similar theaters designed by Edward Eichenbaum of the firm Levy and Klein. The others included the Marbro and the Granada. It was built in the Spanish Baroque style and later revamped and modernized during the 1930s Chicago Century of Progress World's Fair. It had 3,056 seats when it opened. Balaban and Katz took over the Diversey on February 7, 1930. By that time, it was already known as the Century Theater. (Photograph courtesy of Theatre Historical Society of America.)

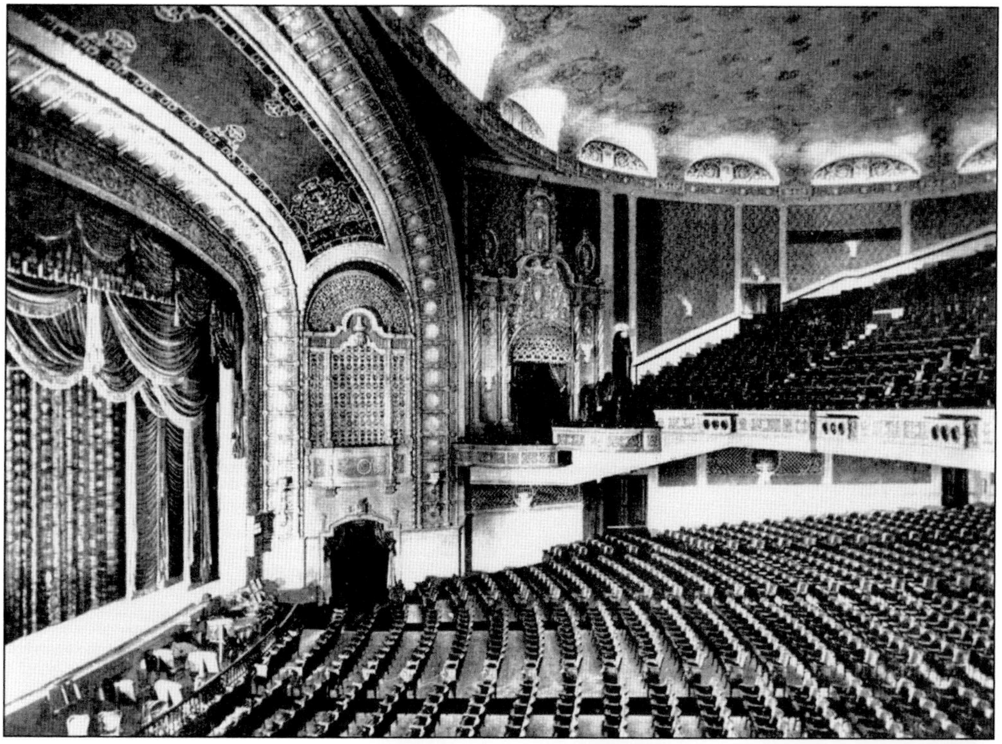

In 1973, the entire Century Theatre was torn out. It became the Century Shopping Center. Later on in 2000, part of the theater was rebuilt as the Landmark's Century Centre Cinema, a multiplex theater. Thankfully, the exterior terra cotta had been saved and still gives the feeling of grandeur of the original theater. (Photographs courtesy of Theatre Historical Society of America.)

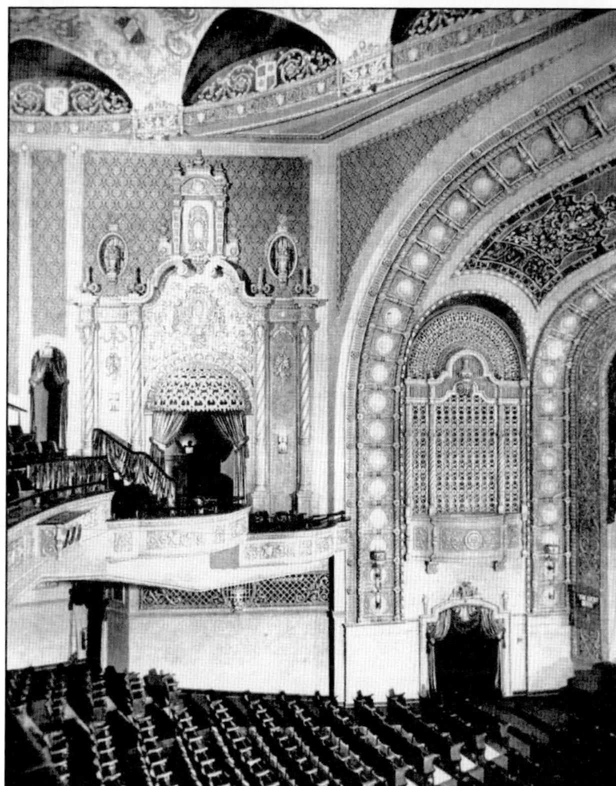

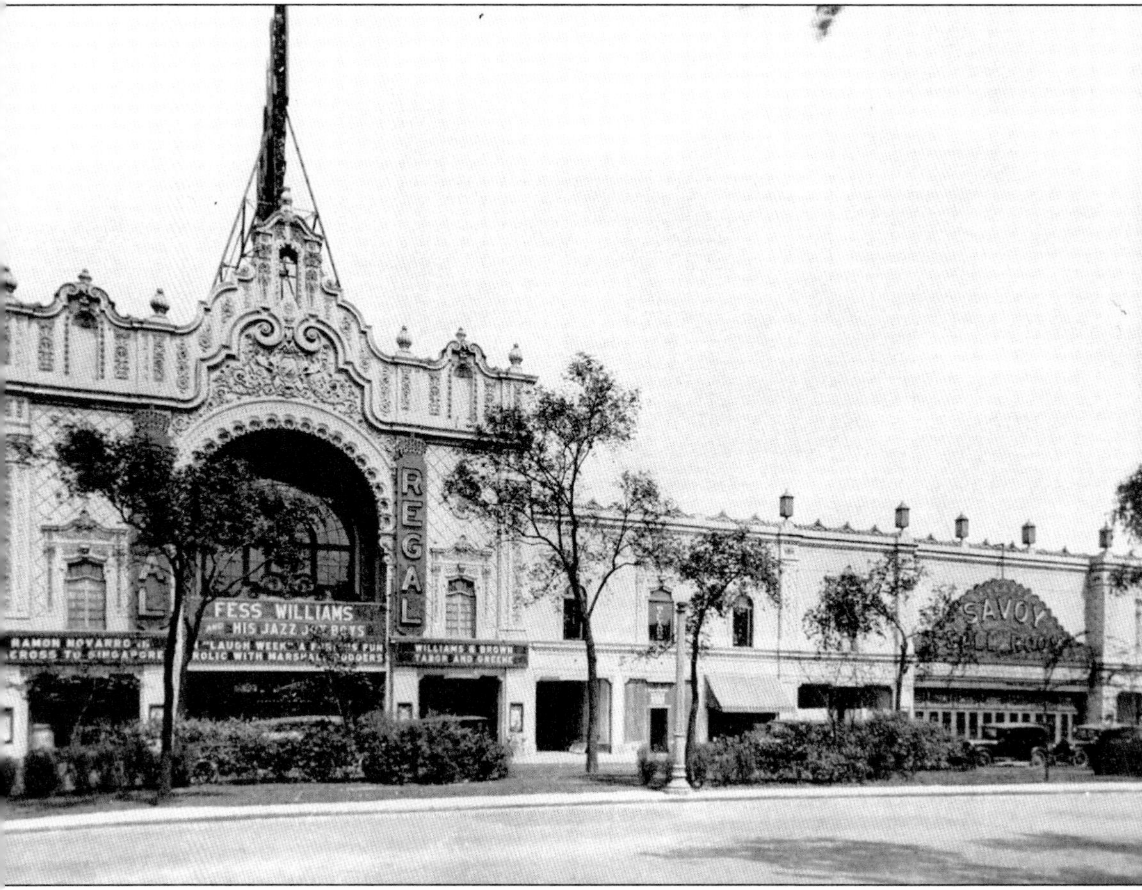

The Regal Theater, located at 4719 South Parkway, opened in 1928 as part of the Lubliner and Trinz circuit. B and K later leased the Regal, marking the first time that Balaban and Katz were in direct competition with the James Coston circuit. Coston ran the Metropolitan Theater, which was located directly across the street. (Photograph courtesy of Theatre History Society of America.)

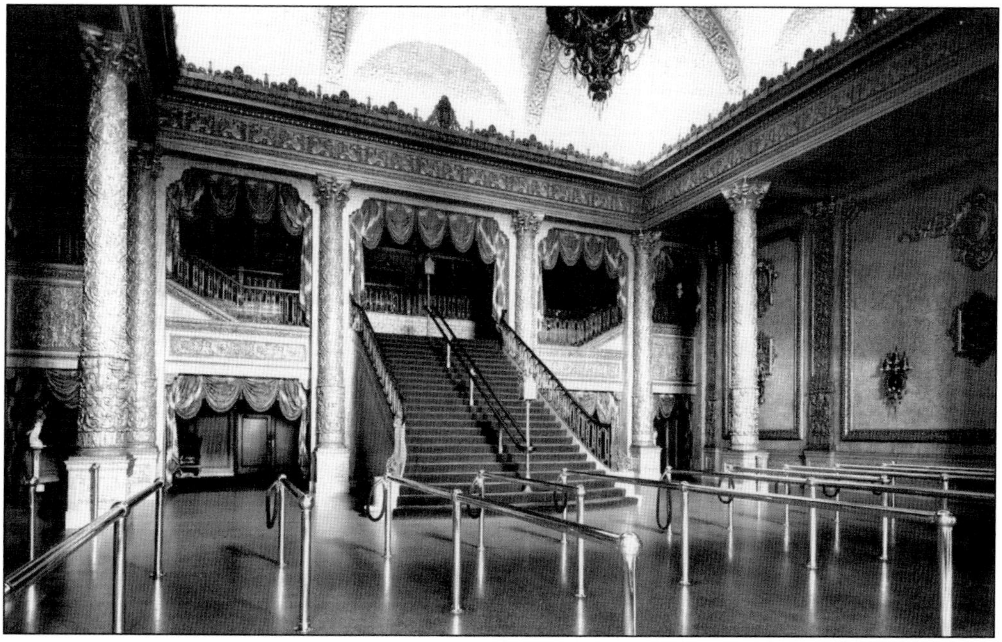

Notice the beautiful marble floors that graced the lobby of the Regal. The theater also featured leather laden seats. The Regal became a showplace for the finest African American talent in the city. There were other famous cultural centers nearby, including the Savoy Ballroom. The neighborhood where the Regal was located hailed as the "Harlem" of Chicago. The Regal's staff was mostly African American when Lubliner and Trinz ran the house, and this practice was continued under Balaban and Katz management. Virtually every famous black musical artist played the Regal. When Balaban and Katz tried to shut it down to save costs, neighborhood residents held massive protests, persuading Balaban and Katz to change their minds. The theater enjoyed many decades of popularity, including the Motown years of the 1960s. It finally closed in 1968. It was torn down a few years later. (Photographs courtesy of Theatre History Society of America.)

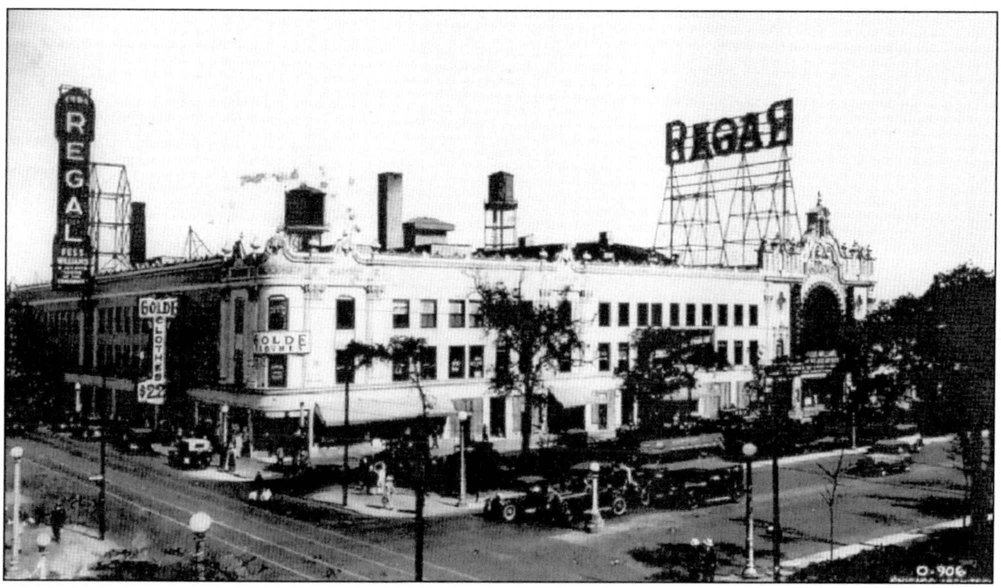

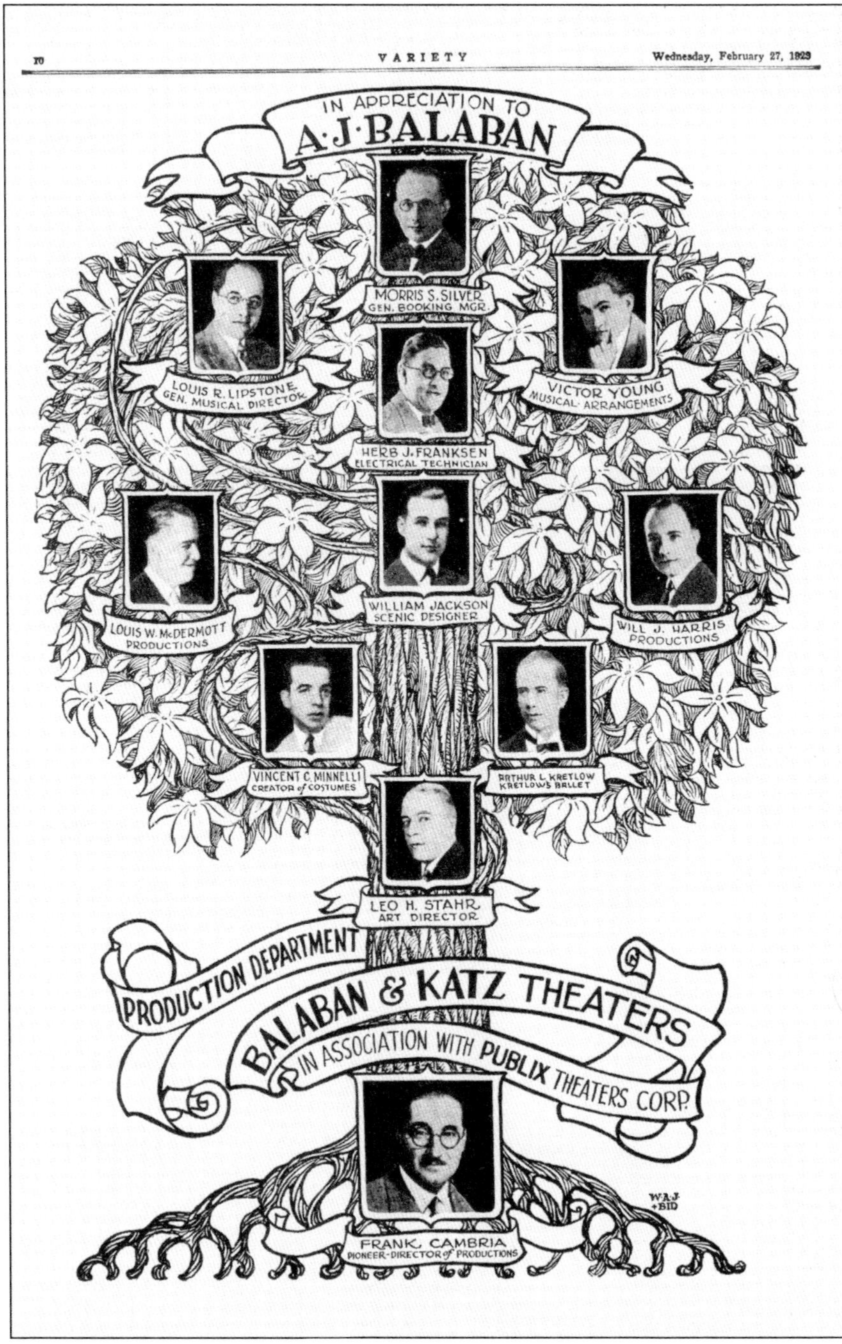

On February 27, 1929, *Variety* magazine, the most famous entertainment journal covering the movie industry, devoted their entire publication to the career of A. J. Balaban. A. J. had retired from the business and moved his family to Europe. Seen here is a page in which the members of the Balaban and Katz live entertainment production department wish A. J. well in his retirement from Balaban and Katz. Vincent Minelli was B and K's costume designer. Vincent, the father of Liza Minelli, went on to a successful career as producer of musicals for MGM. (Image courtesy of Reed Business Information.)

Five

Continuous Performances

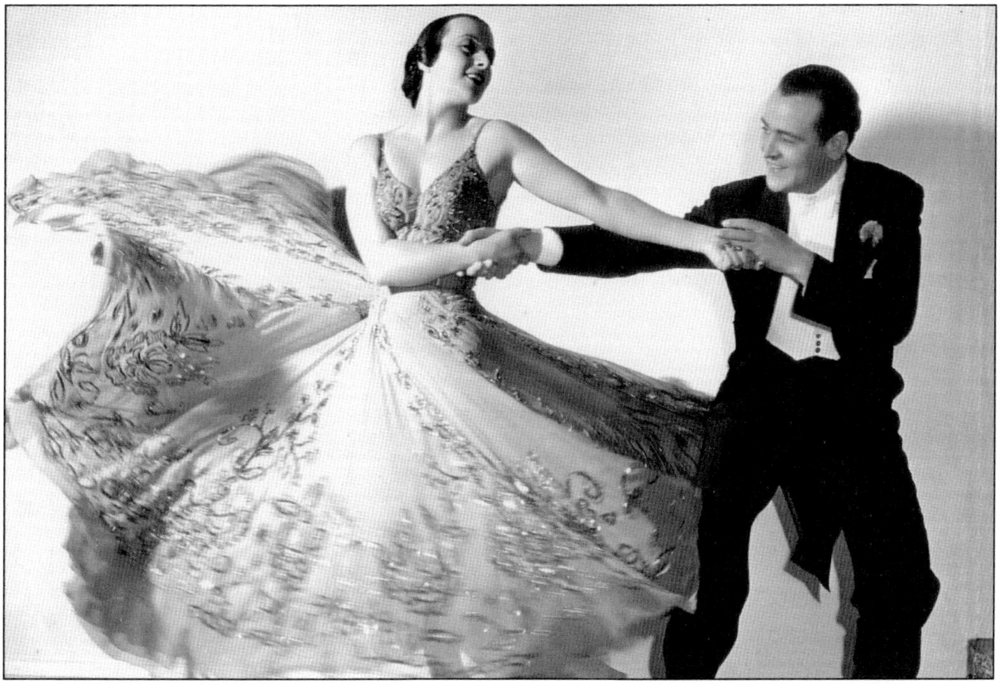

Balaban and Katz employed a "continuous performance" philosophy—providing the finest ongoing entertainment for one low price to patrons. The average cost for evening performances in the 1920s was around 50¢, and for day performances, about 30¢. The shows ran in succession, beginning in the morning, and included movies, short subjects or newsreels, live shows, and musical entertainment such as jazz bands, orchestras, and fully costumed dance revues. In addition, many of the early theaters had grand Wurlitzer organs, which were played in between shows. B and K hired the finest organists, including Jesse Crawford. The orchestras had as many as 40 musicians. The live shows changed once a week. Stage shows ran anywhere from eight minutes to the better part of an hour. There was never a dull moment at the Balaban and Katz movie palaces! In fact, before Balaban and Katz merged with Paramount, they often had trouble getting the newest movies. It was the stage shows and air-conditioning that brought the crowds in. (Photograph courtesy of Balaban and Katz Historical Foundation.)

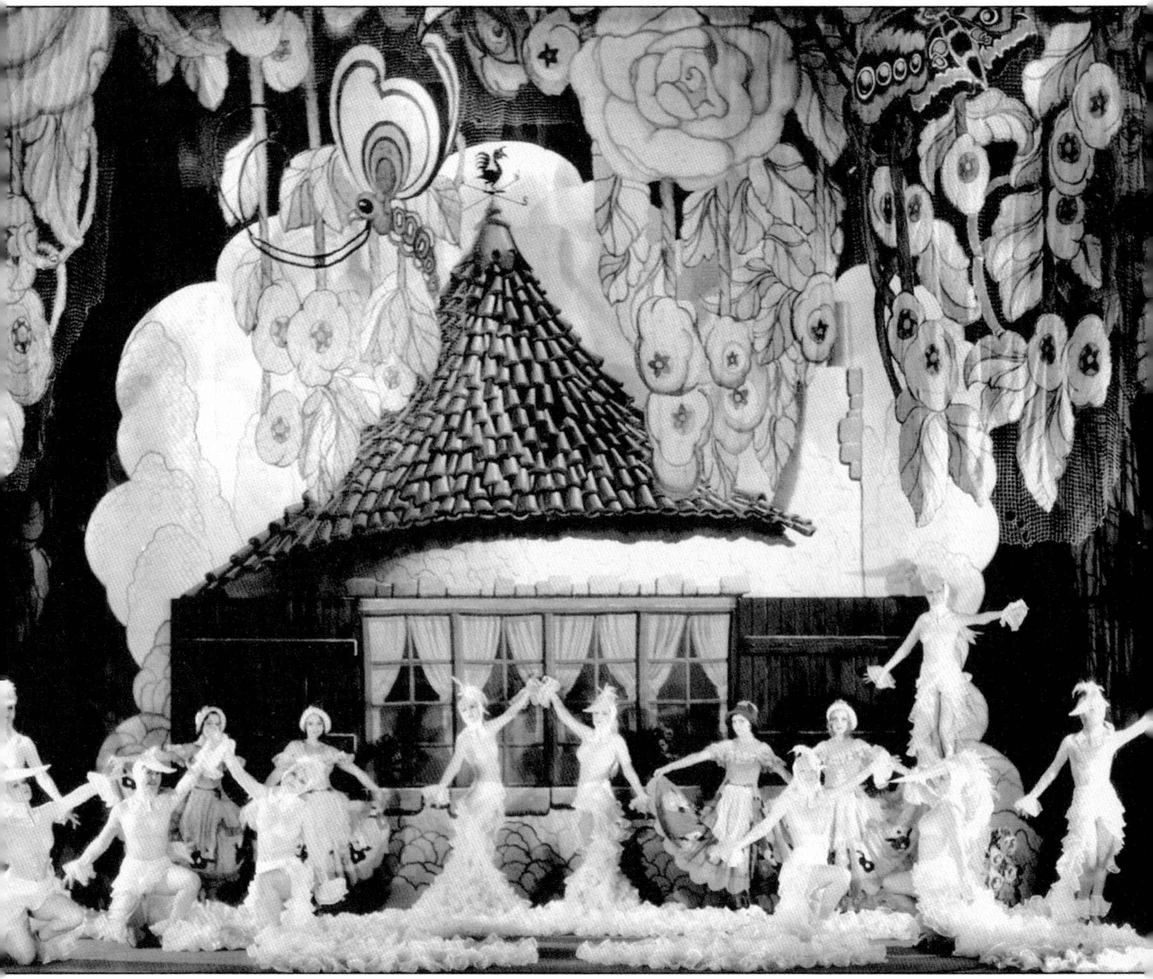

The colorful costumes seen here were the creation of Vincent Minelli. Minelli was hired to enliven the shows. The sets and costumes were created in the set shops located in the Chicago Theatre building. Frank Cambria, a veteran of Broadway shows, oversaw the whole live-show operation and reported directly to A. J. Balaban. (Photograph courtesy of Balaban and Katz Historical Foundation.)

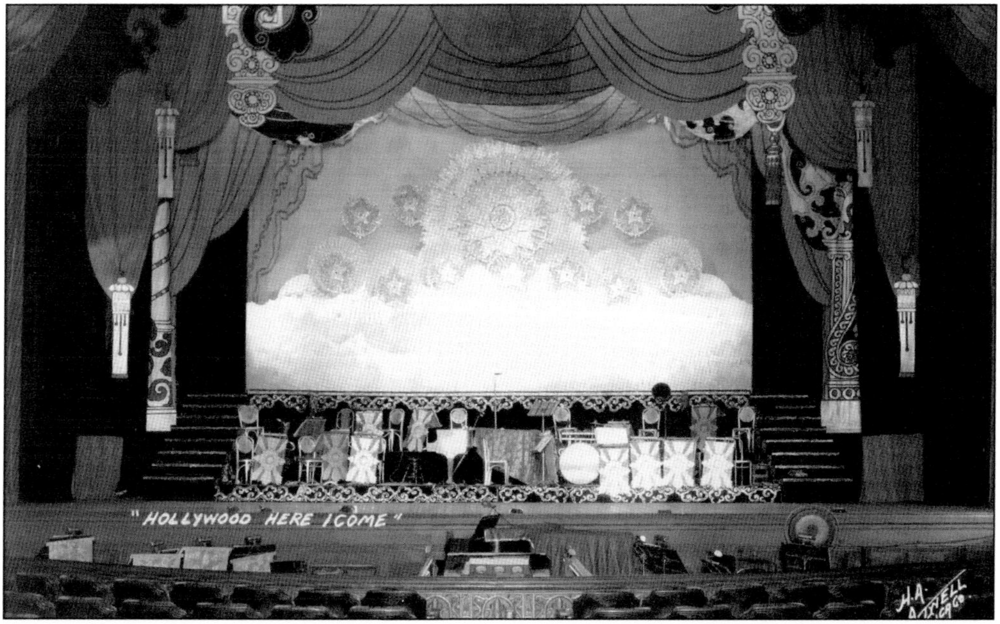

These photographs show live performances at the Oriental Theatre. The live shows rotated between the various Balaban and Katz movie palaces throughout Chicago. This saved on costs and exposed audiences from different parts of the city to a variety of shows. In 1931, the live shows slowed down to a trickle as Paramount ordered a drastic cut in budgets and implemented a "movie only" policy. (Photographs courtesy of Balaban and Katz Historical Foundation.)

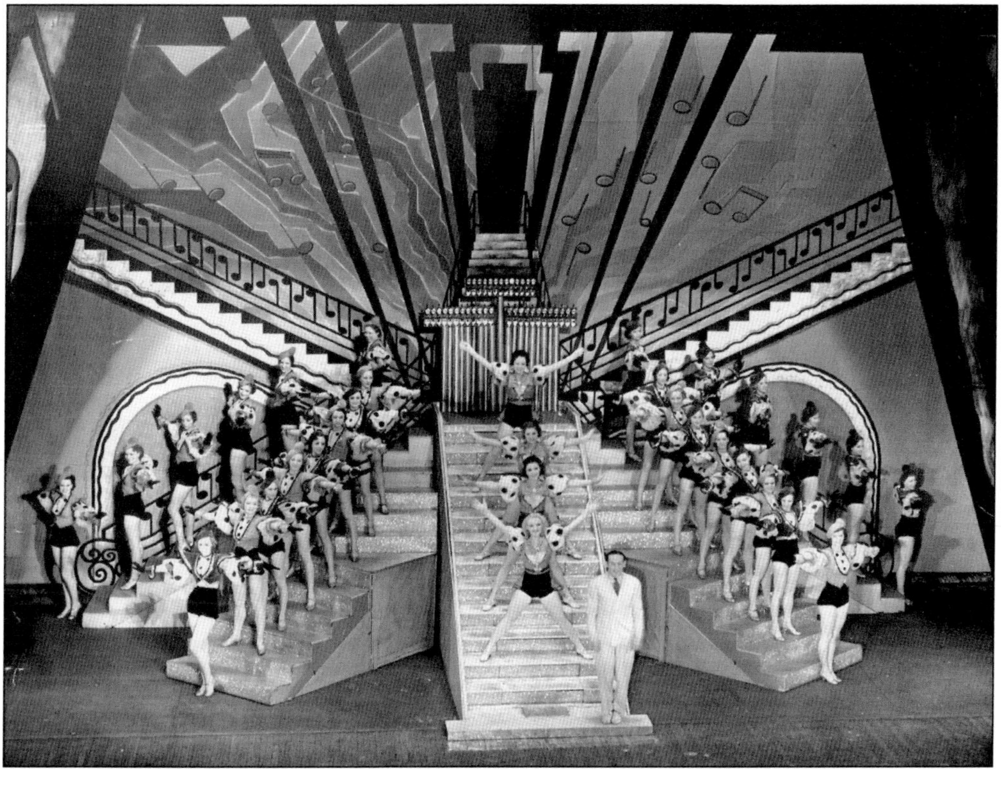

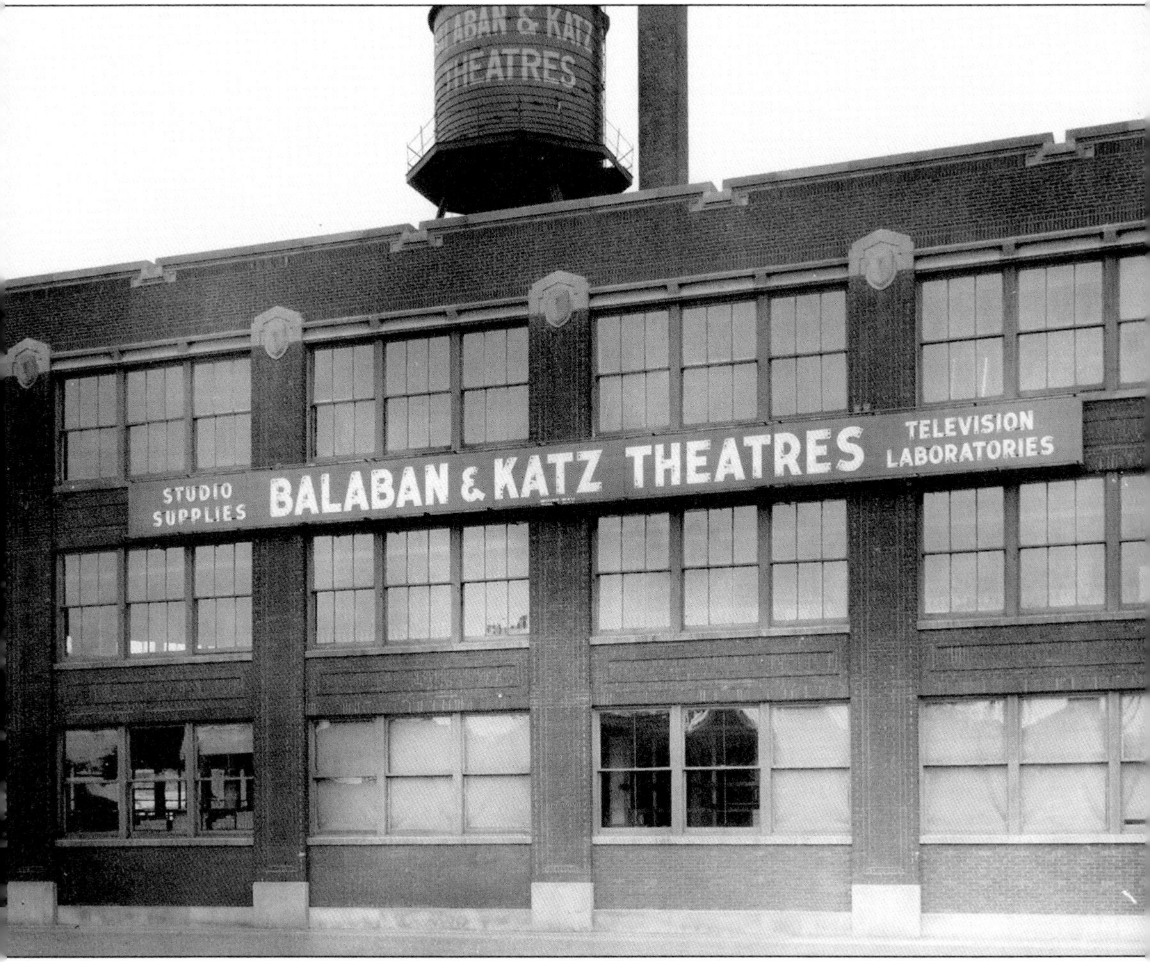

Balaban and Katz produced most of its own scenic props for its live shows in the building adjoining to the Chicago Theatre on State Street. However, when additional fabrication or storage space was needed, they used the warehouse seen here. The address was 408 North Ashland, Chicago. It was also used as a massive popcorn and candy storage space. Notice the television laboratories sign on the right. Balaban and Katz founded the third commercial television station (WBKB) in the country in 1939. Since there was a shortage of suppliers of television studio lighting and equipment, WBKB invented its own at this laboratory. (Photograph courtesy of Balaban and Katz Historical Foundation.)

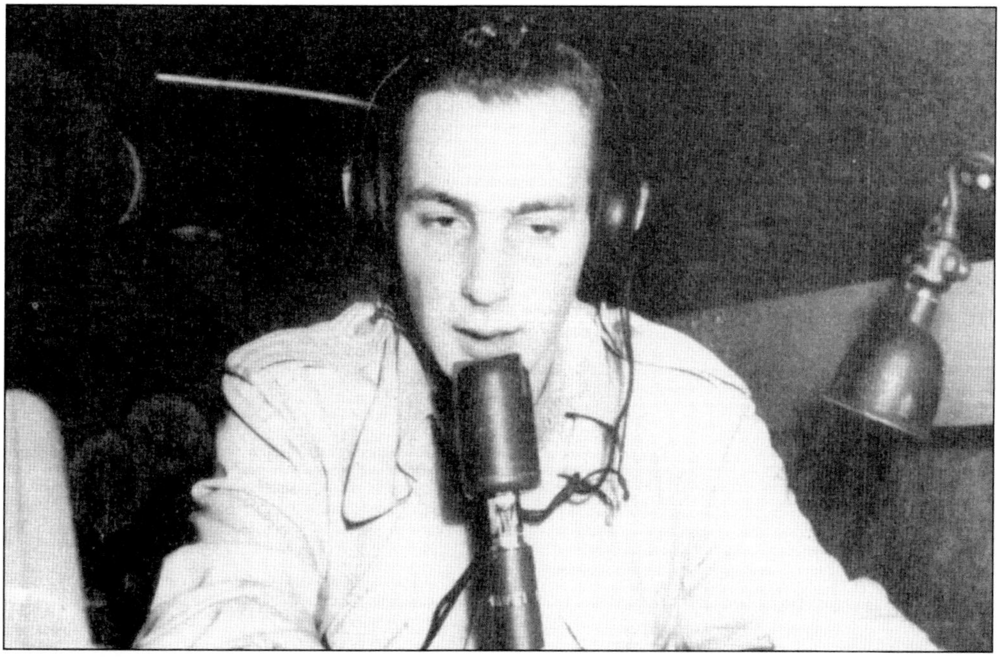

Bill Balaban, son of John Balaban, is seen here at work as a WBKB director. WBKB was at the forefront of the emerging art of television production. Many tools of the trade had to be fashioned in the WBKB television laboratories because there were so few television stations. When the station went on the air in 1941, there were only a few hundred televisions in the whole city of Chicago. (Photograph courtesy of Balaban and Katz Historical Foundation.)

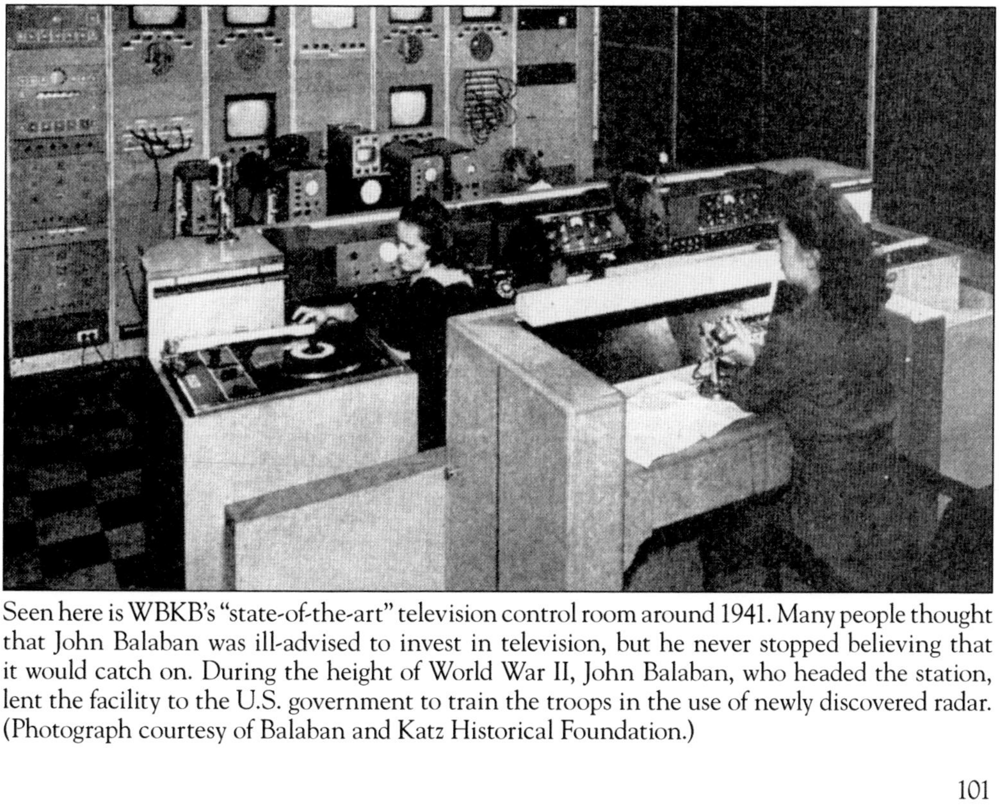

Seen here is WBKB's "state-of-the-art" television control room around 1941. Many people thought that John Balaban was ill-advised to invest in television, but he never stopped believing that it would catch on. During the height of World War II, John Balaban, who headed the station, lent the facility to the U.S. government to train the troops in the use of newly discovered radar. (Photograph courtesy of Balaban and Katz Historical Foundation.)

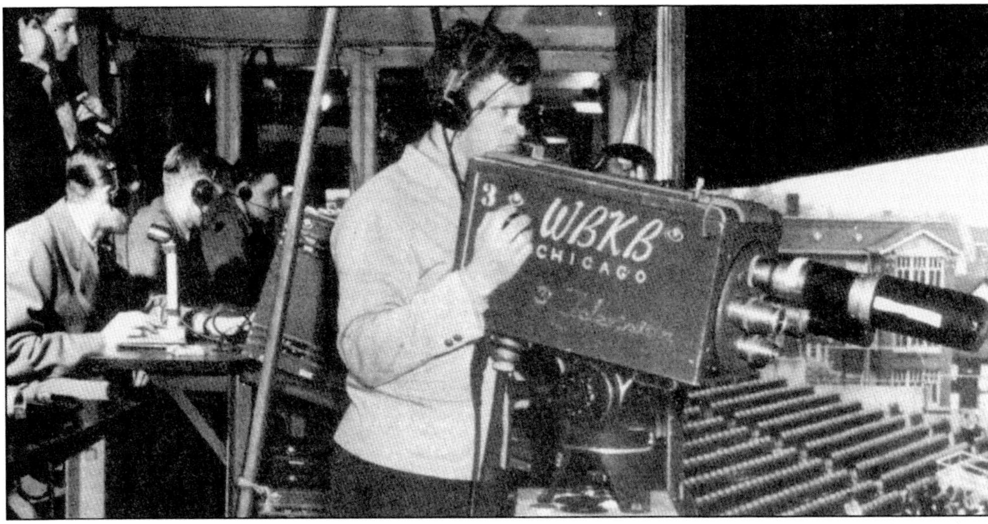

Founded in 1939, WBKB was Chicago's first commercial television station. It was located on the fourth floor of the State Lake building at 190 North State Street. Hugh Downs hosted a 15-minute daily news show. Boxing and wrestling were amongst the first sports shows produced. WBKB also aired movies and westerns. Many local pubs were the first to buy television sets, so programming was geared to a male audience, as their patrons were mostly men. WBKB was the first to broadcast a Cubs baseball game from Wrigley Field and a Notre Dame football game. WBKB hired soon-to-be famous puppeteer Burr Tillstrum to produce the *Kukla, Fran and Ollie* kids' show. It debuted on WBKB October 13, 1947. (Photograph courtesy of Balaban and Katz Historical Foundation.)

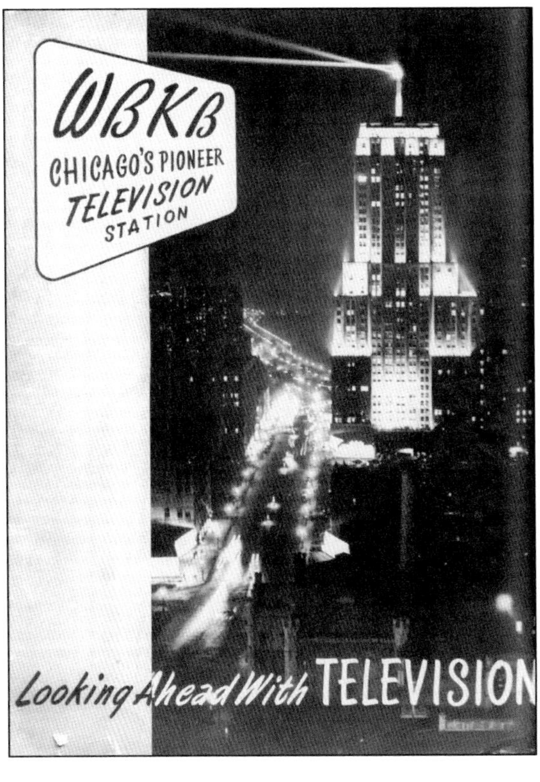

The television news format viewers are used to today got its start on WBKB. The station's engineers invented a device called a "multiscope," which superimposed breaking news information from United Press International on the bottom of the television screen. The news crawl seen today on 24-hour news programs is derived from this early invention. (Photograph courtesy of Balaban and Katz Historical Foundation.)

Six

Famous Players Lasky Corporation and Paramount Publix

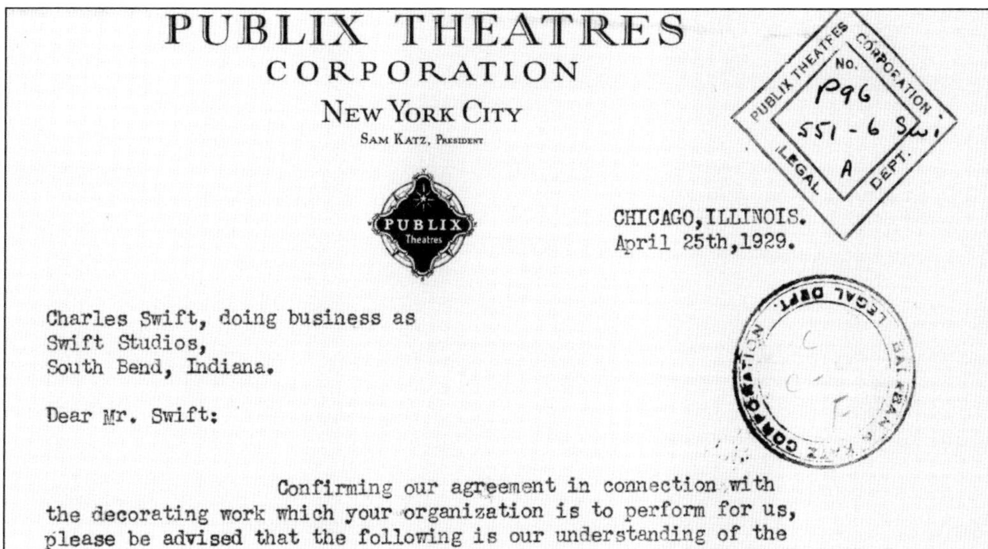

PUBLIX THEATRES
CORPORATION
NEW YORK CITY
SAM KATZ, PRESIDENT

PUBLIX Theatres

CHICAGO, ILLINOIS.
April 25th, 1929.

Charles Swift, doing business as
Swift Studios,
South Bend, Indiana.

Dear Mr. Swift:

Confirming our agreement in connection with the decorating work which your organization is to perform for us, please be advised that the following is our understanding of the agreement:

You are to decorate the Chicago Theatre,

On June 30, 1926, Famous Players Lasky Corporation bought a majority stake in the Balaban and Katz Corporation. Sam Katz and Adolf Zukor had been talking about the idea for a while. The Balaban brothers were hesitant at first but soon gave in. The deal gave Adolf's company a firm hold on film distribution in Chicago. In exchange, all Balaban and Katz stockholders got a number of shares in the new company. Sam Katz moved to New York City with his staff to become president of the newly formed Paramount Famous Lasky and Publix Theatres Corporation. Barney Balaban assumed the role of president at Balaban and Katz to fill Sam's old job. Balaban and Katz executives were offered contracts with Paramount. A. J. and John Balaban both worked in the Big Apple for a while, but John returned to Chicago soon after, and A. J. temporarily retired to Switzerland. (Letter courtesy of Balaban and Katz Historical Foundation.)

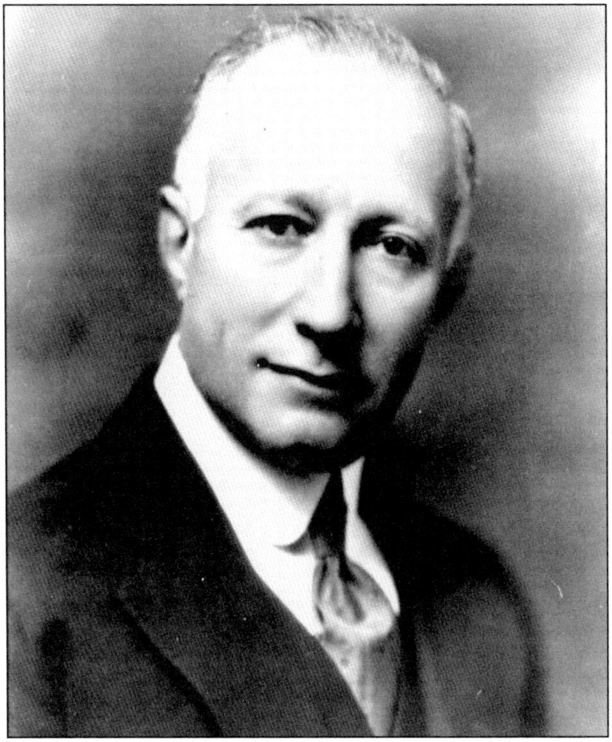

Pictured here is Adolf Zukor. Born in 1873 in Hungary, Zukor founded the Famous Players Company in 1912. He began his movie career as an operator of nickelodeons in New York City. He led many incarnations of the company that became Paramount Pictures in 1936. He died in 1976 at the age of 103. (Photograph courtesy of Quigley Photographic Archive, Georgetown University Library, Special Collections Division.)

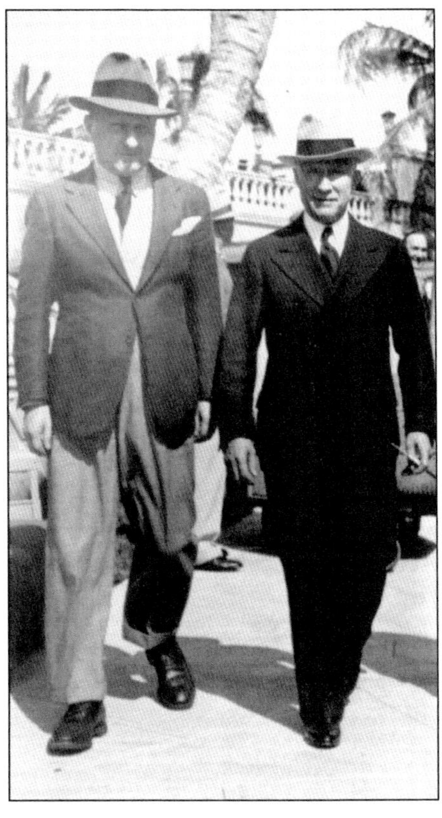

In 1936, Barney moved to New York City to become president of Paramount, under the leadership of Adolf Zukor. John Balaban took charge of Balaban and Katz in Chicago. Sam had left Paramount, and times were bad. Joseph Kennedy (Pres. John F. Kennedy's father) had attempted to take control of the bankrupt Paramount Publix. Paramount Publix was renamed Paramount Pictures. Barney had Zukor appointed chairman of the board of the new company. It was Barney's mission to turn Paramount into a profitable business—which he did and remained at the helm for 28 years. Most of the serious financial decisions regarding Paramount were made out of the company's Times Square office building where Barney had a comfortable office. Pictured here are Adolf and Barney walking to a business meeting in California. (Photograph courtesy of Quigley Photographic Archive, Georgetown University Library, Special Collections Division.)

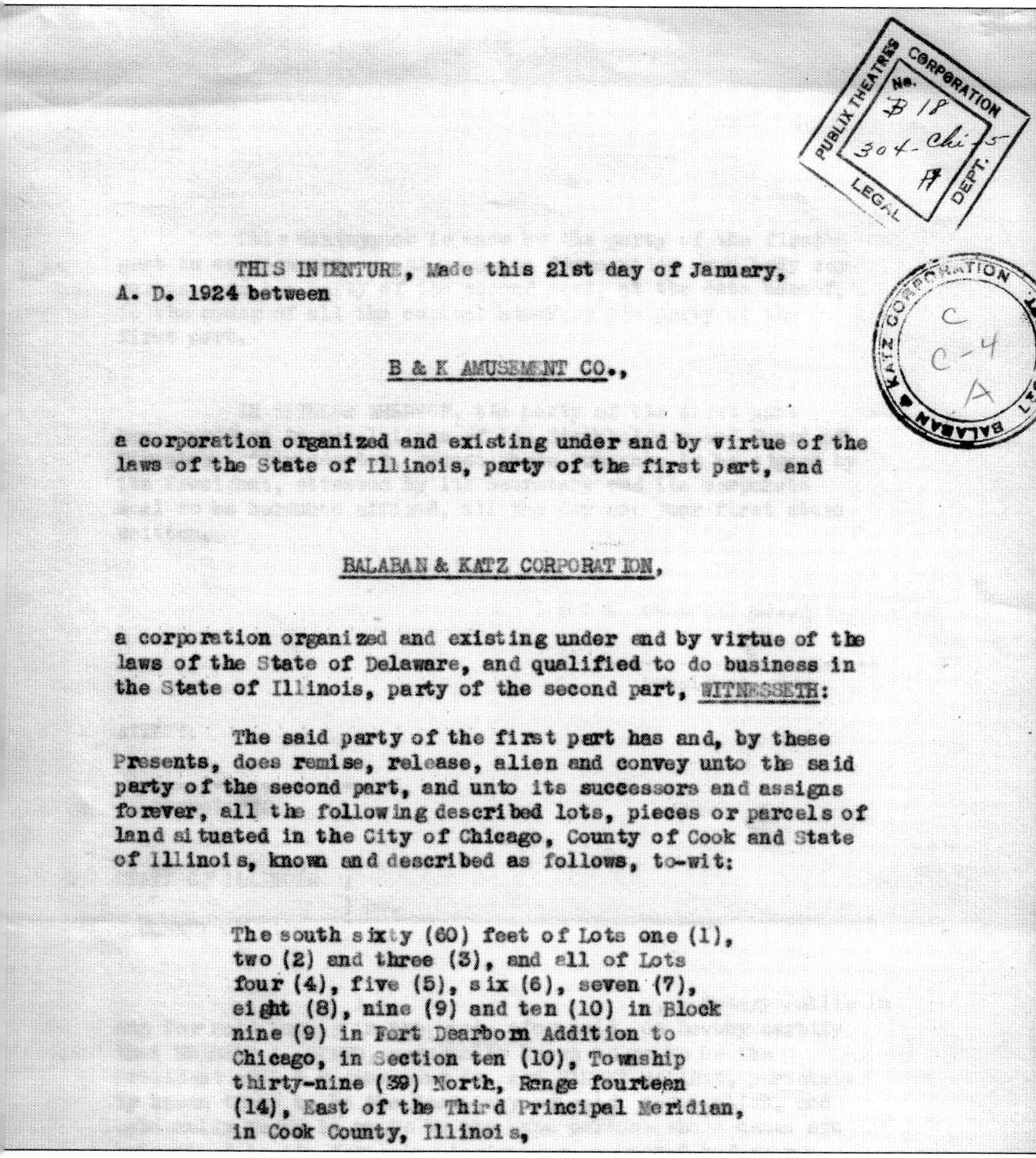

THIS INDENTURE, Made this 21st day of January, A. D. 1924 between

B & K AMUSEMENT CO.,

a corporation organized and existing under and by virtue of the laws of the State of Illinois, party of the first part, and

BALABAN & KATZ CORPORATION,

a corporation organized and existing under and by virtue of the laws of the State of Delaware, and qualified to do business in the State of Illinois, party of the second part, WITNESSETH:

The said party of the first part has and, by these Presents, does remise, release, alien and convey unto the said party of the second part, and unto its successors and assigns forever, all the following described lots, pieces or parcels of land situated in the City of Chicago, County of Cook and State of Illinois, known and described as follows, to-wit:

The south sixty (60) feet of Lots one (1), two (2) and three (3), and all of Lots four (4), five (5), six (6), seven (7), eight (8), nine (9) and ten (10) in Block nine (9) in Fort Dearborn Addition to Chicago, in Section ten (10), Township thirty-nine (39) North, Range fourteen (14), East of the Third Principal Meridian, in Cook County, Illinois,

In 1925, the Publix Theatres Corporation, a division of Famous Players Lasky Corporation and, later, Paramount Pictures headed by Sam Katz, began to transfer ownership of various theater properties to Balaban and Katz. Smaller satellite companies had been set up years before by B and K. Seen here is the article of transfer of one theater property from B and K Amusement Company to Balaban and Katz Corporation, in January 1924. (Image courtesy of Balaban and Katz Historical Foundation.)

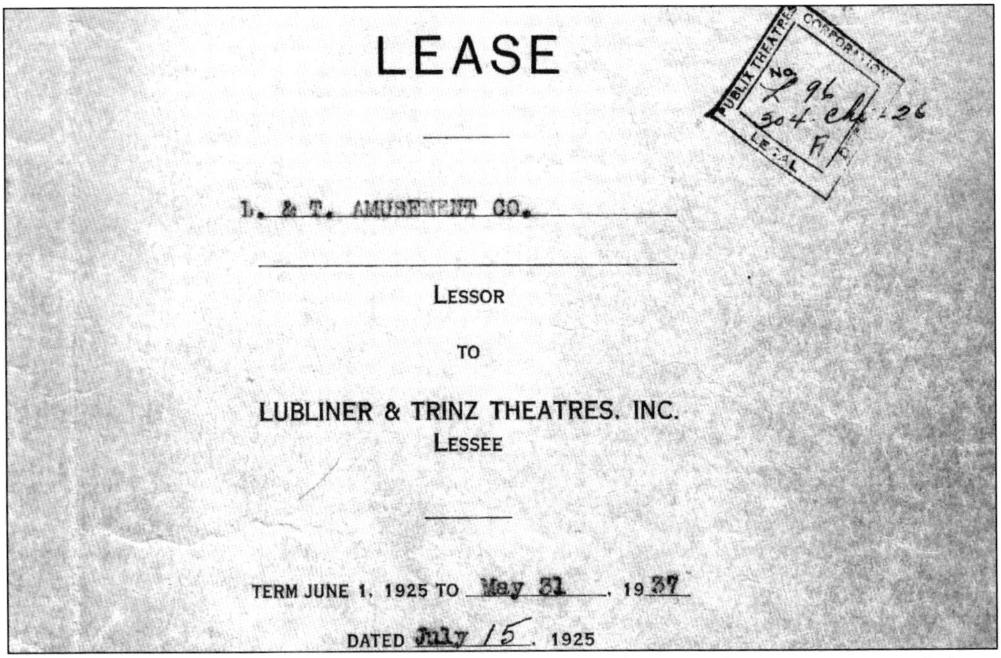

LEASE

L. & T. AMUSEMENT CO.

LESSOR

TO

LUBLINER & TRINZ THEATRES, INC.

LESSEE

TERM JUNE 1, 1925 TO May 31, 1937

DATED July 15, 1925

The Publix Theatres Corporation, a division of Famous Players Lasky Corporation and, later, Paramount Publix, negotiated the takeover of many of Chicago's once-powerful theater chains. Seen here is the cover of the lease agreement for the takeover of the assets of Lubliner and Trinz. Lubliner operated many of Chicago's finest theaters in the 1910s and 1920s, including the Regal and Congress Theaters. Rather than an outright purchase, Publix formed a new corporation called L&T Amusement Company in which Publix shared ownership with Lubliner executives. Balaban and Katz, now a subsidiary of Publix, operated the theaters and shared any profits with the Lubliners. Notice the Publix Theatres Corporation stamp in the top right of the document. (Image courtesy of Balaban and Katz Historical Foundation.)

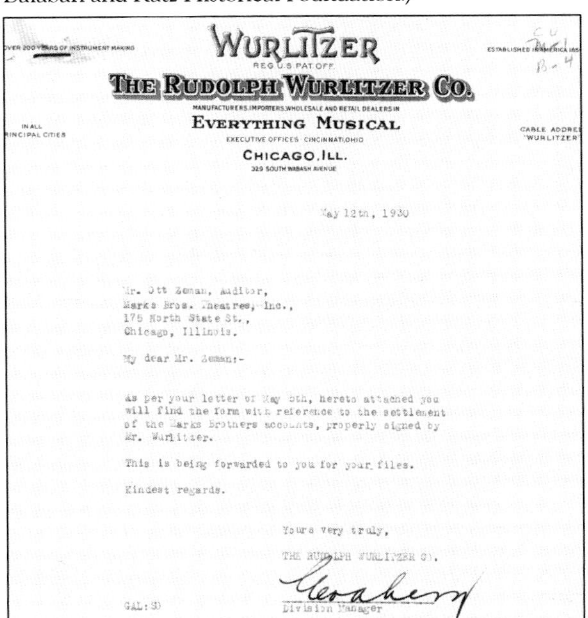

WURLITZER
REG. U.S. PAT. OFF.
THE RUDOLPH WURLITZER CO.
MANUFACTURERS, IMPORTERS, WHOLESALE AND RETAIL DEALERS IN
EVERYTHING MUSICAL
EXECUTIVE OFFICES CINCINNATI, OHIO
CHICAGO, ILL.
329 SOUTH WABASH AVENUE

May 12th, 1930

Mr. Ott Zeman, Auditor,
Marks Bros. Theatres, Inc.,
175 North State St.,
Chicago, Illinois.

My dear Mr. Zeman:-

As per your letter of May 5th, hereto attached you will find the form with reference to the settlement of the Marks Brothers accounts, properly signed by Mr. Wurlitzer.

This is being forwarded to you for your files.

Kindest regards.

Yours very truly,

THE RUDOLPH WURLITZER CO.

Division Manager

GAL:SD

At the left is a letter from the Wurlitzer organ company to the Marks Brothers. B and K kept these files active for many decades. (Image courtesy of Balaban and Katz Historical Foundation.)

Seven

STATE-OF-THE-ART ENTERTAINMENT

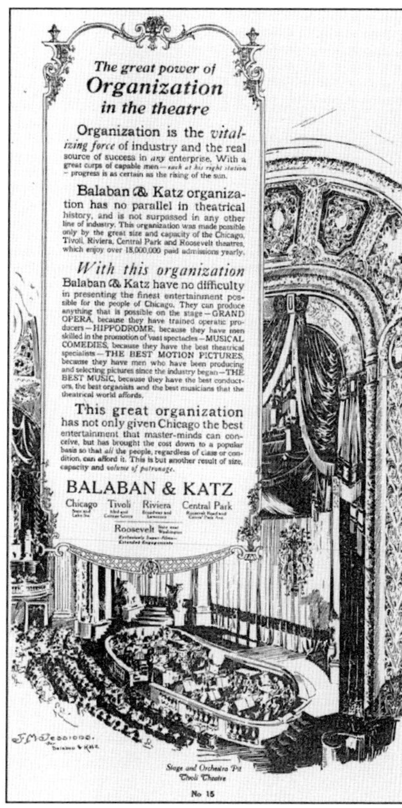

Seen here is a promotional announcement laying out the Balaban and Katz marketing concept. By the mid-1920s, B and K had carved out a broad niche as the premier provider of quality entertainment in the Chicago area. The text here boasts of attracting 18 million customers annually. This was amazing considering that the company only operated five theaters at the time. It was years before the other theater operators in the area learned to compete against the mighty Balaban and Katz business model. (Photograph courtesy of Theatre Historical Society of America.)

AUTOMATIC TELEPHONE DIRECTORY

	Name	Ext.
A -	Abrams, Ethel	43
	Adelman, Sylvia	73
	Advertising Department	12
	Arlen, Dave	91
B -	Bail, Waldo	45
	Balaban, John	51
	Balcony - Lower Foyer	31
	Berry, Elsie M.	10
	Bloom, Abe Z.	80
	Box-office	35
	Brandt, George	95
	Bregenzer, Dick	88
	Burns, R.	69
C -	Candy Counter	70
	Candy Storeroom	86
	Carlson, Myrtle	36
	Carpenter Shop	20
	Checkroom	97
	Conductor's Stand	25
	Conference Room	58
	Cooney, J.	13
	Cook, C.	84
	Crawford, R. B.	38
D -	Danzig, Esther	47
	Davidson, C.	49
	District Managers	95
	Ditto Room	89
	Dromey, John	32
E -	Eichholz, Marion	74
	Electric Shop	22
	Enders, Helen	52
	Engineer	19
F -	File Room	89
G -	Garber, J.	54
	Glass, M.	59
	Goldberg, A.	79
	Goodall, J.	17
	Gora, Ann	48
	Groner, Esther	30
H -	Hachat, Henry	85
	Hoffman, George	52
	Holden, W. B. (D.M.)	95
	Holden, W. H. (Ins.)	37
	Hollander, W. K.	40
	Holtzman, Noreen	43
	Horner, Janet	47
	Horwitz, Sol	49
I -	Immerman, Elmer	66
	Information-6th Fl. Chgo.	14
	" -7th Fl. Chgo.	59
	" -5th Fl. L.E.	34
	" -6th Fl. L.E.	37
J -	Jacobs, E.	81
	Jacobsen, I.	69
	Johnson, W.	13
	Jones, A. W.	71

	Name	Ext.
K -	Kaplan, I.	67
	Kennedy, D. R.	41
	Kinobooth	18
	Klein, Ann	52
L -	Levy, Althea	32
	Lewis, W.	61
	Lost & Found	33
	Lower Balcony	31
	Lustgarten, H.	72
M -	Mail Room	82
	Main Floor Lobby	27
	Malina, S.	12
	Manager's Office	26
	Manig, Kurt	84
	Matron	75
	McBreen, C.	94
	McDougall, Joanne	66
	McPhee, Donald	46
	McPhee, Marie	82
	Meindl, Shirley	37
	Melnick, Faye	62
	Melnick, Rita	34
	Mezzanine Foyer	28
	Mounsey, Cynthia	14
	Musicians' Room	67
O -	Orchestra Leader	15
P -	Payroll Typing	68
	Platt, Abe	64
	Platt, Nate	17
	Porters' Room	96
	Powers, Marcella	55
	Priest, Virginia	77
R -	Raben, Art	52
S -	Screening Room	60
	Seguin, E.	53
	Shayne, Miriam	63
	Shields, J.	81
	Shirey, Joy	95
	Shulman, Lois	49
	Simons, Ruth	39
	Stage Door	23
	Stage Switchboard	24
	Standl, Frank	85
	Stone, Harriet	92
	Stott, Sam	38
T -	Telephone Switchboard	55
	Thompson, Ray	26
	Treasurer's Office	42
	Trebow, A. L.	39
	Twyman, Marion	59
U -	Upton, E. C.	30
	Ushers' Room	21
V -	Van Getson, R.	46
W -	Wallerstein, D. B.	44
	Winsberg, J.	49
	Wohl, J.	85

8-22-55 jg

This is the Balaban and Katz corporate phone list from around 1955. Balaban and Katz was one of the first companies to use a sophisticated intercompany telephone system, which included 100 different locations, from the company president's office (extension 51), to the lost and found of the Chicago Theatre (extension 33). With this system, every employee could be contacted instantly to solve a customer service or technical issue. John Balaban would often randomly call different numbers to check on the attentiveness of employees. (Image courtesy of Paul Jannusch.)

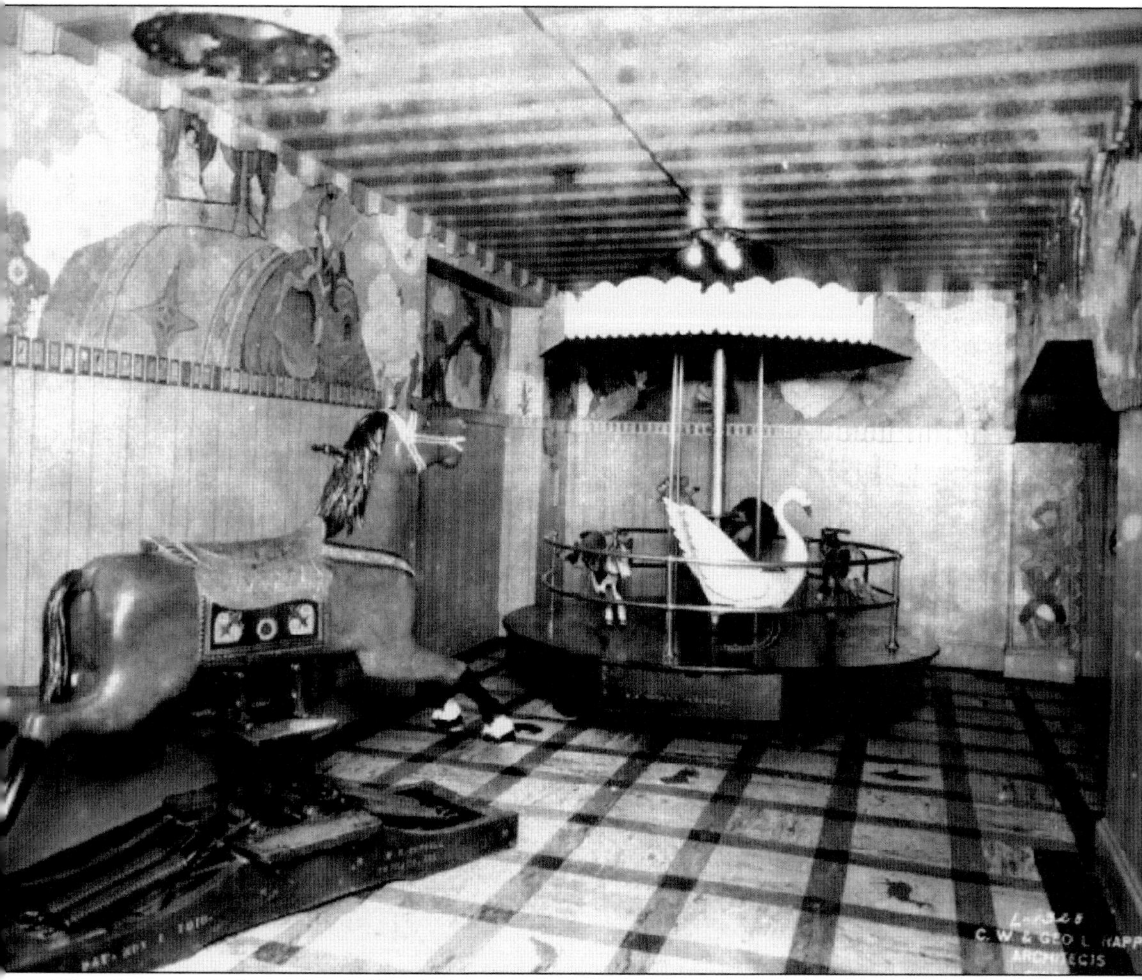

This photograph shows the children's play area at the Uptown Theatre in 1925. Balaban and Katz developed a reputation for offering child care services to enhance the theatergoing experience of mothers with young children. At the Central Park Theatre, "baby carriage service" was first offered, whereby parents could leave their infant with a Balaban and Katz attendant. A notice would go up on the screen notifying patrons that their baby was crying. The Riviera also continued in the babysitting tradition. At the Uptown, the concept developed into a very modern looking indoor playground. Remnants of the wall decorations from the play areas can be seen today at the Theatre Historical Society of America in Elmhurst, Illinois. (Photograph courtesy of Theatre Historical Society of America.)

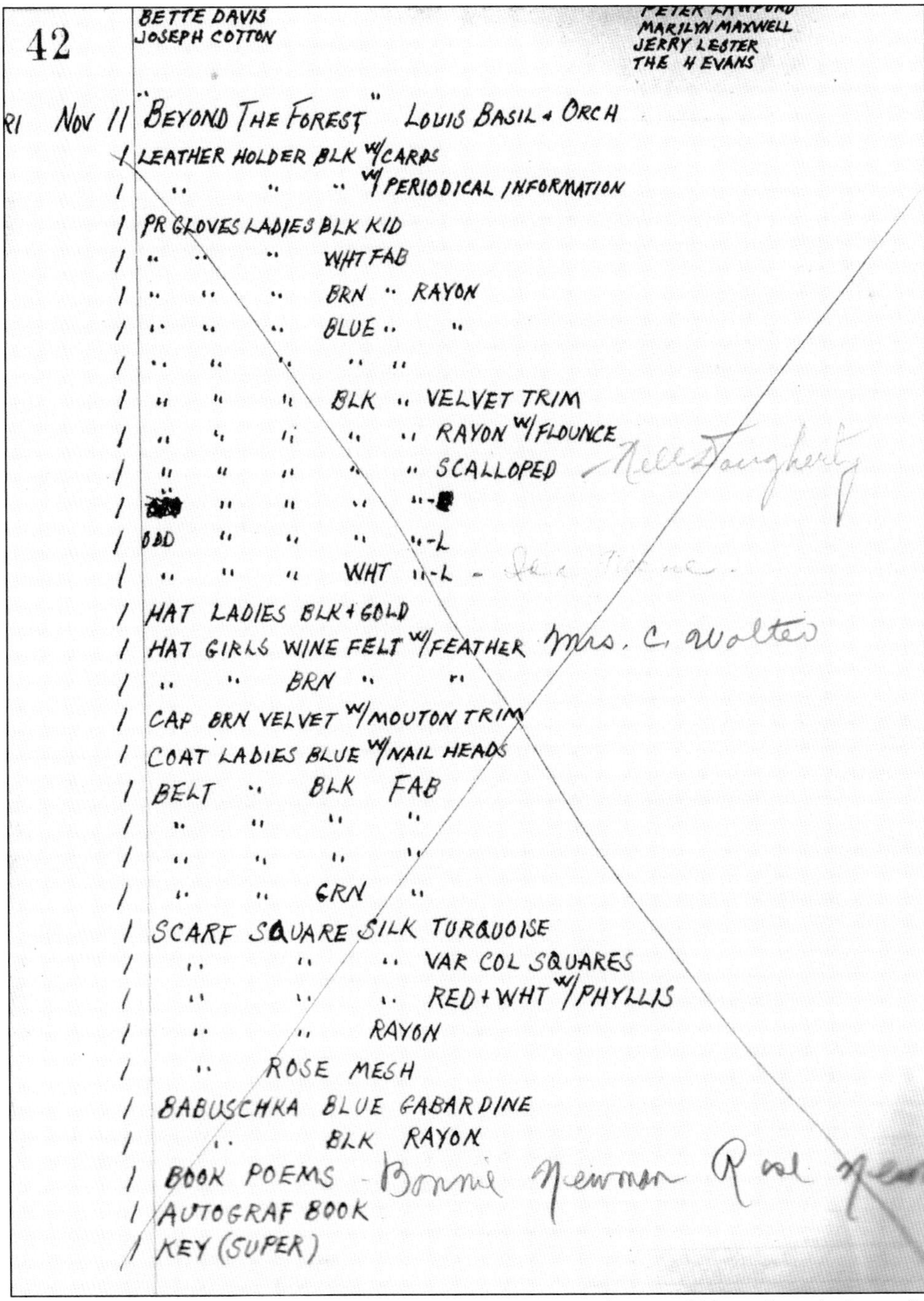

42

BETTE DAVIS
JOSEPH COTTON

PETER LAWFORD
MARILYN MAXWELL
JERRY LESTER
THE 4 EVANS

RI Nov 11 "BEYOND THE FOREST" LOUIS BASIL + ORCH

1 LEATHER HOLDER BLK W/CARDS
1 " " " W/PERIODICAL INFORMATION
1 PR GLOVES LADIES BLK KID
1 " " " WHT FAB
1 " " " BRN " RAYON
1 " " " BLUE " "
1 " " " " "
1 " " " BLK " VELVET TRIM
1 " " " " " RAYON W/FLOUNCE
1 " " " " " SCALLOPED
1 " " " " "-R
1 ODD " " " "-L
1 " " " WHT "-L
1 HAT LADIES BLK + GOLD
1 HAT GIRLS WINE FELT W/FEATHER Mrs. C. Walter
1 " " BRN " "
1 CAP BRN VELVET W/MOUTON TRIM
1 COAT LADIES BLUE W/NAIL HEADS
1 BELT " BLK FAB
1 " " " "
1 " " " "
1 " " GRN "
1 SCARF SQUARE SILK TURQUOISE
1 " " " VAR COL SQUARES
1 " " " RED + WHT W/PHYLLIS
1 " " RAYON
1 " ROSE MESH
1 BABUSCHKA BLUE GABARDINE
1 " BLK RAYON
1 BOOK POEMS - Bonnie Newman
1 AUTOGRAF BOOK
1 KEY (SUPER)

Balaban and Katz provided many services to their customers that would be unheard of in today's fast-paced world. A detailed lost and found book was kept by each theater. In it, items would be logged in and tagged and organized. As customers eventually retraced their steps and picked up their personal items, each log entry was meticulously crossed off. Here is a page from the 1949 lost and found record book from the Chicago Theatre. On each page, the movie stars that appeared in the film shown that day were recorded. Bette Davis and Peter Lawford were the attraction for Friday, November 11, 1949. (Image courtesy of Balaban and Katz Historical Foundation.)

In 1925, Balaban and Katz began distributing a free weekly magazine to its customers. By that time, over a million eager patrons were seeing shows in B and K theaters each month. The purpose of the publication was to promote the upcoming film and live shows that were playing at the ever-growing array of B and K theaters. Pictured here is the beautiful Corrine Griffith and an advertisement for a radio console from Spiegel's catalogue. It came with a free bench, all for $99 (minus the tubes)—such a deal! (Photographs courtesy of Balaban and Katz Historical Foundation.)

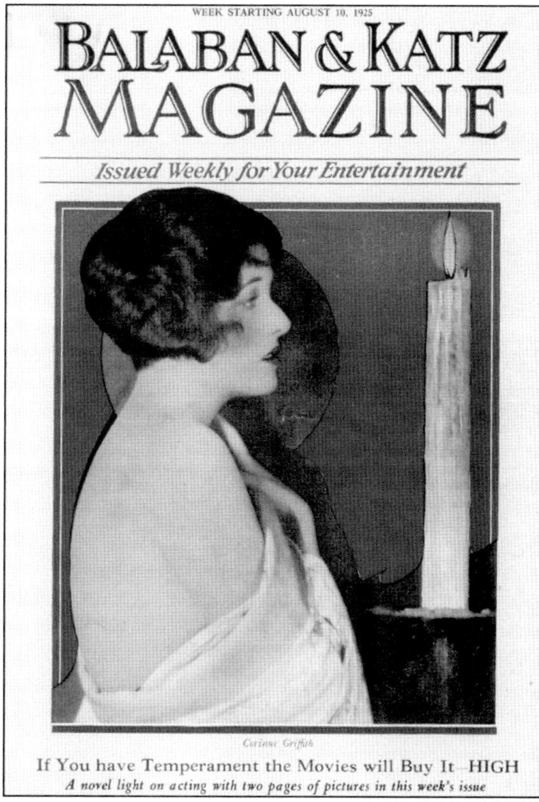
WEEK STARTING AUGUST 10, 1925

BALABAN & KATZ MAGAZINE

Issued Weekly for Your Entertainment

Corinne Griffith

If You have Temperament the Movies will Buy It—HIGH

A novel light on acting with two pages of pictures in this week's issue

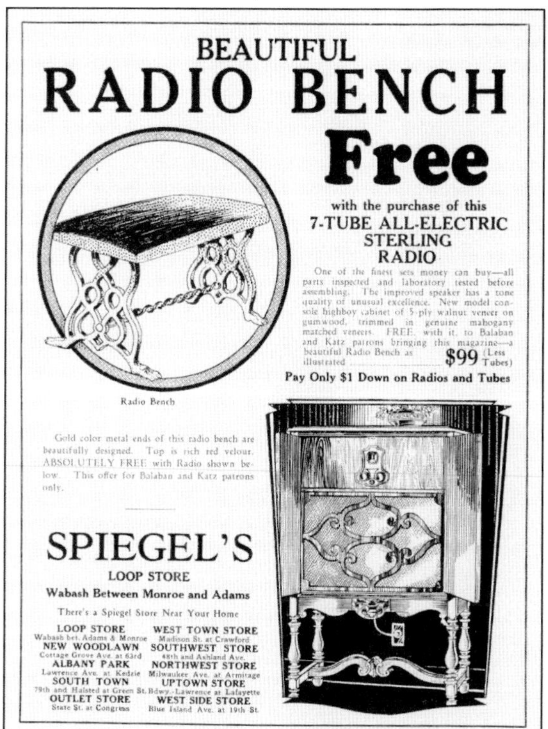
BEAUTIFUL

RADIO BENCH

Free

with the purchase of this

7-TUBE ALL-ELECTRIC STERLING RADIO

One of the finest sets money can buy—all parts inspected and laboratory tested before assembling. The improved speaker has a tone quality of unusual excellence. New model console highboy cabinet of 5-ply walnut veneer on gumwood, trimmed in genuine mahogany matched veneers. FREE, with it, to Balaban and Katz patrons bringing this magazine—a beautiful Radio Bench as illustrated .... $99 (Less Tubes)

Pay Only $1 Down on Radios and Tubes

Radio Bench

Gold color metal ends of this radio bench are beautifully designed. Top is rich red velour. ABSOLUTELY FREE with Radio shown below. This offer for Balaban and Katz patrons only.

SPIEGEL'S

LOOP STORE

Wabash Between Monroe and Adams

There's a Spiegel Store Near Your Home

LOOP STORE Wabash bet. Adams & Monroe	**WEST TOWN STORE** Madison St. at Crawford
NEW WOODLAWN Cottage Grove Ave. at 63rd	**SOUTHWEST STORE** 48th and Ashland Ave.
ALBANY PARK Lawrence Ave. at Kedzie	**NORTHWEST STORE** Milwaukee Ave. at Armitage
SOUTH TOWN 79th and Halsted at Green St.	**UPTOWN STORE** Bdwy.-Lawrence at Lafayette
OUTLET STORE State St. at Congress	**WEST SIDE STORE** Blue Island Ave. at 19th St.

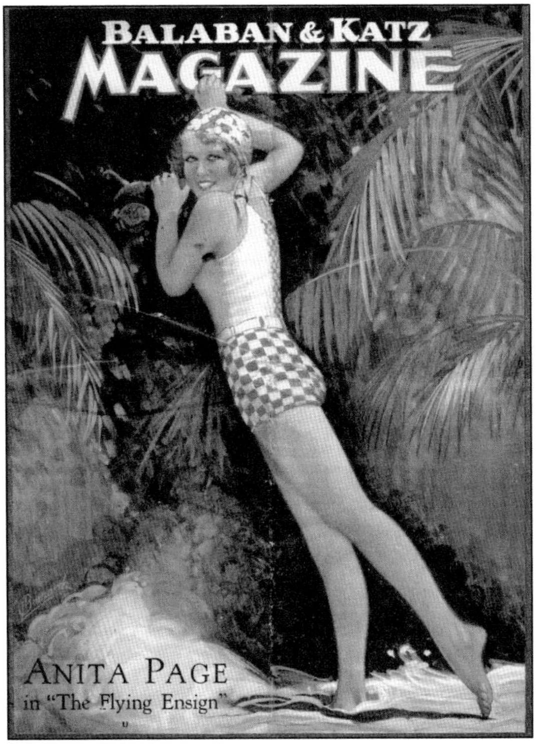

Balaban & Katz Magazine was produced in beautiful, full color. Each week, the portrait of a highly recognizable movie star was featured on the cover. This week's star was Anita Page. Inside the magazine were advertisements for wonder cures and exciting products of the day. Seen below are advertisements for plastic surgery and a cure for gray hair—how 20th century! (Photographs courtesy of Balaban and Katz Historical Foundation.)

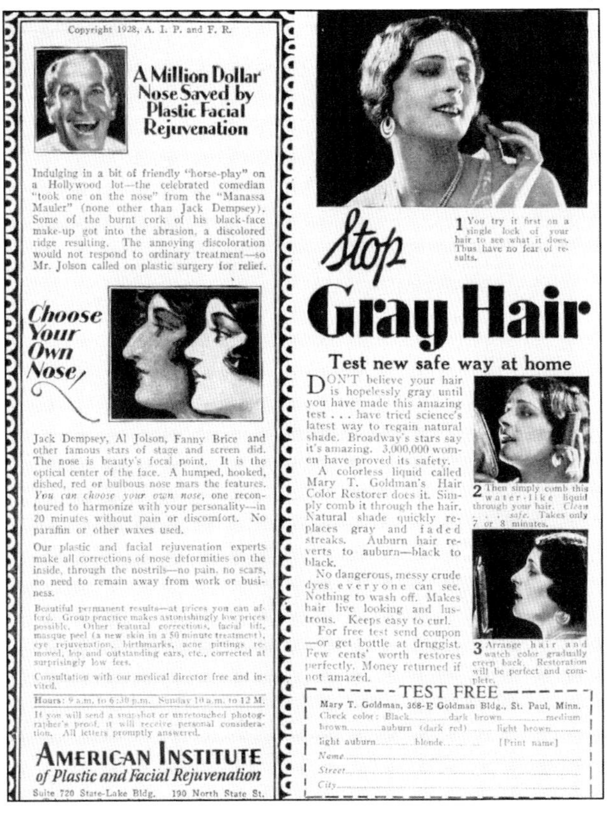

Copyright 1928, A. I. P. and F. R.

A Million Dollar Nose Saved by Plastic Facial Rejuvenation

Indulging in a bit of friendly "horse-play" on a Hollywood lot—the celebrated comedian "took one on the nose" from the "Manassa Mauler" (none other than Jack Dempsey). Some of the burnt cork of his black-face make-up got into the abrasion, a discolored ridge resulting. The annoying discoloration would not respond to ordinary treatment—so Mr. Jolson called on plastic surgery for relief.

Choose Your Own Nose

Jack Dempsey, Al Jolson, Fanny Brice and other famous stars of stage and screen did. The nose is beauty's focal point. It is the optical center of the face. A humped, hooked, dished, red or bulbous nose mars the features. *You can choose your own nose,* one recontoured to harmonize with your personality—in 20 minutes without pain or discomfort. No paraffin or other waxes used.

Our plastic and facial rejuvenation experts make all corrections of nose deformities on the inside, through the nostrils—no pain, no scars, no need to remain away from work or business.

Beautiful permanent results—at prices you can afford. Group practice makes astonishingly low prices possible. Other featural corrections, facial lift, masque peel (a new skin in a 50 minute treatment), eye rejuvenation, birthmarks, acne pittings removed, lop and outstanding ears, etc., corrected at surprisingly low fees.

Consultation with our medical director free and invited.

Hours: 9 a.m. to 6:30 p.m. Sunday 10 a.m. to 12 M.

If you will send a snapshot or unretouched photographer's proof, it will receive personal consideration. All letters promptly answered.

AMERICAN INSTITUTE
of Plastic and Facial Rejuvenation
Suite 720 State-Lake Bldg. 190 North State St.

Stop
Gray Hair

Test new safe way at home

DON'T believe your hair is hopelessly gray until you have made this amazing test . . . have tried science's latest way to regain natural shade. Broadway's stars say it's amazing. 3,000,000 women have proved its safety.

A colorless liquid called Mary T. Goldman's Hair Color Restorer does it. Simply comb it through the hair. Natural shade quickly replaces gray and faded streaks. Auburn hair reverts to auburn—black to black.

No dangerous, messy crude dyes everyone can see. Nothing to wash off. Makes hair live looking and lustrous. Keeps easy to curl.

For free test send coupon—or get bottle at druggist. Few cents' worth restores perfectly. Money returned if not amazed.

1 You try it first on a single lock of your hair to see what it does. Thus have no fear of results.

2 Then simply comb this water-like liquid through your hair. *Clean . . . safe.* Takes only 7 or 8 minutes.

3 Arrange hair and watch color gradually creep back. Restoration will be perfect and complete.

TEST FREE

Mary T. Goldman, 368-E Goldman Bldg., St. Paul, Minn.
Check color: Black........ dark brown........ medium brown........ auburn (dark red)........ light brown........ light auburn........ blonde........ [Print name]
Name........
Street........
City........

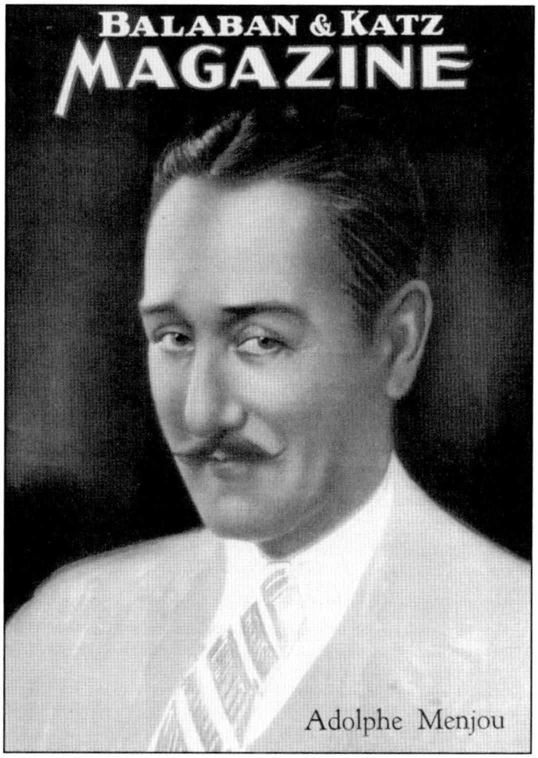

Adolphe Menjou graced this week's *Balaban & Katz Magazine*. The inside cover featured a "racy" bathing suit photographic spread. (Photographs courtesy of Balaban and Katz Historical Foundation.)

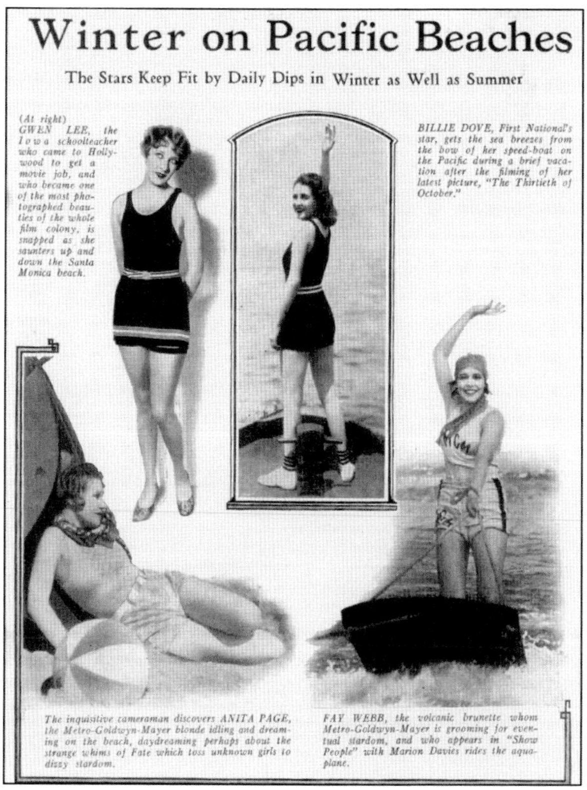

Winter on Pacific Beaches

The Stars Keep Fit by Daily Dips in Winter as Well as Summer

(At right) GWEN LEE, the Iowa schoolteacher who came to Hollywood to get a movie job, and who became one of the most photographed beauties of the whole film colony, is snapped as she saunters up and down the Santa Monica beach.

BILLIE DOVE, First National's star, gets the sea breezes from the bow of her speed-boat on the Pacific during a brief vacation after the filming of her latest picture, "The Thirtieth of October."

The inquisitive cameraman discovers ANITA PAGE, the Metro-Goldwyn-Mayer blonde idling and dreaming on the beach, daydreaming perhaps about the strange whims of Fate which toss unknown girls to dizzy stardom.

FAY WEBB, the volcanic brunette whom Metro-Goldwyn-Mayer is grooming for eventual stardom, and who appears in "Show People" with Marion Davies rides the aquaplane.

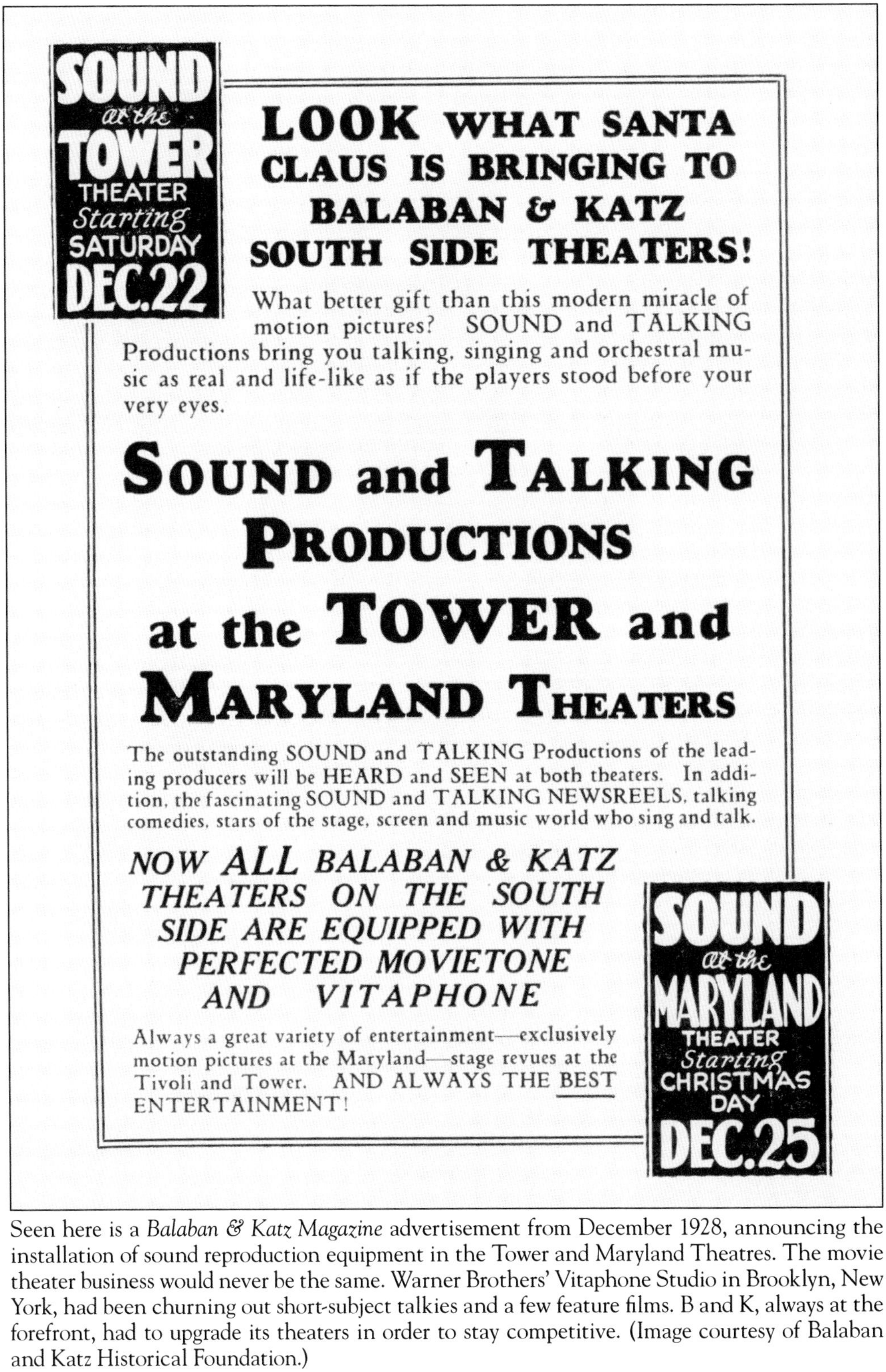

Seen here is a *Balaban & Katz Magazine* advertisement from December 1928, announcing the installation of sound reproduction equipment in the Tower and Maryland Theatres. The movie theater business would never be the same. Warner Brothers' Vitaphone Studio in Brooklyn, New York, had been churning out short-subject talkies and a few feature films. B and K, always at the forefront, had to upgrade its theaters in order to stay competitive. (Image courtesy of Balaban and Katz Historical Foundation.)

In the mid-1930s, Balaban and Katz created an employee publication called *Balabanner*. Pictured here is one of the editions from the early 1940s. The magazine featured news about employee related issues, including promotions, length of service awards, and community news. (Image courtesy of Balaban and Katz Historical Foundation.)

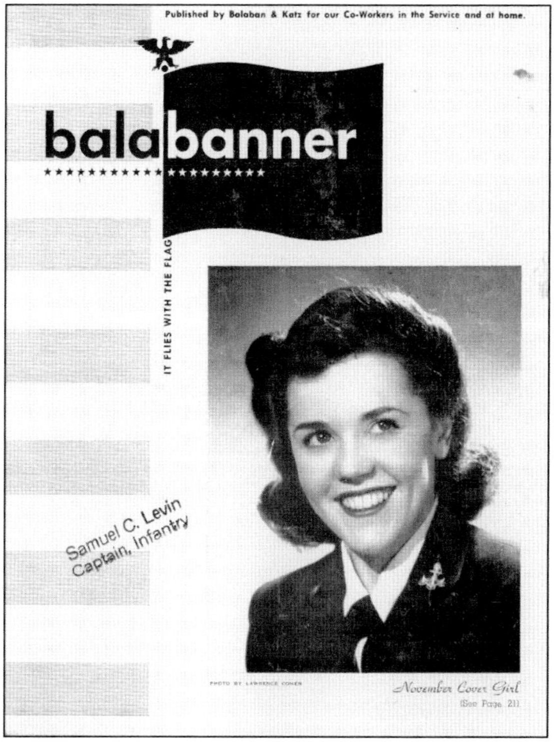

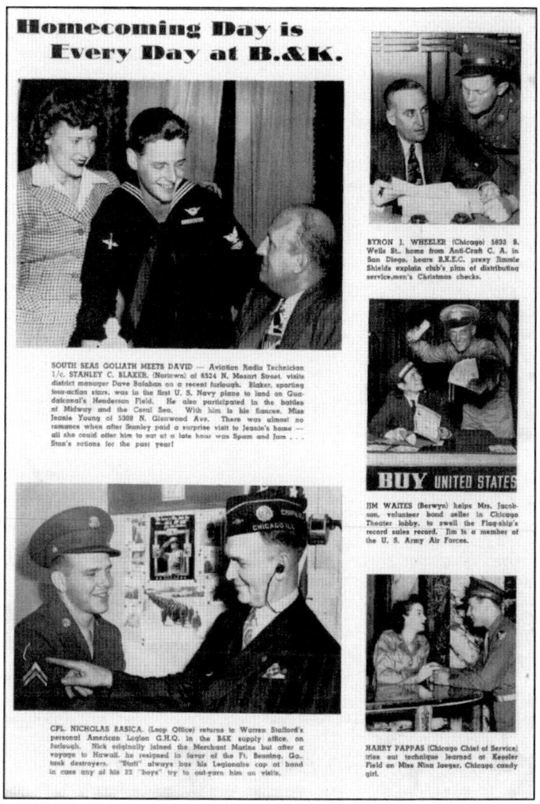

Homecoming Day is Every Day at B.&K.

SOUTH SEAS GOLIATH MEETS DAVID — Aviation Radio Technician 1/c. STANLEY C. BLAKER. (Nortown) of 6324 N. Mozart Street, visits district manager Dave Balaban on a recent furlough. Blaker, sporting four-action stars, was in the first U. S. Navy plane to land on Guadalcanal's Henderson Field. He also participated in the battles of Midway and the Coral Sea. With him is his fiancee, Miss Jeanie Young of 5308 N. Glenwood Ave. There was almost no romance when after Stanley paid a surprise visit to Jeanie's home — all she could offer him to eat at a late hour was Spam and Jam . . . Stan's rations for the past year!

BYRON J. WHEELER (Chicago) 5833 S. Wells St., home from Anti-Craft C. A. in San Diego, hears B.K.E.C. prexy Jimmie Shields explain club's plan of distributing service.men's Christmas checks.

BUY UNITED STATES

JIM WAITES (Berwyn) helps Mrs. Jacobson, volunteer bond seller in Chicago Theater lobby, to swell the Flag-ship's record sales record. Jim is a member of the U. S. Army Air Forces.

CPL. NICHOLAS BASICA. (Loop Office) returns to Warren Stafford's personal American Legion G.H.Q. in the B&K supply office, on furlough. Nick originally joined the Merchant Marine but after a voyage to Hawaii, he resigned in favor of the Ft. Benning, Ga., tank destroyers. "Staff" always has his Legionaire cap at hand in case any of his 22 "boys" try to out-yarn him on visits.

HARRY PAPPAS (Chicago Chief of Service) tries out technique learned at Keesler Field on Miss Nina Jaeger, Chicago candy girl.

Balabanner offered an additional opportunity for the company to portray itself as people- and community-driven. During the World War II years, the magazine featured patriotic B and K employees proud to serve and protect their country. Seen here are a number of employees back from their overseas service mingling with their fellow employees back home. Notice David Balaban, then a district manager, socializing with Stanley Blaker of the Nortown Theater. David Balaban had been manager of the Nortown years before. (Image courtesy of Balaban and Katz Historical Foundation.)

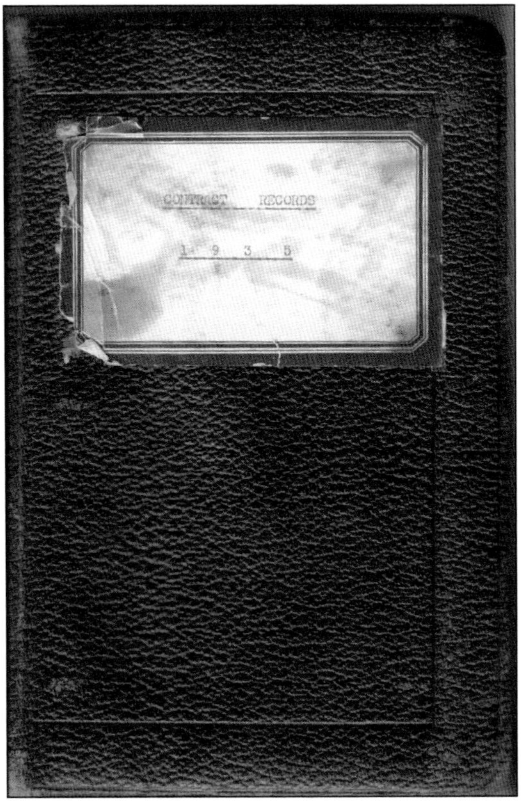

Here is the cover from the 1935 Balaban and Katz talent book. These books include the exact financial arrangements for every live performer that played in the Balaban and Katz theaters in Chicago. The inside page is from the 1948 talent book. The contracts were handled by a division of Balaban and Katz called Theater Booking Incorporated. They were stored in the Balaban and Katz corporate offices in the Chicago Theatre building on State Street. The salaries have been removed for inclusion in this book. Up until 1941, the B and K house orchestras and internal shows rotated between different theaters. The special artists hired for isolated weeks did not. These books show the financial arrangements and schedules for the limited-engagement artists. Specific types of acts were booked into different theaters depending on the neighborhood and clientele that frequented that theater. (Images courtesy of Balaban and Katz Historical Foundation.)

(R) B&K

NAME	SALARY	ENGAGEMENT	THEATRE	DATE	COMM
ROLLY ROLLS (ANDRE RENAUD)		2 weeks	STATE-LAKE	1-30-48	2½%TBO-AB
PHIL REGAN		1 week	"	2-27-48	2½%TBO-ABI
"		"	"	3-5-48	" "
THE RAVENS & SHOW		1 week	REGAL	3-26-48	2½%TBC-ABI
LINA ROMAY		1 week	STATE-LAKE	4-30-48	2½% TBO-ABI
"		1 week	"	5-7-48	"
BUDDY RICH ORCH (J. MOORE BLAZERS & SHOW)		1 week	REGAL	5-7-48	
SUE RYAN		1 week	STATE-LAKE	5-14-48	2½%TBO-ABB
CY REEVES (SAMMY KAYE SHOW)		1 week	STATE-LAKE	5-21-48	
ROCHELLE & BEEBE		2 weeks	STATE-LAKE	6-11-48	2½%TBO-ABB
JUNE RICHMOND (ANDY KIRK SHOW)		1 week	REGAL	7-2-48	
ROSS & LA PIERRE		1 week	CHICAGO	7-16-48	2½%TBO-ABB
" "		3 weeks	"	7-23-48	" "
PAUL REGAN		1 week	"	9-10-48	2½% TBO-ABB
"		1 week	"	9-17-48	"
MICKEY ROONEY & SHOW		1 week	CHICAGO	10-22-48	2½% TBO-ABB
"		1 week	"	10-29-48	2½% TBO-ABB
ROSEMARIE		2 weeks	CHICAGO	11-19-48	2½%TBO- ABB
RENALD & RUDY		2 weeks	CHICAGO	11-19-48	2½% TBO-ABB

Here is a page out of the Balaban and Katz Theatres orchestra book. Theater mangers kept track of the musical arrangements that were played at each B and K theater in this book. This prevented duplication of arrangements, since many theatergoers would go to a show at a different house every night. (Photograph courtesy of Theatre Dreams Chicago LLC.)

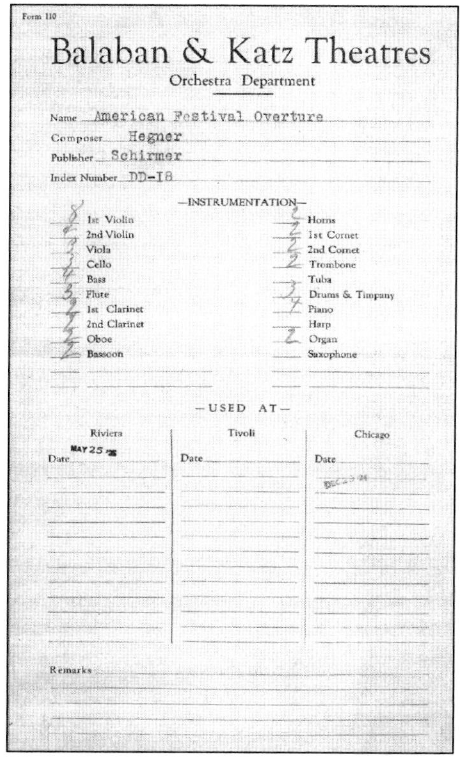

Form 110

Balaban & Katz Theatres

Orchestra Department

Name American Festival Overture

Composer Hegner

Publisher Schirmer

Index Number DD-18

—INSTRUMENTATION—

8	1st Violin	5	Horns
8	2nd Violin	2	1st Cornet
3	Viola	2	2nd Cornet
3	Cello	2	Trombone
4	Bass		Tuba
3	Flute	3	Drums & Timpany
2	1st Clarinet	1	Piano
2	2nd Clarinet		Harp
2	Oboe	2	Organ
2	Bassoon		Saxophone

—USED AT—

Riviera	Tivoli	Chicago
Date MAY 25 '25	Date	Date DEC 3 '26

Remarks

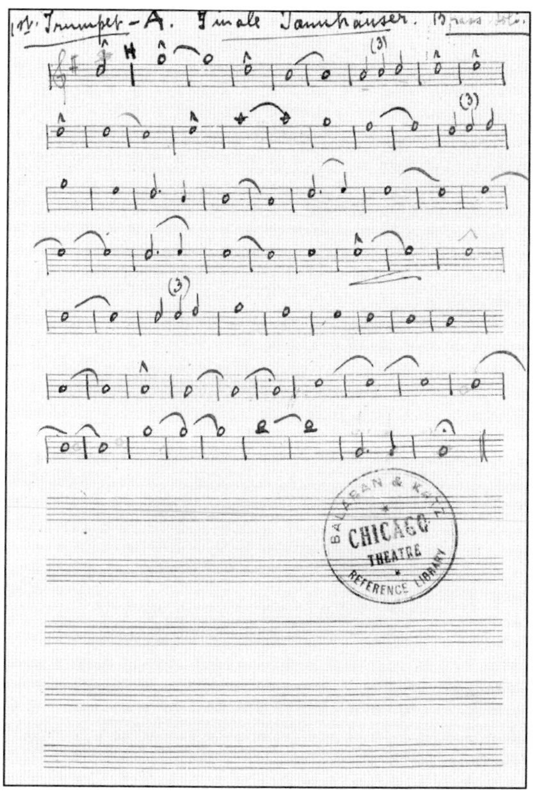

This piece of sheet music was used at the Chicago Theatre in the 1920s. This "stock" arrangement gave detailed musical instructions for each instrument in an orchestra. Many of these arrangements were from popular songs from "Tin Pan Alley" publishing houses. Tin Pan Alley referred to a block in lower Manhattan in New York City where many bands originated in the late 1890s. Tin Pan Alley publishing houses distributed sheet music as a major source of income before radio and phonograph records became popular. (Photograph courtesy of Theatre Dreams Chicago LLC.)

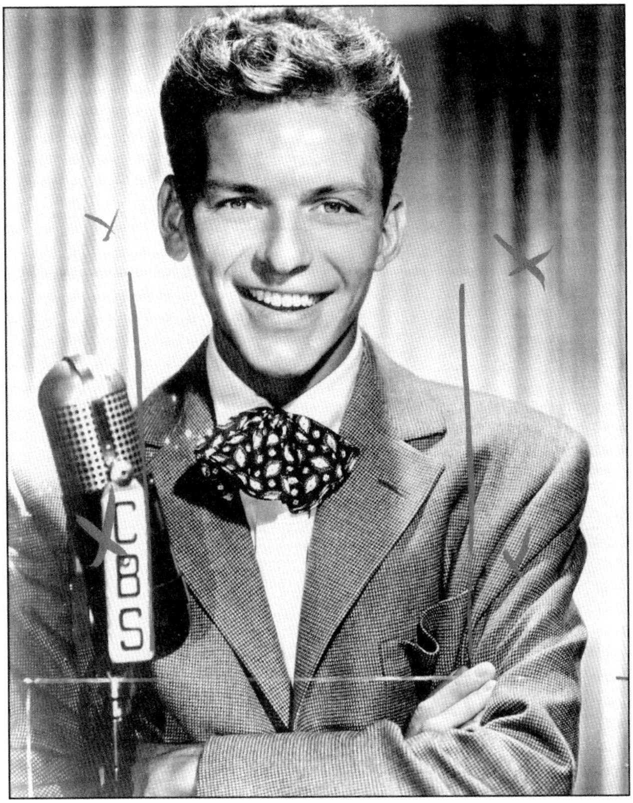

Movie stars that were also singers and live entertainers often made appearances in Balaban and Katz theaters to promote their film projects. Frank Sinatra caused a near riot of young bobby sock–wearing girls whenever he came to town. Here is a promotional picture for one of his live performances in the 1940s. The above photograph was released for use in newspaper advertisements and bears black marks from the advertising department. Sinatra headlined the bill at the reopening of the Chicago Theatre in 1986. Seen below is a promotional photograph for the Marx Brothers. (Photographs courtesy of Balaban and Katz Historic Foundation.)

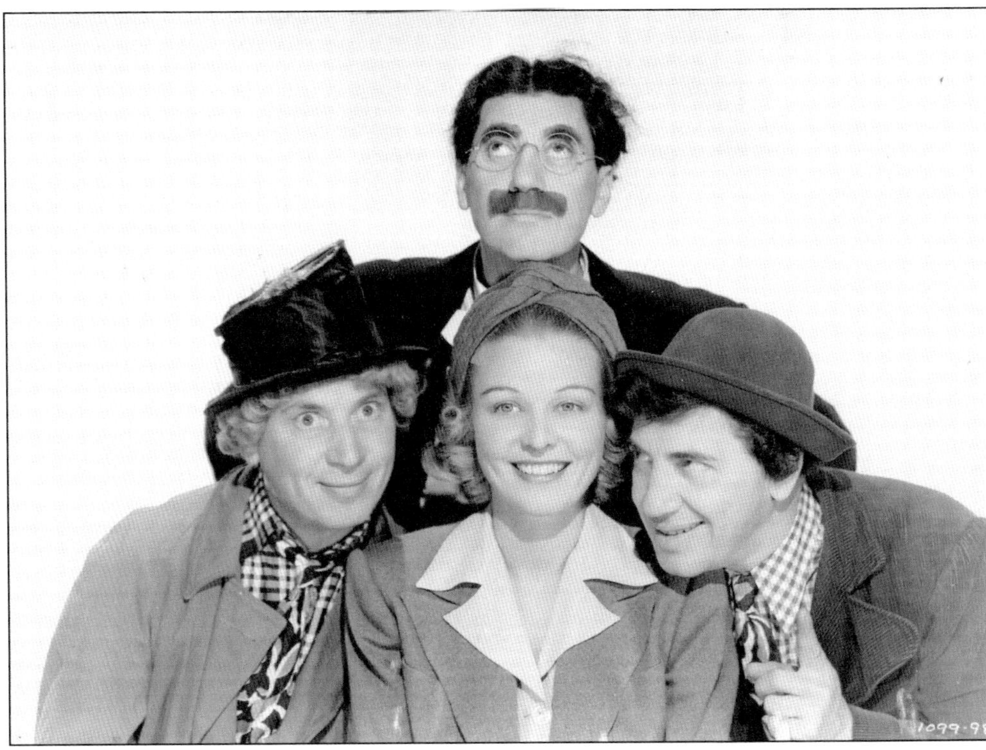

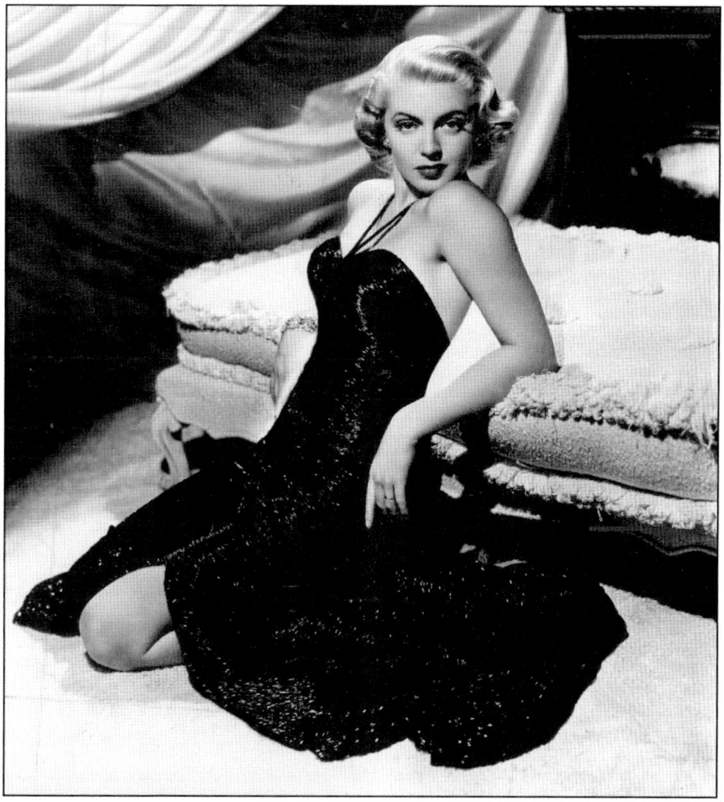

Many stars made live appearances at Balaban and Katz movie palaces to coincide with their new movie being released. Seen above is a promotional photograph for the sensual Lana Turner, and below is a promotional photograph of Jimmy Stewart. (Photographs courtesy of Balaban and Katz Historic Foundation.)

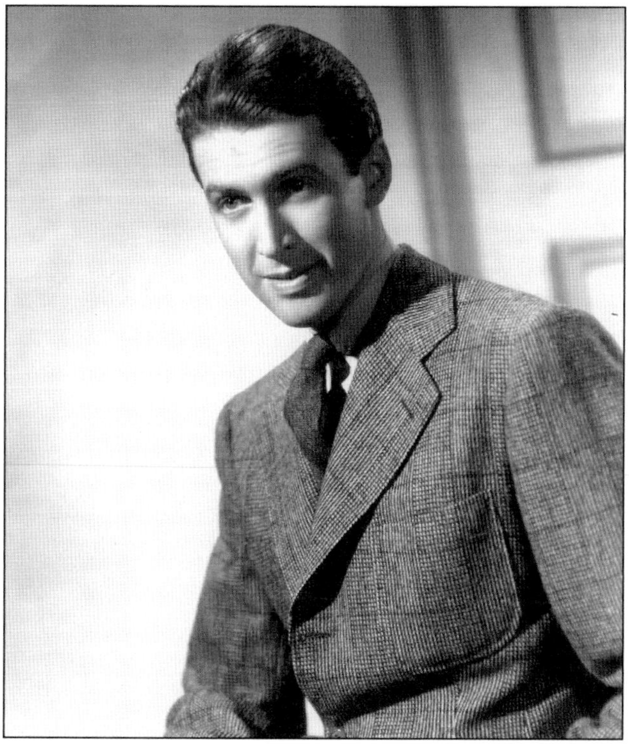

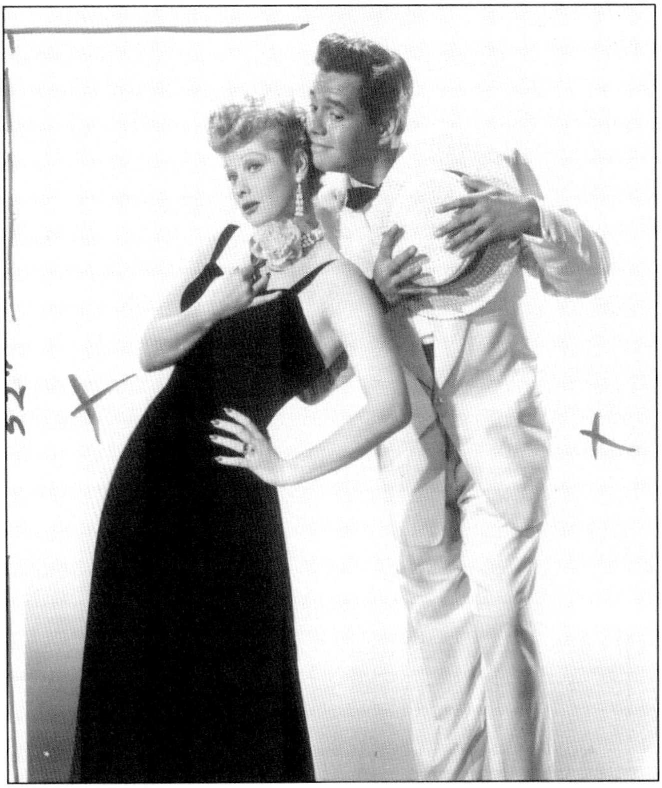

The list of movie stars and live performers that appeared at B and K theaters was almost endless. Seen here are two unique publicity photographs of Lucille Ball and Desi Arnaz and Laurel and Hardy from the Balaban and Katz advertising archives. (Photographs courtesy of Balaban and Katz Historic Foundation.)

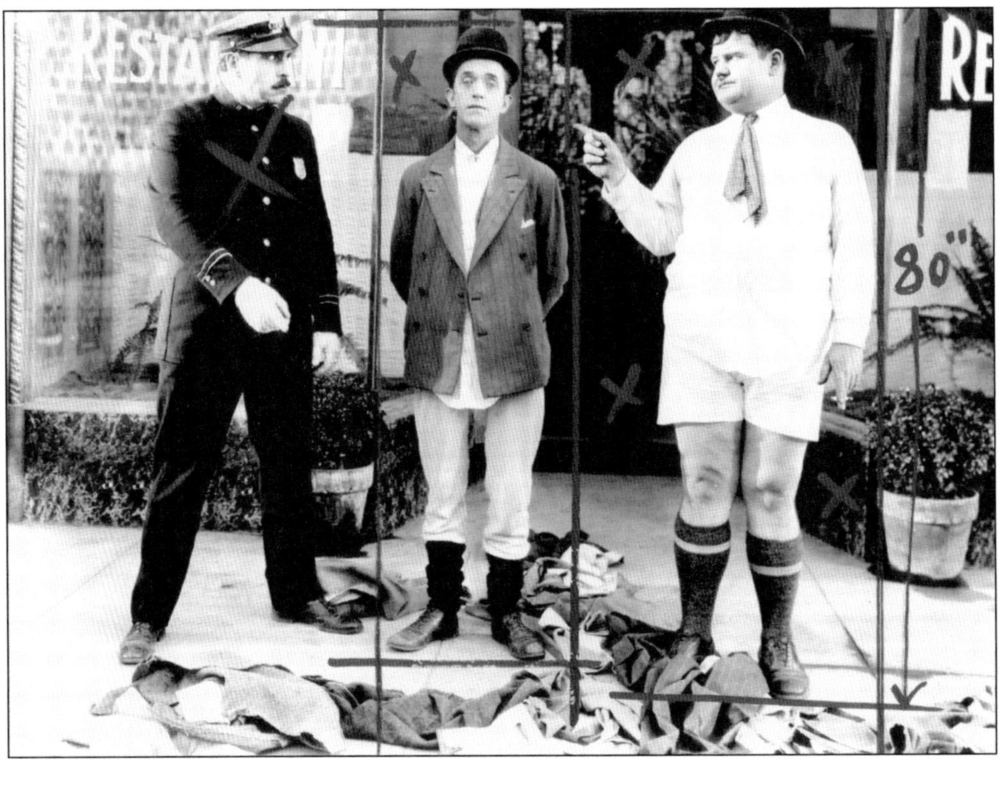

Eight

Many Palaces Vanish . . . Some Remain

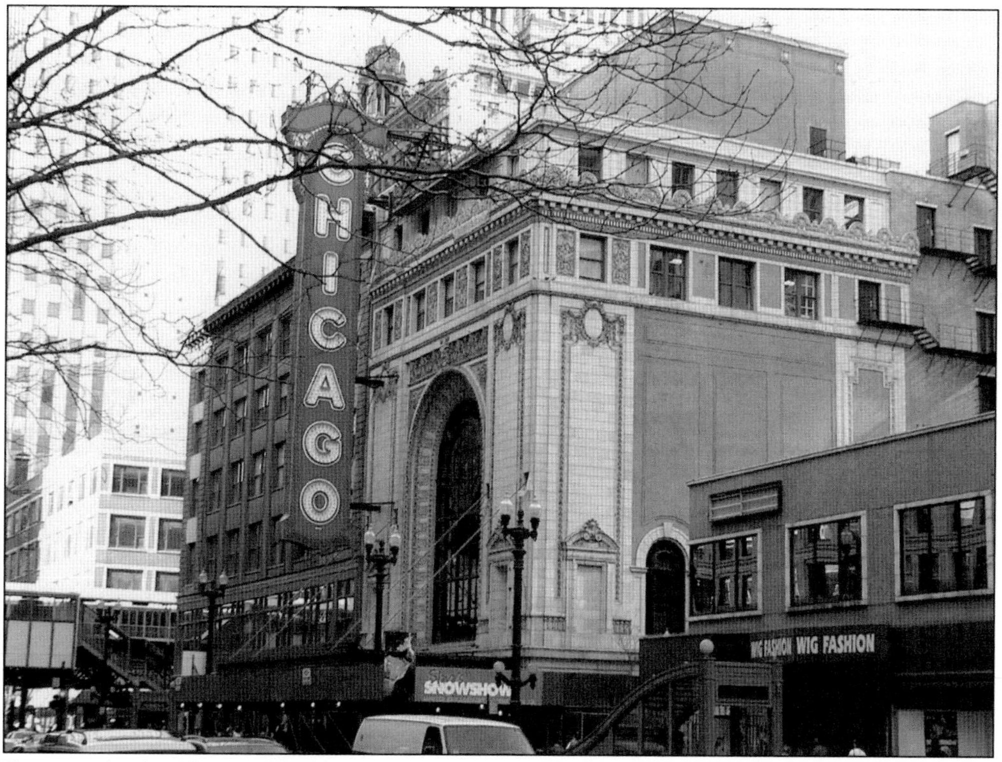

Fortunately, the Chicago Theatre at 175 North State Street still stands. The Chicago was restored to its 1920s condition in 1986 by Chicago Theatre Restoration Associates, with assistance from the City of Chicago. Frank Sinatra played for the exciting grand reopening on September 10, 1986. Ownership of the Chicago Theatre was taken over by Theatre Dreams Chicago LLC on April 1, 2004. It offers a variety of entertainment, including stage events, concerts, dance, comedy, and special events. (Photograph courtesy of David Balaban.)

Status of Balaban and Katz Theaters in Chicago

Theater	Status
Admiral	Open/adult shows
Alba	Closed/demolished
Alvin	Closed/retail use
Apollo (United Artists)	Closed/demolished
Apollo (New Chicago)	Closed/demolished
Belmont	Closed/demolished
Belpark	Closed/banquet hall
Biltmore	Closed/demolished
Broadway Strand	Closed/demolished
Central Park	Closed/used as church
Chicago	Open/restored/live shows
Cine	Closed/restaurant use
Circle	Closed/demolished
Congress	Open/restored/live shows
Crystal	Closed/demolished
Garrick	Closed/demolished
Gateway	Open/cultural organization
Granada	Closed/demolished
Harding	Closed/demolished
Howard	Closed/demolished
Iris	Closed/used by church
Lakeshore	Open/used by dinner theater
Landmark's Century Centre Cinema (originally the Diversey)	Open/building radically altered
Luna	Closed/demolished
Manor	Closed/demolished
Marbro	Closed/demolished
Maryland	Closed/demolished
McVickers	Closed/demolished
Norshore	Closed/demolished
Oriental (Ford Center)	Open/restored/live shows
Paradise	Closed/demolished
Regal	Closed/demolished
Riviera	Open/used for concerts
Roosevelt	Closed/demolished
Senate	Closed/demolished
Southtown	Closed/demolished
State Lake	Closed/demolished
Terminal	Closed/demolished
Tivoli	Closed/demolished
Tower	Closed/demolished
Uptown	Closed/fate unknown
Woods	Closed/demolished

Most Balaban and Katz movie palaces are now gone. This table shows the status of the Balaban and Katz theaters in Chicago. The information is current as of December 2005. (Information from Balaban and Katz internal documents and www.cinematreasures.com.)

The magnificent Uptown Theatre at 4814 Broadway Street still stands vacant as the largest theater in Chicago's Uptown neighborhood. It has suffered a twisted fate of ownership changes, false promises, and shifting demographics since 1981, when it closed down. It had been operated as a concert hall and movie theater by the Rabiela family, who bought it from Plitt Theatres in 1975. As of this writing, there are a few proposals before the city government to finally save this one-of-a-kind Balaban and Katz movie palace. David Balaban, the author's grandfather, managed this theater as well as the Riviera across the street. (Photograph courtesy of David Balaban.)

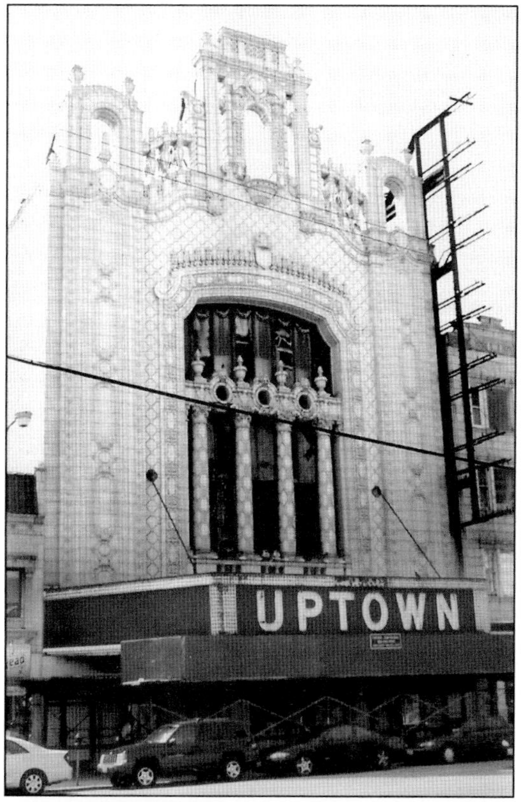

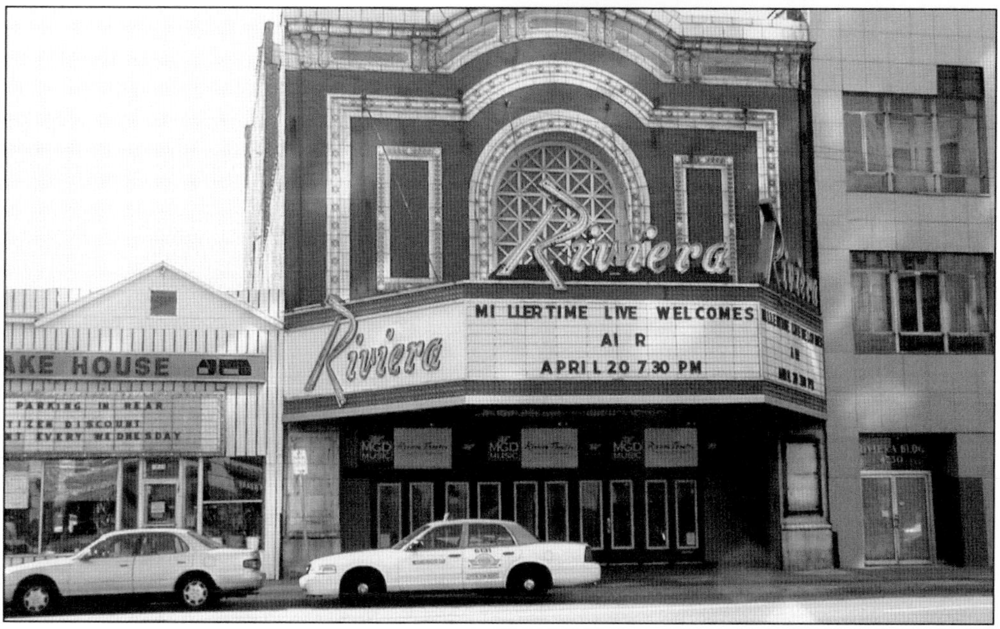

The beautiful Riviera Theatre at 4746 North Racine Avenue is one of few Balaban and Katz theaters that remains open today in any capacity. The Riviera closed as a movie theater in the 1980s. It became a nightclub, and today is one of Chicago's most popular concert halls. Most of the seats have been removed. (Photograph courtesy of Alan Gresik.)

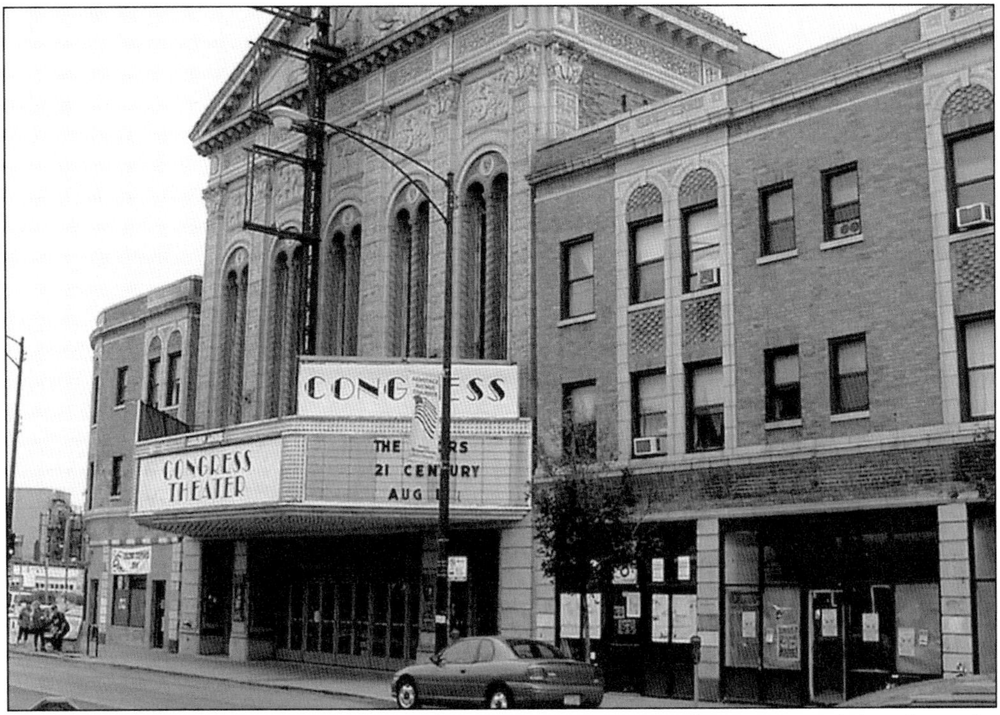

The Congress Theater at 2135 North Milwaukee Avenue escaped an attempted demolition by a developer after concerned community members protested. It is one of the few surviving B and K movie palaces from the 1920s. Its interior has been beautifully restored. Today the Congress features music concerts, movie festivals, talent shows, and other special events. (Photograph courtesy of the Congress Theater.)

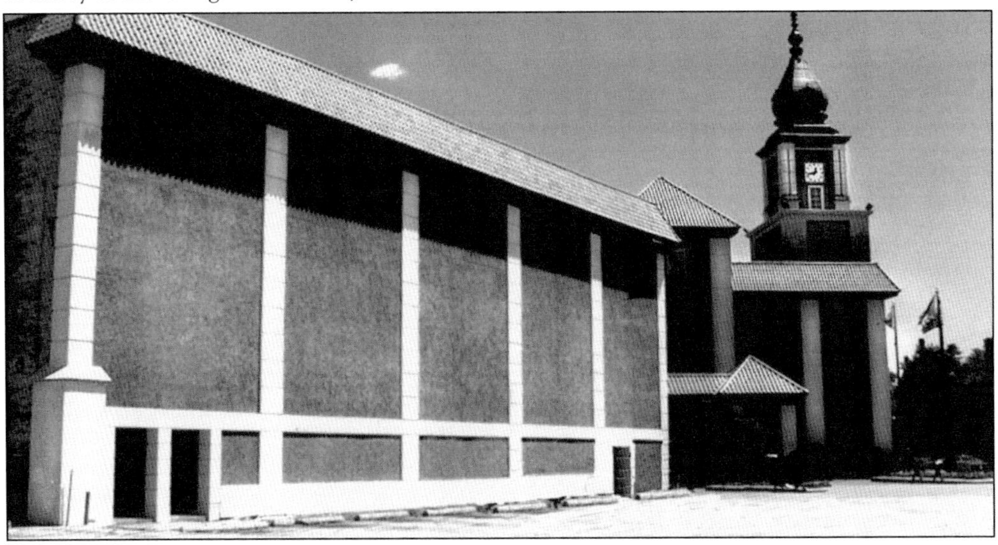

The Gateway Theatre at 5218 West Lawrence Avenue was purchased by the Copernicus Cultural and Civic Center in Chicago in the mid-1980s. It rarely shows movies now. It mainly serves as a meeting place. The Silent Film Society of Chicago featured shows there from time to time until recently. This theater is in danger of being torn down as of this writing. A developer wants to build condominiums on the site. (Photograph courtesy of Copernicus Cultural and Civic Center.)

Since 1971, the Central Park Theatre at 3535 West Roosevelt Road has been owned by the House of Prayer Church of God in Christ. They have been struggling to renovate the structure while maintaining its practical use as a house of worship. Recently the building has hosted silent film festivals and speakers who have gathered to celebrate the first Balaban and Katz movie palace's rich cultural heritage. (Photograph courtesy of Ken Roe.)

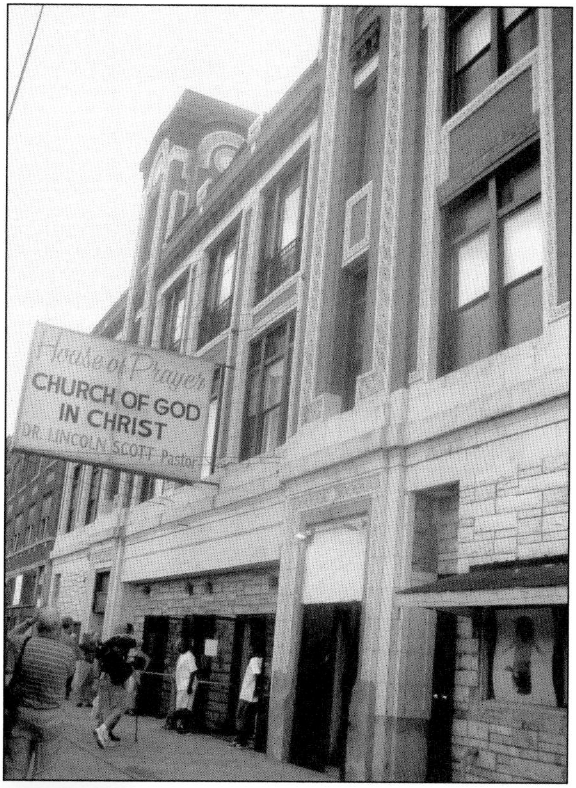

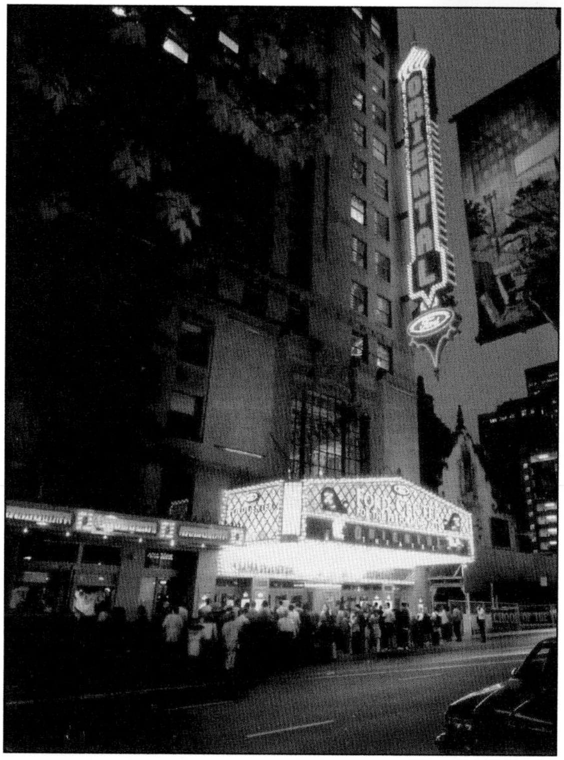

The beautiful Oriental Theatre at 20 West Randolph Street was saved from destruction in 1996 when it was completely restored. It reopened in 1998 as part of a circuit of theaters called "Broadway in Chicago." It is also known as the Ford Center for the Performing Arts. It features many types of family oriented entertainment. (Photograph courtesy of Broadway in Chicago.)

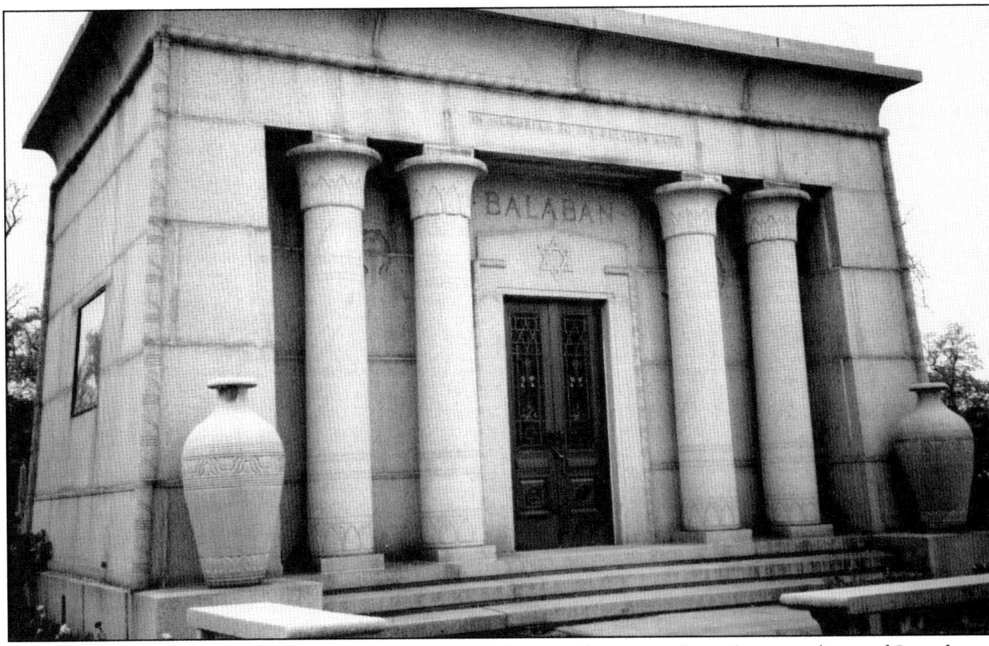

The Balaban family built this Egyptian-inspired mausoleum so that the members of Israel and Augusta Balaban's family would be remembered always. It is located in the Waldheim Jewish Cemeteries at 1400 South Des Plaines in Forest Park, Illinois. The mausoleum was designed by Rapp and Rapp, designers of the Balaban and Katz movie palaces. It is reminiscent of the hundreds of beautiful structures the Balaban brothers contributed to the American landscape. It is the largest mausoleum in that area of the cemetery. Inside the sanctuary are lighted pictures of Augusta and Israel and their offspring. The grand design of this structure says to the world, "We are the Balabans, we made an impact!" (Photographs courtesy of Karen Colizzi-Noonan.)

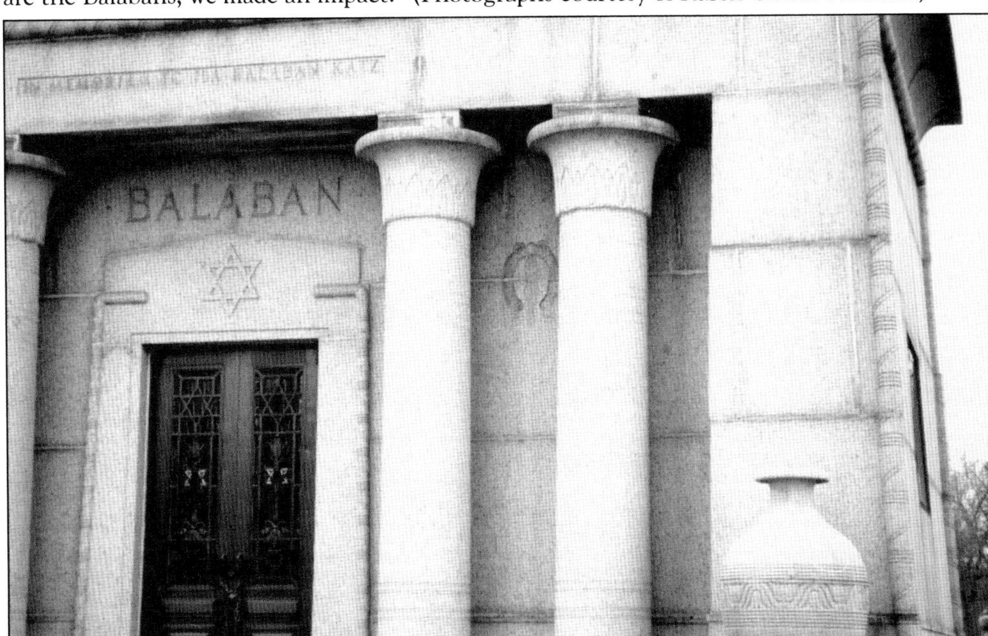

Bibliography

American Theatre Organ Society. (June 30, 2005). http://www.atos.org.

Balaban, Barney and Sam Katz. *The Fundamental Principles of Balaban & Katz Theatre Management*. Chicago: Balaban and Katz Corporation, 1926.

Balaban, Carrie. *Continuous Performance: The Story of A. J. Balaban*. New York: A. J. Balaban Foundation, 1964.

Balaban, John. "History of the Balaban and Katz Theatre Circuit." Internal Balaban and Katz company document, 1936.

Berkow, Ira. *Maxwell Street: Survival in a Bazaar*. Garden City, NY: Doubleday, 1977.

Bernstein, Arnie. *Hollywood on Lake Michigan: 100 Years of Chicago and the Movies*. Chicago: Lake Claremont Press, 1998.

Cinema Journal 18, no. 2 (Spring 1979).

Cooper, Gail. *Air-conditioning America: Engineers and the Controlled Environment, 1900–1960*. Baltimore: Johns Hopkins University Press, 1998.

Dick, Bernard F. *Engulfed: The Death of Paramount Pictures and the Birth of Corporate Hollywood*. Lexington, KY: University of Kentucky Press, 2001.

Eddy, William. *Television: The Eyes of Tomorrow*. New York: Prentice Hall, 1947.

Goldenson, Leonard H. and Marvin J. Wolf. *Beating the Odds*. New York: Scribner, 1991.

Gomery, Douglas. "The Growth of Movie Monopolies: The Case of Balaban and Katz." *Wide Angle* 3, no. 1 (1979).

———. *Shared Pleasures: A History of Movie Presentation in the United States*. Madison, WI: University of Wisconsin Press, 1992.

Grove, Lori. *Chicago's Maxwell Street*. Charleston, SC: Arcadia Publishing, 2002.

Hall, Ben M. *The Best Remaining Seats: The Golden Age of the Movie Palace*. New York: De Capo Press, 1988.

http://www.cinematreasures.org.

http://www.jazzagechicago.com.

Irwin, Will. *The House that Shadows Built*. Garden City, NY: Doubleday, Doran, 1928.

Kramer, Stanley with Thomas M. Coffey. *A Mad, Mad, Mad, Mad World: A Life in Hollywood*. New York: Harcourt Brace, 1997.

May, Lary. *Screening out the Past: The Birth of Mass Culture and the Motion Picture Industry*. Chicago: University of Chicago Press, 1980.

Naylor, David. *American Picture Palaces*. New York City: Prentice Hall, 1981.

"Paradoxes in Paradise: Elements of Conflict in Chicago's Balaban and Katz Movie Palaces," *Marquee* 27, no. 2 (1993).

Schatz, Thomas. *The Genius of the System: Hollywood Filmmaking in the Studio Era*. New York: Henry Holt, 1988.

Variety Daily. A. J. Balaban special edition, February 27, 1929.

Zukor, Adolf with Dale Kramer. *The Public Is Never Wrong: My Fifty Years in Motion Pictures*. New York: G. P. Putnam and Sons, 1953.

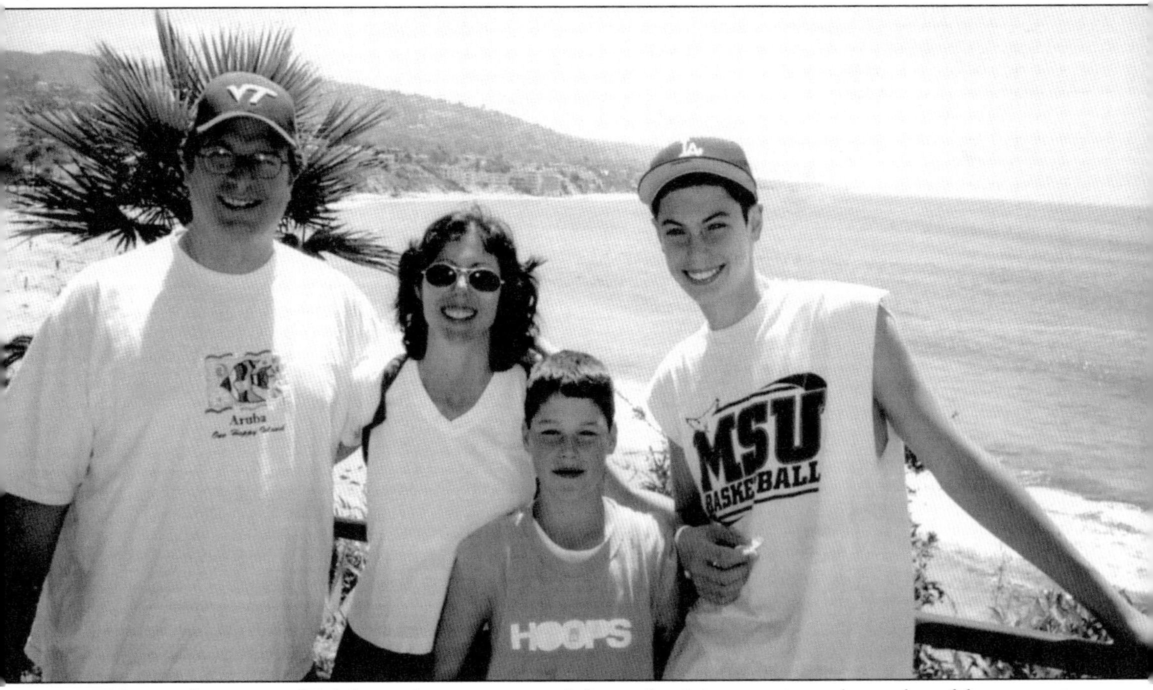

Here is the group of Balabans that encouraged the author's journey into the realm of documenting the lives of previous and contemporary Balabans. From left to right are author David Balaban, his wife, Barbara, and their sons, Sam and Danny Balaban. This Pacific Ocean photograph was taken in Laguna Beach, California, in July 2004 on their trip to Paramount Studios for the production of the Balaban and Katz documentary. For more information, please visit the Balaban and Katz Historical Foundation Web site at www.balabanandkatzfoundation.com.